D1213042

BOOM

BOOM

BRIDGING THE
OPPORTUNITY GAP
TO REIGNITE
STARTUPS

CRAIG HALL
with Linden Gross

Foreword by Mark Zandi, PhD
Chief Economist at Moody's Analytics

SAVIO
REPVBLIC

A SAVIO REPUBLIC BOOK
An Imprint of Post Hill Press

Boom:
Bridging the Opportunity Gap to Reignite Startups
© 2019 by Craig Hall with Linden Gross
All Rights Reserved

ISBN: 978-1-64293-108-2
ISBN (eBook): 978-1-64293-109-9

Cover design by Sara Lovas, HALL Group graphic designer
Interior design and production, Greg Johnson/Textbook Perfect

posthillpress.com
New York • Nashville

Published in the United States of America

This book is dedicated to aspiring entrepreneurs.
May you find hope and opportunity
to pursue your start-ups.

Author's Note

The intent of this book is to discuss the current environment for entrepreneurship. And while the emphasis is on the challenges entrepreneurs may face and how the private and public sectors can and should work together to solve them, it is not intended to discourage anyone from becoming an entrepreneur. If you are considering becoming an entrepreneur, do not wait for an easier or better environment.

On the contrary, my advice: Jump in! Give Entrepreneurship a try! What is the worst thing that can happen to you? It can be immensely satisfying, and you can make a positive difference in the world around you. You will never know if you do not try.

Good luck!

CONTENTS

Foreword

By Mark Zandi, PhD
Chief Economist at Moody's Analytics

Entrepreneurship is what makes the American economy tick. But in recent years, this engine of growth has sputtered. There is no one better than serial entrepreneur Craig Hall to diagnose the problem and determine how to fix it.

German industry is known for its precision craftsmanship and engineering, and Japanese manufacturers for their practical efficiency. Chinese businesses benefit from the country's low business costs. Every economy has its comparative advantage. The American economy's edge is its entrepreneurship. Hundreds of thousands of new businesses start each year, each entrepreneur working overtime to develop and sell a new idea.

Smartphones, video streaming, driverless cars, drones, online retailing, tweeting (I could go on and on)—all began in American startups. Each is the ultimate fruit of the efforts of one or two people: entrepreneurs.

These heroes of our economy are rightly revered. The most successful are celebrities, the subjects of movies and books. When I was growing up, to be successful meant becoming a doctor or perhaps a lawyer. Not today. Our best and brightest want to be entrepreneurs.

It is thus surprising that entrepreneurship has sputtered in recent years. The number of startups peaked twenty years ago at the height of the internet boom and has declined ever since. No industry has been immune to the falloff in business formation, and the number of jobs created at new companies is way down.

There are good reasons to be worried. Unless this turns around soon, it is difficult to see how our economy will truly get its groove back. Economic growth will remain disappointing, complicating all of our problems, from poverty to how to pay for Social Security and Medicare. The political and societal implications are arguably even more disconcerting.

Craig Hall is one of the foremost entrepreneurs of our time, but you wouldn't know that if you met him. He isn't a showman. He is humble and unassuming. But it is immediately evident that he is a person who gets things done. This started at a very early age. In a particularly riveting story, he recounts how as a college student he was able to finagle the purchase of a property that he fixed up and rented to his classmates. He was off and running, becoming one of the largest private apartment operators in the country.

Given the string of successful businesses he has started since—the first for-profit HMO, health clubs, software and energy companies, real estate and financial services firms, and even a winery or three—he has many stories to tell. He also has a wealth of experiences to draw upon to identify what has gone wrong with entrepreneurship in America.

As you can imagine, it's not just one thing. At the top of his list is the dearth and concentration of capital. Venture capitalists and private equity firms are focused on technology startups in Silicon Valley or perhaps in Boston, New York, and Washington, D.C. It is striking how much of their attention is fixated on just a handful of areas and how they have forgotten about the talent in much of the rest of the country.

The collapse in house prices and the loss of homeowners' equity in the wake of the housing crash have also hurt. Budding entrepreneurs often cash in that equity to finance their new enterprises. That's what I did to pay the early bills for the economic consulting firm I ultimately sold to Moody's Analytics, where I'm currently the chief economist.

Startups are also facing rising barriers created by increasingly massive multinationals and financial institutions. These behemoths are attracting talent and resources, and willing to pay up for intellectual property. For a startup to survive, it has to navigate under the radar for as long as possible.

With a diagnosis of what ails American entrepreneurship in hand, Craig then turns to how to cure it. Our entrepreneurialism has long been financed by small community banks, who suffered severely during the 2008 financial crisis. Reviving community banks and creating more small-business investment companies—Small Business Administration-licensed institutions that provide small businesses with loans and equity—will go a long way toward reviving new business formation.

Cities also need to engage in what Craig calls supportive entrepreneurship, providing resources to help new companies figure out complicated zoning restrictions, inspections, and other regulations. He recommends that policymakers ease the heavy student loan burden. If millennials who were in their twenties when the financial crisis hit are going to start companies in their thirties, as their baby boomer parents did, they need help with their student loans. Help to support homeownership, such as a tax incentive to promote saving for a down payment, would also eventually boost entrepreneurs.

Entrepreneurship has been troubled for some time, and it will take time to get it back on track, particularly if policymakers continue to pull back on immigration and global trade. Immigrants tend to start companies at a much higher rate than residents. Trade also creates competition, which breaks down barriers and disrupts entrenched multinationals. Nothing will stymie startups more than anti-immigration and antitrade policies.

My son once had the good fortune of hearing Craig recount some of his awesome life story. He is now renovating and renting apartments to college students. Do you think this is a coincidence? I don't. Read this book and you will be impacted as deeply as my son and I have been by Craig Hall.

Introduction

Fifty Years of Entrepreneurial Perspective

I'm a serial entrepreneur. I start things. I build things. I take risks. Over the years, my companies have created more than ten thousand jobs, and owned and operated more than one hundred thousand apartments and ten million square feet of office space across the U.S., along with hotels and industrial real estate. I've launched and run financial institutions, cofounded a health maintenance organization (HMO), and built various software companies that sold to big public companies. I've also drilled for oil and owned part of an airline company as well as part of the Dallas Cowboys football team. Inspired by the love of my wife, Kathryn, for the wine business, she and I started three wineries from scratch in Napa Valley and Sonoma, California. We now own three wine brands and thousands of acres of land and vineyards.

I consider myself one very lucky person. It didn't hurt that I was born a white male in the U.S. Although I grew up without wealth or social privilege, I had strong Midwestern values and a lot of opportunity.

I've been rich. I've lost it all. I was forced into bankruptcy. I was so broke that almost no one thought there was any hope. And I came back.

If I were starting out today, I'd like to think that I could make it, but I worry that it's a lot harder these days. This concerns me a great deal. Our country has provided me with freedom, hope, and opportunity.

I will forever be grateful. But too many today are not getting the same chance.

Ironically, entrepreneurship has never been more popular in the U.S. Just look at *Shark Tank* and its six million weekly viewers. While "the Fab Four" were the kings of popular culture in the '60s and '70s, we now look up to Bill Gates, Steve Jobs, Jeff Bezos, and Mark Zuckerberg. Not only are they the subjects of books and films, but they are inspiring a whole generation of kids to be entrepreneurs just like them.

Entrepreneurship has become contagious. A 2014 study by Babson College and Baruch College found that optimism about becoming an entrepreneur in this country had reached its highest level in more than fifteen years, with more than 50 percent of the adult population believing that good opportunities exist for starting a business.

And yet, paradoxically, we are living in one of the hardest times to be an entrepreneur, which is defined by Webster's Dictionary as "a person who starts a business and is willing to risk loss in order to make money."[1] U.S. entrepreneurship has largely been on the decline for more than three decades, spanning five presidencies. Despite an amazing amount of positive energy in the nonprofit sector and the groundswell of university programs geared toward entrepreneurship, only half as many businesses start up annually as they did a generation ago.[2] Data from the Census Bureau's Business Dynamics Statistics (BDS)[3] reveals that in 2015, the nation's 414,000 startup firms generated 2.5 million new jobs. Contrast those numbers to the pre–Great Recession level of startup activity. From 2002 to 2006, an average of 524,000 startup firms and 3.3 million new jobs per year were created. According to the Ewing Marion Kauffman Foundation, "New economic research demonstrates that the entrepreneurship deficit is tied to stagnant productivity, job loss, inequality and growth, which means lower wages and living standards for Americans."[4]

A shocking lack of available capital across much of the U.S. is partly to blame, especially when you consider the fact that the vast majority of capital is concentrated in just a few locations—Silicon Valley, New York, and Boston—and in a single sector. While there is plenty of capital for technology startups, traditional startups are not getting adequate access to capital. But, as we'll see, that's just part of the problem.

Not only have business startups (defined here as companies less than five years old)[5] been declining for the better part of four decades, as we'll see in Chapter 1, but the situation is even worse for women and people of color.

In looking at U.S. entrepreneurship through the lens of my fifty years of entrepreneurial experience, I realize that the system today is stacked against startups and small businesses. Our playing field is not as fair or level as it has been historically. As a result, national entrepreneurship is declining in terms of the numbers of new businesses. For people like me who have already grown their companies, having less competition is a selfish advantage. But it hurts the country at large in many ways.

Ironically, entrepreneurship in the 1960s and early 1970s was not nearly as popular as it is today, but it was a given. There were simply more opportunities, and it was much easier to start a new business. Even though I had no relevant skills or background and very little money, I never questioned whether I could start a business. I simply knew it was my right as an American.

Television shows, movies, books, newspaper and magazine stories, advertising campaigns, and oral legends all teach American children that they can succeed at anything if they work hard and earn that success. But as this book will show, taking the risk and making a viable living as an entrepreneur has increasingly moved out of reach for many.

These days, most entrepreneurs' and small-business owners' success is hampered by too many roadblocks. To me, entrepreneurial success means taking an idea—or taking on a project—and creating a viable and profitable business that improves people's lives. But starting a business requires a willingness to take a risk, which is challenging for many of us. It also requires startup capital, which for many these days is in short supply.

Money has become very scarce for all but big high-tech deals or other grand slams, making it almost impossible for entrepreneurs or small businesses to get loans or equity from traditional investing or lending sources. Once they clear that hurdle, they have to deal with mushrooming regulations, increasing bureaucracy, and a cost-prohibitive legal system in which startups can get smashed before they ever get going. Moreover, in my observation, many industries have experienced massive consolidation, which contributes to a more difficult environment for smaller companies. Then there's the colossal economic power in the hands of the tech giants, and the resulting efficiencies and disruptions derived from the internet and the digitization of data. Add to all of this the dramatic geographic factors that we'll explore in Chapter 1, and we can clearly see how two different worlds exist for entrepreneurs in the U.S. today.

In short, we have created a huge opportunity gap for many aspiring entrepreneurs who are not in technology or part of the country's booming ecosystems.

The freedom to start and grow a business is one of the fundamentals of the American psyche and the American dream. The American dream means different things to different people. To some it means owning their own home. To others it means starting a business. To most of us, the American dream is about a personal sense of hope, liberty, and happiness, and the freedom to be whomever and whatever we want to be if we work to earn it. That's always been the promise inherent in entrepreneurship. That promise, however, has been under attack for some time, and aside from some noteworthy exceptions in a small number of urban markets—or with many technology or biotech-related business startups—that attack is accelerating.

This is a big issue, one that's critical to America's future. Entrepreneurship is the engine that drives job creation, tax revenue, quality of life, and innovation.[6] And if the futurists are right, it's poised to be an even bigger issue in the next decade or two, as globalization and technology make more and more jobs obsolete and displace more and more people from what we have historically known as work.

This is not a problem for just would-be entrepreneurs and small businesses. We can no longer afford to turn a blind eye to the decline of

U.S. entrepreneurship. We need to challenge that status quo and begin to implement short- and long-term solutions, and we need to do it now.

This book certainly won't solve every ailment related to entrepreneurship, but I hope it shines a light on the problem and helps spark awareness, dialogue, and change. *BOOM: Bridging the Opportunity Gap to Reignite Startups* could be longer and crammed full of statistics, but it's not intended to be an academic work. It's also not intended to be one of those self-serving, "I'm about to run for office" books. I'm neither a professor nor a politician. I'm a concerned citizen and a proud entrepreneur who has benefited from the opportunities I've had throughout my career. So in most of this book, I'll share my sense of how entrepreneurship has changed since I jumped in at age eighteen, as a way of providing some perspective on today's state of entrepreneurial affairs.

As I look back on my five-plus decades in business, there's no question that over time, things have become more challenging for startups. In addition to exploring why, I'll spotlight potential solutions to this problem that are unfolding across the country. I'll also share a few of my own ideas about what we need to do to create an environment that will foster startups and support small business.

A groundswell of positive entrepreneurship is right there on the surface if entrepreneurs could just break free. But we've shackled them by making it harder and harder to raise capital and through increasing, unnecessary government interference. The change in the environment for startups between when I started as an entrepreneur in the 1960s and today has contributed to the current tanking of American entrepreneurship.

As this book was being written, research was being released and academics, along with some in Congress, began to debate this subject. A few people are happy with the current situation, but most others familiar with the statistics regarding U.S. entrepreneurship share my concerns. And while this is a hot topic in a few circles, it has yet to become part of the broader dialogue. After talking with many people about the contents of this book and considering many anecdotes—my own as well as others'—I believe that the country at large, including most policymakers and the public, remain unaware of the problems related to U.S. entrepreneurship.

Hopefully this book can serve as a wake-up call that leads to widespread awareness of the problem and adoption of the actions that will truly level the playing field. Just as our nation decided years ago that we needed to ensure fairness by protecting ourselves against monopolies, we need private and public policies that encourage and protect more business startups in the United States. This idea is important because the health of entrepreneurship matters for jobs. It matters for innovation. And it matters for citizenship.

Entrepreneurship is a critical part of what has made America great. We need to make sure that we safeguard it for today's generation and for generations to come.

PART I

THE PROBLEM

The Business Environment Is Stacked Against Most Startups

Albert Einstein is quoted as saying: "If I had an hour to solve a problem, I'd spend 55 minutes defining the problem and five minutes on the solution." Consider Part I our 55 minutes.

We live in a revolutionary time in the U.S., when technology and innovation have really taken hold and entrepreneurship should be booming. However, the fact is that in all but the field of technology and certain geographical areas of the country, U.S. entrepreneurship is struggling. The rate of company formation on an annual basis is roughly half of what it was four decades ago.[1]

The problems for most Americans who want to be entrepreneurs are complex, with many conflicting trends. Even though many positive factors shape today's entrepreneurial landscape, for most people, opportunities are few and far between. That's because the environment for starting new businesses today, including factors impacting risk taking, is stacked against the average entrepreneur. Our economy today is structured to support big companies over new, fledgling startups.

In Part I, we will take our "55 minutes" to define the entrepreneurship environment of today. We will look at the challenges today's startups face through my lens as an entrepreneur with more than fifty years of experience. Hopefully we will do Albert Einstein's 55 minutes some justice as we define the problems.

CHAPTER 1

There's Something Happening Here

I wasn't an obvious candidate for entrepreneurial success. Even though I was a lower-middle-class kid with epilepsy who struggled academically and socially, it never occurred to me that I could not start a business. It seemed to me that all Americans had that right if they were willing to work hard. I had no experience, and my family had no history of entrepreneurship, yet the preservation of the American dream and freedom was part of what my mother and father both fought for when they served in the Navy during World War II. My parents believed in giving my brother and me access to whatever would enable us to fashion the kinds of lives we wanted. I wonder how they would view today's future versus the one they worked to provide. I wonder how I would have reacted had I come of age in this decade.

What's different?

Just about everything, as I would discover in August 2011.

One morning in Napa Valley, my wife, Kathryn, and I were chilled by the still and crisp air from the evening before (typical for the region) as we walked up to the Vintage Inn lawn. It would be eleven o'clock or even later before the sun would completely break through the cloud cover, prompting us to seek shelter under great umbrellas erected over the long tables that would host a fabulous luncheon. The group of 250 or so individuals—mostly donors to the Democratic Congressional Campaign Committee, along with a number of members of congress and new candidates—had been mingling out on the lawn or sitting at tables finishing their continental breakfast from the buffet. Now they began to wrap up their conversations and grab coffees before gathering inside, where the panel discussions would begin. Little did I realize on that day that my economic worldview—or at least one of my key assumptions about it—was about to get torpedoed.

Let me digress and state at the outset that this is not a book praising one political party over another. While I am a Democrat, I do not believe that either party has really shown leadership regarding the important issues tackled in this book. Frankly, these are American issues, and the solutions should be embraced by elected officials from both sides of the aisle. Now, back to the story.

I always enjoy this group and this annual meeting, which is not a fundraiser per se but rather a venue for people who have already donated to discuss policy issues. A series of panels is filled with standout speakers and inspiring conversations. I particularly appreciate the Saturday-morning discussion on the economy, which for many years has included Moody's Analytics' chief economist Mark Zandi, a bright straight shooter who every year talks about the state of our economy and tells it like it is.

As I waited for the first panel to start, I couldn't help but remember the night before. There I was, out on our patio overlooking Napa Valley and our vineyards as people streamed through our home with glasses of Sauvignon Blanc, Chardonnay, and Pinot Noir in hand, just as they always do on the initial evening of this weekend event.

"Craig, how's business?" Mark Zandi asked, walking up to where I stood.

After hearing my complaints in 2008, three years earlier, he had greeted me with a different question in 2009 and 2010. "Things better yet?" he would ask.

My business team, Kathryn, and I managed to survive the second-worst business crisis in my career. Even though that proved a lot easier than the 1980s downturn, it still took a lot of hard work to get through what can be described only as an uncertain and depressing time. While business improved as the years went on, it remained far from normal, a condition that plenty of other people who suffered during the Great Recession have also experienced.

As aware as I was of our own and others' struggles, I don't think I had fully realized the overarching national toll the Great Recession had taken until Mark's presentation at the 2011 meeting.

"Entrepreneurship is in trouble," he announced.

Mark is a big thinker. I have gotten to know him fairly well during these annual events in Napa and often see him on CNBC discussing various economic topics. So I knew that the statistics and information he presented had been carefully prepared. Even so, I had a hard time believing what I heard.

Startups Are Declining

"American entrepreneurship has been declining for decades," Mark said.

It turns out that entrepreneurship has been in trouble for several decades. In fact, entrepreneurship—as measured by new businesses versus all businesses—has been in decline since at least 1978.

Is this because of some older industries that are outmoded? I wondered.

The Hamilton Project, the economic and well-being think tank that's part of the Brookings Institution, published the chart (shown on page 6) in June 2018. It clearly shows that from 1979 to 2014, startups in every industry materially declined. Similarly, the Heritage Foundation refers to the "startup-deficit" crisis in 2017, stating that "restoring a pro-growth climate and reducing the costs of regulatory compliance should be a top priority for policy makers at the federal, state and local levels."[1] As both liberal and conservative think tanks point out, the number of new businesses in the U.S. is falling, and that trend has been going on for decades.

As if that isn't dismal enough, the decline accelerated following the Great Recession of 2008. Although things have improved from when they hit rock bottom, for the first time in recorded history, the period after the Great Recession saw more firms dying and going out

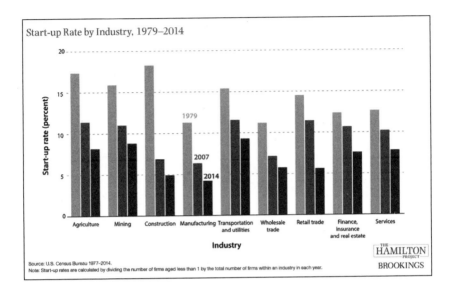

Start-up Rate by Industry, 1979–2014

Source: U.S. Census Bureau 1977–2014.
Note: Start-up rates are calculated by dividing the number of firms aged less than 1 by the total number of firms within an industry in each year.

THE HAMILTON PROJECT

BROOKINGS

of business than new firms starting. As the chart opposite shows, from 2008 to 2011—for the only time in recorded history—more U.S. businesses died annually than new ones started.

The situation is even more dire for women and people of color.

It turns out that female entrepreneurs, despite often outperforming men, made up only 4.4 percent of aggregate venture capital deals and only 2.2 percent of venture capital funding in 2017.[2] In addition, their loans were approved 33 percent less often than those of their male counterparts. That has clearly taken a toll. The dip from 44 percent of female entrepreneurs in 1997 to just 37 percent in 2016 means we're closing in on a historic low.[3]

People of color are faring worse than that. The Small Business Association (SBA) reports that "Black/African American-owned firms... [are] 81% less likely to be employers than nonminority firms. Similarly Hispanic-, Native American-, and Pacific Islander-owned firms are about 40% as likely to be employers."[4] Perhaps that statistic is related to the findings of an article published in the *Journal of Empirical Legal Studies*, which reveals that "African-American-owned firms have lower access to capital than white-owned firms. They are rejected with an

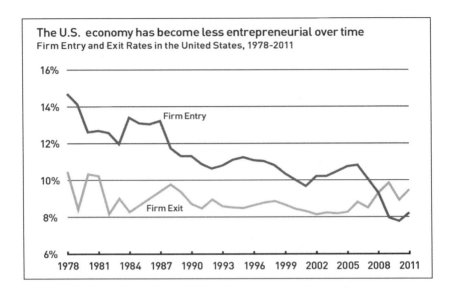

The U.S. economy has become less entrepreneurial over time
Firm Entry and Exit Rates in the United States, 1978-2011

approximately 30 percent higher probability than similar white-owned firms."[5] According to the U.S. Department of Commerce's Minority Business Development Agency, the chances of being granted loans are so much lower for people of color than for those of nonminority firms that many minority business owners often won't bother to apply. When they do receive business loans, they're usually forced to pay higher interest rates.[6]

Of course, as Dr. Amy Gannon—director of entrepreneur development and cofounder of Doyenne, a nonprofit organization dedicated to eliminating the gender gap in the entrepreneurial community—points out, generations of racism and discrimination, coupled with generations of policy that has prevented wealth building in the black community, mean that people of color don't usually have a friends-and-family round of dollars to draw upon.

Haitian-born Carl Dorvil knows all about these concerning national trends, even though his own history as an entrepreneur has been successful. After immigrating to the U.S. with his parents and getting into Southern Methodist University in Dallas, Carl turned a job tutoring younger students into a business while still in school. Carl's business, Group Excellence, grew, and ultimately he sold it. When the buyers ran it into the ground, he bought it back, as many entrepreneurs would have done, eventually turning it into a nonprofit and moving on. He recently ran a public company, GEX Management, which recruits employees for companies looking to outsource staffing for cafeterias and other food service businesses. That required very expensive financing. In order to help pay for these costs, he sold his control of the public company to a new investor and stepped aside as CEO. He has recently purchased another company.

Throughout his years in business, he has seen the good and the bad of being an entrepreneur as a person of color. On the plus side, several large companies make a real effort to contract with companies with diverse leadership. Since there aren't that many around, that can provide great opportunities to minority business owners. On the flip side, businesses capital at both the equity stage and even later, when business owners are profitable, is extremely problematic, since as a rule banks don't seem to trust people of color. The lack of access to traditional capital markets has driven many of these entrepreneurs to use factoring, credit cards, and other high-cost providers to secure the working capital they need.

"A lot of them do not to realize they are paying 36 percent to 60 percent interest rates to run their businesses," Carl told me. He explained that they'll have a contract that provides for staffing services or cleaning services or any number of products and services. The cash flow will come in sixty or so days later than the expenses and operating costs for the business. They take the receivables from the contracting and factor them at a 3 percent discount, which on a thirty-day receivable constitutes a 36 percent interest rate. "That's not uncommon," he concluded.

The 2017 Kauffman Foundation *State of Entrepreneurship* report states that "blacks are almost three times more likely than whites to have profits negatively impacted by access to capital" and "more than twice as likely to be negatively impacted by the cost of capital."[7] Aside from being downright unjust, this too contributes to a decline in American entrepreneurship. The Kauffman Foundation reports that "if minorities started and owned companies at the same rate as whites, the

U.S. would have over one million more businesses and up to an extra 9.5 million jobs."[8]

That's far from the only sector not performing up to entrepreneurial capacity. In his eye-opening presentation, Mark Zandi pointed out that the rate of business formation by Americans ages twenty to thirty-four had just fallen sharply (remember, this was in 2011) and that millennials were not starting as many new enterprises as baby boomers of that age had done.

What?

As an entrepreneur headquartered in Dallas, I had seen my share of ups and downs, but generally, even in the post–Great Recession era, it seemed to me that entrepreneurship was alive and well. Alarm bells began ringing in my head. Mark hadn't just surprised me, he had hit me over the head with a sledgehammer. I realized all too clearly that floundering entrepreneurship could have dire consequences for our national economy and our future as a world leader.

Wow, is this really something that we want to just let happen? I asked myself with an increasing sense of urgency. *Why are the policymakers not all over this and getting it fixed?*

Mark's comments haunted me. So I set off to begin my own research into the state of U.S. entrepreneurship. I had to know. Was he right?

The answer to that is yes, he was right, and we definitely have problems when it comes to U.S. entrepreneurship and opportunity. But these problems are not without nuances, and everything about the current state of entrepreneurship is far from black and white.

I now know enough to conclude that these are the best of times for some entrepreneurs and the worst of times for others. The difference comes down to geography, industry, demographics, and many more factors that we'll discuss throughout this book. The good news is that the U.S. leads the world in innovation, and we are in the midst of an incredible technological revolution that's making life and work faster, cheaper, and better. At the same time, unparalleled efforts to support startups (which, following the Kauffman Foundation's lead, I'm defining as companies less than five years old) are in play all over the country.

This is, of course, great. And it's a far cry from what I experienced when I was launching my career in the late 1960s.

So how bad can it be when we have so many good programs supporting entrepreneurship? I wondered. The answers to that question would lead me back to a mixed set of facts and the view that what's happening is anything but clear.

As I suspected, the news isn't all bad. In technology and other big industries, grand slams like Apple, Facebook, Uber, Google, and Tesla are launched and everyone wants to invest in early on. These are doing just fine. Make no mistake, there is tons of money chasing technology and big ideas, so these grand-slam startups, many of which tend to be based in Silicon Valley, had and continue to have funds to draw on. As of 2016, funding to the tune of $175 billion had helped launch 229 unicorns (those exceedingly rare tech startups valued at more than a billion dollars) that are now worth $1.3 trillion.[9] No problem there. The businesses that are struggling are the smaller non-tech, service-based companies—or those that provide a product—that are likely to create base-run rather than grand-slam returns for investors.

While it's hard to quibble with a grand slam, there are some serious negatives to not giving small startups a chance, especially since a lot of good things begin small and then grow. But that growth isn't happening, in part because most funding sources are focused on grand-slam startups.

These underfunded startups fall into two general categories:

- Startups with good ideas that can fill a need in the market and deliver solid singles or doubles but will likely never scale, so will never be grand slams.

- Specially created startups in economically depressed parts of the country that can't take advantage of an ecosystem inherent in established startup areas like Silicon Valley or even new advancing areas like Dallas or Austin, Texas.

Combined, these two segments that we'll talk about a lot more in the pages to come represent the majority of our country's startups.

Which means that despite lip service at the federal level about entrepreneurs and despite the Small Business Administration, the majority
of this country's startups are struggling with issues ranging from raising
capital to dealing with regulation, a lot of red tape, and huge barriers to
entry. And all too often, they're failing.

A chart produced by Mark Zandi for one of our annual meetings,
presented a couple of years after the one that prompted me to start my
research, focuses on a narrower time frame: 1990 to 2013. Note the
decline before the Great Recession. While that devastating downturn
certainly didn't help, it also didn't cause the problem, though it may
have made it worse.

The resulting deteriorating entrepreneurial spirit has left a mark.
Forbes magazine defines entrepreneurial spirit as "an attitude and
approach to thinking that actively seeks out change, rather than waiting
to adapt to change. It's a mindset that embraces critical questioning,
innovation, service and continuous improvement." Unfortunately, a
drop in that entrepreneurial spirit translates to a drop on the job front.

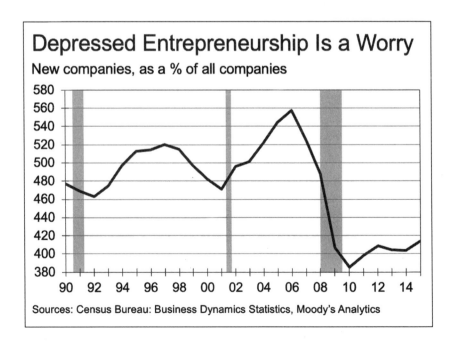

Depressed Entrepreneurship Is a Worry
New companies, as a % of all companies

Sources: Census Bureau: Business Dynamics Statistics, Moody's Analytics

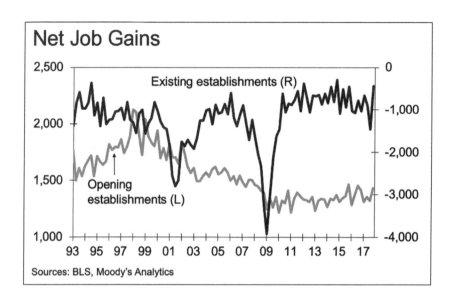

Net Job Gains

Sources: BLS, Moody's Analytics

History shows us that most American net job gains come from businesses less than five years old.[10] Whereas older businesses tend to trade workers, shedding as many as or more than they add, new businesses hire as they grow. Unfortunately, fewer startups have led to a steady decline and low stagnation in net job gains from new establishments (see the chart above), which, as noted above, is typically where most of our net job gains come from. This poses a clear long-term problem for our economy.

Don't let impressively low unemployment numbers fool you. People's dropping out of the workforce artificially lowers those numbers. They also don't account for all those workers whose earnings have been slashed when a change in employment opportunity has forced them to take jobs they're overqualified for, a problem that's likely to be aggravated in the future because of automation—everything from robotics to AI (artificial intelligence) to blockchains (a digitized, decentralized ledger in which transactions made in bitcoins or another cryptocurrency are recorded chronologically and publicly).

This book will explore all of these, starting with blockchains.

The Impact of Blockchain

In Silicon Valley, the environment has been, and still is, on fire in terms of creating new technology companies and numerous entrepreneurial opportunities. Since I grew up in a time and place that was far from the epicenter of a lot of the technological revolution, my adaptation to these changes has admittedly been slow. As those around me will quickly tell you, I'm a bit of an old-school dinosaur when it comes to technology.

Notwithstanding my lack of engineering or similar skills, I can see where blockchains could be the next big thing. Blockchains are transparent, worldwide databases that will potentially eliminate a lot of middlemen in business, resulting in transactions that are faster, cheaper and, frankly, better. In many ways, this will democratize capital and valuations.

Clearly, we not only have been but continue to be in an exciting time of revolutionary changes. The whole area of blockchains and its impact on cryptocurrency and other areas seems incredible. As I was completing this book, I began to study the offshoots of blockchains and how this whole area could open up new entrepreneurial opportunities. It remains to be seen whether this will further the trends of big getting bigger or, instead, help new and smaller companies.

Either way, the sooner we start addressing this disparity, the better off we'll all be.

What's Going On?

It is hard to fathom that during one of the longest economic recoveries in modern history, with the stock market at all-time highs and with record low unemployment as of this writing, an ever-widening opportunity gap for entrepreneurs and startup businesses is also a reality. Although people are employed, our workforce—in terms of labor participation—has shrunk. In addition, as Economic Development for Central Oregon CEO Roger Lee points out, "The national labor participation rate for the emerging workforce is very alarming—a fraction of our youth aged sixteen to twenty-four are working." Many people are also underemployed. These challenges go hand in hand with weakness in startups.

A combination of factors—including tech innovation and the resulting creative destruction (which we'll talk about in Chapter 2), the concentration of economic power in fewer hands, productivity gains, and the offshoring of manufacturing jobs—has led to where we are. The lack of a real awareness of these issues by most Americans just makes everything worse, since by not discussing the problems, we are delaying the solutions and allowing the opportunity gap to expand.

Since the late 1970s, almost fifty years now, the number of new companies that are one to five years old has shrunk. In trying to figure out what's behind this decline, I've realized that one issue is that we have become a nation that favors and is increasingly geared toward big business. To be clear, I am not against big business per se; I am against policies that favor big business at the expense of startups.

It's not just that we're funding large, sexy ideas rather than solid, utilitarian startups. The trend toward big, bigger, biggest is also fueled by a compulsion to solve every potential problem with yet another regulation, which strangles startups and small businesses while creating unintended protections for existing companies. That's the last thing a fledgling company needs.

Additionally, a growing number of "not in my backyard" activists (NIMBYs) often wind up in fights that, however unintentionally, hurt startups and small businesses, since those companies have less staying power when they have to contend with these all-too-often constant fights in today's business world. In my experience, this has gotten worse over time and particularly in recent years. Politicians' reactions to these extreme positions isn't helping.

Too often our political representatives wind up adopting positions demanded by the loudest voice in the room rather than asserting leadership by choosing the right policy and defending it. Senator John

McCain was an example of a true leader who would not be swayed in this manner. He said:

> We seem convinced that majorities exist to impose their will with few concessions and that minorities exist to prevent the party in power from doing anything important. That's not how we were meant to govern. Our entire system of government—with its checks and balances, its bicameral Congress, its protections of the rights of the minority—was designed for compromise. It seldom works smoothly or speedily. It was never expected to. It requires pragmatic problem-solving from even the most passionate partisans. It relies on compromise between opposing sides to protect the interests we share. We can fight like hell for our ideas to prevail. But we have to respect each other or at least respect the fact that we need each other.[11]

Unfortunately, Senator McCain was an exception, and too many extremists with loud voices are hurting the playing field for startups.

Impeding the growth of new companies serves big business and big entrepreneurs who are as successful as I've been fortunate enough to be. Most large companies today are embracing innovation almost entirely via acquisitions of young, small businesses—the very "competitors" that restrictive policies and regulation tend to drive out of business in their early and most vulnerable years. So most of these large companies like the system the way it is today. But this is shortsighted, and it's time for all of us to level the playing field.

Instead, the opposite has happened. The Great Recession widened the resulting opportunity gap even more,[12] something I've observed on a firsthand basis. As you'll read about, while that experience hurt my company in the beginning, arguably it helped us because we now have fewer new competitors. Growth by hurting others is not in our interest as a country, so we all should care about this.

Despite my struggles during and following the Great Recession, I was lucky compared to smaller businesses. I sold one of my software companies to Oracle in July 2008 for $240 million, and the sale helped me pay down debt and get through the recession in one piece. As the recession began to give way to growth, my company was one of the earliest to be able to start constructing office buildings again in North Texas. In 2011, we went ahead and began construction on a two-hundred-thousand-square-foot office. Few people could get the money for a building that did not have preleasing in place (that is, tenants committed to move in) after the Great Recession. We followed that with five-hundred-thousand-square-foot and three-hundred-thousand-square-foot buildings.

In short, my company changed and adapted and got back to business. But if my company had been a new startup trying to compete with companies that were already established, forget it. I wouldn't have stood a chance.

I ended up not only surviving but benefiting from low interest rates. In fact, the beneficiaries of the public policy designed to help the country recover from the Great Recession, whether intended or by accident, were people like me. We have been able, for example, to refinance many assets at much more favorable interest rates.

The recovery has also helped our lending business. The regulators, understandably, compelled banks to greatly enhance their loan quality and take fewer risks in underwriting. Those tightened bank regulations meant that you couldn't borrow money at all unless you were extremely big and extremely creditworthy. In fact, startups that could have gotten loans in other cycles couldn't find money to borrow at any percentage. So the low interest rates didn't help them as they did me. If you can't *get* a loan, it doesn't matter how low the rate is.

As a result, the competition that my company usually has when constructing new buildings simply wasn't there anymore, because competitors couldn't get any financing. So we did well.

Even now, getting funding is more difficult at all levels than it used to be. While I was writing this book, we built a three-hundred-thousand-square-foot building, and the market is still not what it once was. However, that building leased up very quickly. Where there once was a lot of competition, now we have almost none. Indeed, it has become a market where only the biggest players can find financing.

While selfishly, the fallout from how the government dealt with the Great Recession has been fine for HALL Group, I don't believe that selfish goals should be the yardstick, especially when the nation's well-being is at stake.

These days financial challenges still prevent most entrepreneurs from successfully pursuing business ownership, with more than a third reporting that they can't qualify for a loan due to their credit scores.[13]

No wonder new players are either waiting longer to jump in or not jumping in at all. That's especially true with the younger generation.

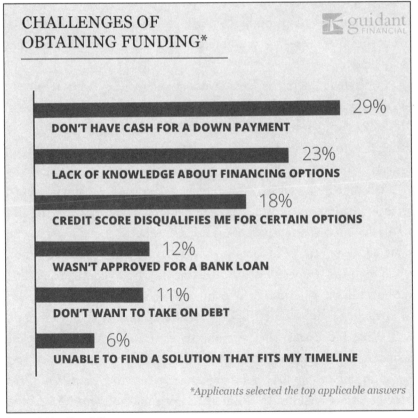

CHALLENGES OF OBTAINING FUNDING*

DON'T HAVE CASH FOR A DOWN PAYMENT — 29%

LACK OF KNOWLEDGE ABOUT FINANCING OPTIONS — 23%

CREDIT SCORE DISQUALIFIES ME FOR CERTAIN OPTIONS — 18%

WASN'T APPROVED FOR A BANK LOAN — 12%

DON'T WANT TO TAKE ON DEBT — 11%

UNABLE TO FIND A SOLUTION THAT FITS MY TIMELINE — 6%

*Applicants selected the top applicable answers

Source: Guidant Financial[14]

The Millennial Problem

Historically, Americans ages twenty to thirty-four have been big creators of new businesses. This was certainly true for my generation—the baby boomers. But millennials, who according to Kauffman research could best lead an entrepreneurial recovery, are not starting new businesses like boomers did. In fact, the number of people under thirty who own a business has fallen by 65 percent since the 1980s and is now at a quarter-century low, according to a *Wall Street Journal* analysis of Federal Reserve data.[15]

The rate of business formation by this group of young Americans, which by 2020 will constitute the country's largest age segment, has always been disappointing, but it has plunged since 2013.[16] In part, this is because their rate of home ownership—historic loan collateral for many entrepreneurs—has plummeted, while their amount of debt has skyrocketed.

Ironically, millennials have an innate edge. They were raised on technology, which, in my view, is a critical part of every new business. This advantage suggests that millennials should be the record-setting generation for new startup creation. Yet up until now, the opposite has proven to be true.

As I thought about why millennials, as opposed to baby boomers, are not creating new businesses, I remembered a story from the late 1970s that may illustrate part of the difference between today versus the same age group thirty to forty years ago. In 1978 at age twenty-eight, while my primary business was apartments, I was rapidly expanding various other businesses of my own, which included building a chain of racquetball clubs called Sports Illustrated Clubs, a joint venture with Time Inc. That's when a group of seven individuals looking for financing approached me through a friend. Although they all worked for nonprofits in the health-maintenance sector, they wanted to form a for-profit national health maintenance organization (HMO). At the time, it usually took two years and some $2 million to get a federal license, but they promised they could accomplish that in ninety days and spend only $100,000.

"We'll work full time and take no salary until the company breaks even," they proposed.

Even at that point, everyone would get very low, modest salaries.

I had already started doing angel investing in entrepreneurial businesses at that point, so I gave them $111,000, the only cash in the deal. I also provided the new company with a picnic table and eight chairs—one for each of them and one for me—and Independence Health Plan, as we called it, was born.

It wasn't easy, and it took more than ninety days. Actually, it took more like nine months. That was just for the licenses. Break-even didn't occur until late in the second year, which was annoying to me and punishing to them. So how did everyone stay alive and feed their families? The answer was simple and complicated. Most of the seven were homeowners. In those days, it wasn't that hard to get a second mortgage or home equity line of credit on your house, which they all promptly did before they quit their jobs.

They didn't take salaries for the first two and a half years. Long hours and no pay ultimately led to a couple of divorces. But when we took the company public in 1983, everyone became incredibly wealthy and, having created a lot of jobs, went on to have great lives as contributors to society. (I didn't do too badly myself. My $111,000 turned into $65 million at one point, and eventually I sold for $33 million in profit.)

Here's the catch when it comes to millennials: Due to the housing collapse and subsequent increase in home values, they don't own homes to the same extent as previous generations. That means they don't have tangible assets from which to draw during lean startup years. To make matters worse, between 2001 and 2014, the number of millennial "severely burdened" renters—those who spend over half their income on rent—has grown by more than 50 percent. Without home equity, a major support for starting and financing businesses is missing.[17]

That's only part of the problem. An avalanche of historically unprecedented student debt has also made it difficult for many to get credit or borrow in order to start a business. A study conducted by the University of Pennsylvania and the Federal Reserve Bank of Philadelphia found that there is "a significant and economically meaningful negative correlation between changes in student debt and net new businesses employing one to four employees, the firms most dependent on personal debt for financing. Based on our model, an increase of one standard deviation in student debt reduced the number of businesses with one to four employees by 14 percent between 2000 and 2010. The effect on larger firms decreased with firm size, which we interpret to mean that these firms had greater access to outside capital."[18]

According to John Lettieri, the cofounder and president of the Economic Innovation Group, "millennials are on track to be the least entrepreneurial generation in recent history." In his testimony before the Senate Committee on Small Business and Entrepreneurship, Lettieri explained that the number of student borrowers grew 89 percent between 2004 and 2014, and the average debt held by student borrowers rose 77 percent.[19]

No wonder millennials aren't starting businesses as much as baby boomers did.

Demographically, one ray of hope is that the oldest millennials have just hit their mid-thirties, and new research from the National Bureau of Economic Research shows that the average age of founders of the fastest-growing startups over the past decade is forty-five.[20] So while the impact of the Great Recession (when a large segment of millennials entered the workforce) has left many at a severe financial disadvantage, this generation has not yet hit its peak age for successful startup formation.

As a country, we need to explore how public policies can get things back on track by the time this generation reaches peak startup age. We'll look at that in the second part of this book. First, we need to continue to fully understand where we are and what has gone wrong. And I guarantee you this next section will shock you as much as it did me.

Then There's Geography

The fact that we have only half as many companies starting up every year than we used to[21] is bad enough. But half of those startups are happening in just twenty counties—or .006 percent of the country. If you look at the chart below, you'll see that when it comes to startups, California, Texas, Florida, and New York, with Illinois, Arizona, and Nevada peppered in, are the places to be.

Splitting the remaining half of the country's startups among the nation's 3,141 counties[22] and county equivalents (parishes, boroughs,

20 COUNTIES GENERATED HALF OF NET NEW ESTABLISHMENTS				
Rank	County	Metro Area	Increase in Est.	Population Rank
1	Los Angeles County, CA	Los Angeles	14,540	1
2	Miami-Dade County, FL	Miami	6,790	8
3	Kings County, NY (Brooklyn)	New York	6,510	7
4	Harris County, TX	Houston	5,990	3
5	Orange County, CA	Los Angeles	4,430	6
6	Queens County, NY	New York	4,210	10
7	San Diego County, CA	San Diego	4,160	5
8	Travis County, TX	Austin	3,790	39
9	Palm Beach County, FL	Miami	3,610	28
10	Broward County, FL	Miami	3,010	18
11	Maricopa County, AZ	Phoenix	2,980	4
12	Cook County, IL	Chicago	2,960	2
13	Santa Clara County, CA	San Francisco	2,900	17
14	Collin County, TX	Dallas	2,890	73
15	Orange County, FL	Orlando	2,700	35
16	Tarrant County, TX	Dallas	2,630	15
17	San Francisco County, CA	San Francisco	2,600	67
18	Clark County, NV	Las Vegas	2,430	13
19	New York County, NY	New York	2,330	20
20	Dallas County, TX	Dallas	2,190	9

The 20 counties that generated half of net new business establishments in the United States from 2010 to 2014.

Source: Economic Innovation Group

and the District of Columbia) leaves a huge amount of the country in
the no-action category. Add to that the fact that only 73 counties in the
U.S. have made up half of the net increase in jobs since 2010, and you
can see how we're becoming geographically polarized with haves and
have-nots, and with areas—including the Midwest, where I grew up—
being left behind.

I understand why the Midwest is in trouble. For the past fifty years,
it has been on a downward slide caused by shuttered businesses and job
losses, resulting in a lack of entrepreneurial spirit. It had always been
all about the auto industry in a big way. Then came globalization, and
manufacturing plants and jobs were shipped overseas. That eliminated
many small support businesses for industries like the auto industry that
were so critical to the region. Add in the fact that artificial intelligence
and other technologies have replaced a lot of service businesses, and
you have the makings of a monster geographical opportunity gap. For
a time, it was argued that the internet would bolster rural areas, since
companies would be able to operate from anywhere, but as we've
seen, the facts simply don't reflect this. Instead, entrepreneurship has
remained an urban phenomenon, with startups and workers clustered
in hubs anchored by big cities and great universities. In the '80s, 20
percent of U.S. companies started in rural areas. That percentage shrunk
to 12.2 percent in 2017.[23]

So yes, I understand why parts of the Midwest and South are in
trouble. But part of the reason I had trouble understanding Mark
Zandi's overarching concerns about U.S. entrepreneurship was that
Dallas, the headquarters for most of my businesses, happens to have
a vibrant entrepreneurial economy (although as I have learned, it too
lacks capital for startups). Despite our national problems, the three
adjoining Texas counties—Tarrant, Collin, and Dallas counties—on
the above chart are all places where I do business.

What's the difference?

As we'll see in the second half of this book, ecosystems (which
are built over years) with strong universities, forward-thinking local
governments, a talent pool filled with people who have technological

backgrounds, and business support systems all play a major role. It's pretty hard to successfully start a business without access to people with that kind of training, who don't tend to congregate in rural communities and small towns. But a lot of this entrepreneurial opportunity gap is profit-driven, especially when you consider that nearly 80 percent of all venture capital goes to just a few big urban markets. We all think of Silicon Valley and San Francisco, but add New York, Boston, Chicago, Los Angeles, Miami, Las Vegas, Phoenix, and Houston, and you have the big success stories. Perhaps a surprise to many, I would add that Detroit is a unique success story in process.

Many new restaurants and retail stores in a small town have trouble raising money, but there will always be plenty of funding for a potentially scalable grand-slam technology business in the key urban markets. That's just the reality. There's so much money available for tech deals that crazy ideas are getting funded. Meanwhile, we in the U.S. have not made it a priority to level the playing field and help that would-be small restaurant or store owner. That we've allowed almost all the investment capital to get sucked into the grand-slam opportunities in Silicon Valley and other technology centers means we've basically left almost all of U.S. business in a lurch. Frankly, we have not even put this issue on the table for discussion.

Walmart Ate Main Street, and Now Amazon Is Taking Over

The discussion about why there are fewer startups than there used to be would not be complete without mentioning the maturing of businesses and corporate Darwinism that's changing the face of virtually every industry.

Take retail.

When I was a little kid in Ann Arbor, Michigan, I lived next door to George Wild, whose daughter Andrea was in my class at school. George owned and managed Wild's Men's Shop,[24] just as his father and grandfather had before him. This is where my dad, brother, and I all got our clothes. Nobody shops there now, because it's out of business.

My wife, Kathryn, grew up stocking shelves in one of her family's three drugstores in Berkeley, California, which were started by her great-grandfather and then run by her grandfather and finally her father. At a certain point, the "chain" of three stores that carried the family surname was sold by Kathryn's father, who was ready to retire. That turned out to be a great personal and business decision. Over time, the new owners couldn't compete with the big chains, and that was that. No more Walt Drugs.

Corporate Darwinism—benefiting Walmart, Costco, Sam's Club, and the like—has put a lot of Main Street Ma-and-Pa businesses out of business. As *The Atlantic* points out, "three drug stores—CVS, Walgreen's, and Rite Aid—own 99 percent of the national market. Two companies—Amazon and Barnes & Noble—sell half of the country's books. If it is not quite a new Gilded Age for America's monopolies, it is certainly a new dawn for its oligopolies."[25]

Now these predators are facing Amazon, the faster, cheaper, and more convenient solution for customers.

That's retail's story. Most business sectors in this country can tell a similar one.

Concentrations of capital and the efficiency of having publicly traded real estate investment trusts (REITs) or other types of public companies have made apartment ownership, like many other forms of real estate, a situation in which the big have a sizable advantage over the medium or small. Eventually, the smaller business usually gets crushed, either becoming absorbed into a bigger company or just getting driven out of business. This changing of the guard has some definite advantages for the consumer, including lower-priced products. That said, we need to realize that it's also changing the fabric of our communities. So we need to ask ourselves as a country whether we want to do something to level the playing field. Since our communities, economy, and, I believe, part of our soul as a country, rely on entrepreneurship, do we want to provide some incentives to small startup companies? If you have a new restaurant or a new local business, you're not exactly on everybody's hot list, so it's pretty hard to raise money. And yet our communities need those startups, so perhaps we ought to think about providing incentives to make that happen.

There are several ways to turn things around, a few of which we'll discuss in this book. But they all start with admitting that we're in trouble. If you're drinking too much but you don't want to admit that you're an alcoholic, you're not going to get better. Similarly, if we don't recognize that we have a problem, U.S. entrepreneurship will continue to struggle rather than thrive. And that's going to seriously cost us on many levels.

CHAPTER 2

Startups Should Be Booming!

Do you want to know the crazy part of this whole entrepreneurial equation?

We have never been better positioned to succeed as a country, in part because we are in what is clearly a very transitional time in terms of technologies leading to changes in almost every industry. A groundswell of positive entrepreneurship is right there, just below the surface. Indeed, we are set to boom if we embrace and encourage broad-based startups launched by a broad base of people, especially since some of these potential newbies will inevitably create innovations that improve our standard of living and economic well-being. But instead of soaring, traditional entrepreneurship in this country is just limping along, which makes the problem all the more concerning.

Ironically, the tools to start a new business have been improving even as startups have been declining over recent decades. While the culture of innovation and technology has a dark side, it also offers a potential revolution of opportunity. At many levels, technology, assuming entrepreneurs tap it, allows them the ability to run businesses more efficiently and more economically than in the past. I know that from personal experience.

What a Difference!

In 1985, when my company owned more than seventy-two thousand apartments across the United States, we had huge problems keeping control of all of it. There was no such thing as technology that could give us real-time information. We didn't even have a property management accounting system that could let us know how various properties were doing.

We obviously needed to fix that. You can't run a business if you can't get an accurate financial picture of what's going on. So in 1985, we decided to develop a system that would allow us to manage the accounting process for all the apartments that we owned. It took 160 people working full time to develop that software and cost more than $10 million (the equivalent of close to $24 million in 2018). Today, you can buy a software package for $10,000 that does a faster, better job than what they came up with. You might even be able to find a comparable software program online for free.

Over the past three decades in particular, technology and the internet have enabled companies to become bigger and actually manage their inventories and their financials on a real-time basis. That has helped promote the overall consolidation of industries that, coupled with automation and globalization, has stripped away jobs in certain areas, displaced entire industries, and eliminated many small businesses that are no longer needed. On the plus side, however, technology has dramatically increased productivity and our standard of living.

Along the way, it has also made starting new, job-creating businesses a whole heck of a lot easier. Financial systems that collect information from disparate locations required major efforts twenty, thirty, forty years ago. Today, you don't have to have a lot of employees. Thanks to technology, you can do a lot of things with very few people. And thanks to email and electronic filing, you can even save on the cost of paper and postage.

That's just the start of how much the world has changed when it comes to starting or running a company.

Architectural Automation and Virtual Reality

We live in a time of phenomenal change that's incredibly exciting. Not only has technology made doing business cheaper, but technology changes have improved the quality of products and services in a multitude of industries. Take the architectural industry. Not long ago, architects would create and draw architectural designs by hand. Today they sit in front of computers and move walls and change the number of floors in a building in seconds. My company's team members often end up with three or four architects sitting in a room literally designing a building on a screen right then and there. While we all watch the design ideas materialize and look at the different proportions of the building, the lead design architect tells the technician what to change and we instantly get to see that.

That automation could impact the field in a very human way. I have heard lead architects in the largest firms talk about how in the next five to ten years, the number of architects will be greatly reduced, as machines will do more and more of what they're currently doing. Due to new startup programs and artificial intelligence, a lot of work in creative areas can increasingly be handled without the human touch that at first glance seems essential. Machines aren't just rendering architectural drawings, for example; they're doing everything from determining the color palette to optimizing the layout of a space.

As a result, technology has revolutionized everything about the way we build.

Adjacent to a new luxury hotel my company is constructing in Dallas, we are also building an exclusive twenty-eight-story, fifty-home residential tower. As we're erecting what will be the highest-quality condominium building ever built in Dallas, we are doing things that just a few years ago we wouldn't have even conceived. For example, cameras on the roof of our adjacent office building look down at the construction site. So 24/7 we can see everyone working on the site as well as the two cranes that are hoisting large tools, steel, concrete, and other building materials. We have a permanent second-by-second record of everything that is going on in terms of construction at this site. The cost of this new technology was zero for us, as the company that's developing it wanted to use our building as a marketing sample. We're told the cost might have been something in the range of $90,000 for the full three years of construction—a bargain by any standard.

This kind of technological advancement extends past construction and into sales and marketing. Let's say you're trying to sell an apartment that's still being constructed. In the past, you could rely only on drawings and models to see what the building was going to look like inside and out. Today, my company can help buyers of our high-rise homes experience what it would be like to live in their residence-to-be. Using virtual reality glasses, they can do a partial walk-through. Even more impactful, if they want to see the view from the master bedroom on the twenty-second floor—*boom*, we've got it. We have a drone that shot the views from every terrace, living room and master bedroom in the building. A year or two ago, all of this was totally unaffordable, but the price has already come down, and in another year or two it'll be even cheaper. We have a large interactive screen that provides virtual answers to many of a prospect's questions before they're even asked. As more and more people take advantage of being able to communicate with potential clients in this way, sales and marketing will improve, which will help new entrepreneurs progress quickly in the development world.

More Unbelievable Advances

Yes, real estate is changing dramatically, which is ironic because, like wine, which we'll talk about later in this chapter, it has been a fairly archaic, staid kind of business. Over the decades, what it takes to build an office park has changed very little. That said, people today are looking at new technology to help them improve the quality, speed, and hopefully price of construction.

Take the type of glass used on jobsites. Not long ago, the big considerations were single, double, or triple pane, or perhaps whether you wanted interior glass instead of drywall. Now glass is getting to be smart.

These days you can install glass that at any moment can adjust its darkness, thereby improving how much heat or coolness is transferred through the pane. You can program the glass to change with the weather, or you can control it from your iPhone. Interestingly, the technology is not new; it was actually invented fifty years ago. What's new is the technology that has enabled scaling it, refining the quality, and dropping the price. This glass still costs more than traditional glass, but those costs will continue to come down. I believe there will be a time when all glass will be created this way.

And this is just the beginning. Transparent television screens embedded into glass now allow you to watch a movie on one glass panel and the stock exchange on the other without anyone on the outside knowing that you're watching anything at all.

Before long, glass will also become your security alarm, since, thanks to facial recognition, your glass will know who is entering the premises. It will even get to know you in order to help you organize your life. And you'll be able to talk to it, just like you talk to Alexa, Siri, and Google Home.

Artificial Intelligence

If this sort of robotics-meets-artificial intelligence reminds you of *The Jetsons*, just wait until you hear what's in store when it comes to transportation. In July 2018, my company worked with local private-sector partners, the city, and a local multicounty agency to launch the nation's first autonomous on-demand car service in Frisco, Texas.[1] The car scans the area, so it knows what that location should look like. If an object comes into view that's not consistent with that area, like a person walking in front of the car, it knows to stop. While the car has a form of radar, so to speak, it also has the ability to read colors, so it can tell if a traffic light is red, green, or yellow. So far, so cool, right? But wait. This car actually learns every day, so, like younger drivers, it gets better over time. It not only constantly picks up new information as it's driving, it learns even when it's not on the road. At night all the newly acquired information gets sent back to Silicon Valley and is shared with the other cars. Of course, all the other cars are doing the same thing. So every day, the entire fleet of cars gets smarter and smarter when it comes to driving ability. That's more than we can say about a lot of humans' driving ability. And the cars never drink.

Over time, this kind of artificial intelligence will handle more and more of the workload in more and more fields. After analyzing two thousand-plus work activities for more than eight hundred occupations across the U.S. in 2016, worldwide management consulting firm McKinsey & Company "showed that currently demonstrated technologies could automate 45 percent of the activities people are paid to perform and that about 60 percent of all occupations could see 30 percent or more of their constituent activities automated, again with technologies available today."[2]

A McKinsey & Company study the following year assessed the impact of automation on the workforce and forecast that by 2030, almost a third of American workers—which translates to some seventy million people—will need to train for another occupation.[3,4] In fact, 65 percent of today's elementary school students will end up in a career that doesn't exist yet.[5]

This colossal shift will dramatically change startups' needs as well as the startups themselves. And it's right around the corner.

As truck drivers and taxi drivers begin losing their jobs to autonomous vehicles, and other industries suffer job losses in favor of artificial intelligence, there will be a great need for new forms of employment. Since startups generate all net new jobs, we need to prepare for the dramatic changes that are coming. We also need to prepare for the next recession and the one after that, since the current excessive amounts of government and corporate debt will help to squeeze out other forms of borrowing. It's critical now more than ever that we foster an environment that encourages startup creation.

Accelerated Change

Clearly, applications of the technological changes we've discussed in this chapter will increasingly impact every industry. As of today, however, perhaps no industry has been more dramatically transformed than the wine industry.

I often look at the five-thousand-year-old wine industry and say that in the past five years and perhaps in the upcoming ten or fifteen years, we will have more change than in the preceding 4,990 years. Hopefully this will allow us to deliver a higher-quality product at a more reasonable price.

It used to be that everyone talked about how they handpicked the grapes and very carefully put them into the fermentation tanks. Sounds romantic and great, doesn't it?

Now here's the truth: Machines are being developed that can sort grapes more quickly, gently, and with greater accuracy than humans can. It used to be that at HALL Wines, six to eight people would stand alongside a conveyor belt and pick out the imperfect grapes. Then we bought a very smart machine that selects the grapes that match the exact criteria provided by our winemakers for the harvest from a particular area of the vineyard.

When the grapes that have just been picked land at the winery, the winemakers select two hundred of them that typify the characteristics they want for the juice from that vineyard block. Once the machine has logged the two hundred chosen samples, it goes through the rest of the batch as it's turned onto the conveyer belt and unerringly detects the grapes that don't fit the profile. A puff of air blows the discards, which will be used for making less expensive wines or sold to other wineries, off the conveyor belt.

While sadly this kind of automation eliminates jobs, it also eliminates the possibility of human error, allowing us to produce better wine more efficiently and at a lower cost. Well, maybe not exactly less expensively at this point. Like a lot of developments, early technology can be pricey, and that $400,000 machine wasn't exactly a money-saving move. In the long run, however, you can bet that prices will drop, and we already know that the quality will rise.

The dramatic changes related to how we conduct our wine business don't stop there. We have all kinds of new equipment that monitor each of the fermentation tanks, along with a lot of computers that keep records and allow us to get better and better all the time at production analysis. Every year in the vineyard operations and in the winemaking production area, we experiment with new ideas and methodologies to improve the quality of our wine. These are proprietary, so I won't go into detail. Suffice it to say that our goal is to always be on the cutting edge of new techniques. This year, among other things, we're experimenting with different colors and types of shade cloth to shield certain parts of the vineyards from the sun. We're also testing new machines and equipment that can potentially pick grapes better than humans and then sort them in the vineyard, which will change all of the developments I described above that are only a few years old. The bottom line is that exciting new machines and equipment are being developed for the wine industry, just as in other industries, and our vineyard and production operations will never be the same.

Actually, the whole vineyard operation is already in the process of being transformed. Eventually, through satellites and other technology, we will be able to water each vine separately so that it receives the optimum amount of water. We can monitor the sunlight and ascertain when to cut which leaf in order to perfect the amount of sun and nutrients that each vine gets. Again, the whole process will lead to a much higher-quality, better-tasting wine.

These changes even extend past production. On the promotion front, for example, the internet in many industries, including wine, has lessened the value of the middleman. It used to be that several people put their hands into the pricing of any given product before it reached the consumer. These distributors and middlemen, consolidated though they may be, are still serving some purpose in the wine business, but more and more high-end luxury wines are being sold directly to consumers. This enables those higher-quality wines to be offered at a lower price, a win for both the consumer and the producer.

How does all of this impact the new entrepreneur who aspires to enter the wine business? A lot of improvements in the growing and production of wine that simply didn't exist five years ago will be taken for granted. Meanwhile, smaller wineries can be more profitable by using efficient systems and avoiding the middleman in the distribution chain. This will allow those who otherwise would not have fit into the traditional producer-distributor-retailer model, or three-tier system, as we call it, to get into the business and stay in it by making profits—even in this traditionally labor- and input-intensive industry.

On the other hand, in the short run these new technologies, while helpful, can also be a big minus for the aspiring entrepreneur entering the wine business. Today, they are expensive and, like other trends in the wine industry (which I will discuss in later chapters), are a barrier to entry, since it's harder for most startups to fund these machines that aren't absolutely necessary but are eminently desirable. While this new, fancy equipment may ultimately yield an economic benefit, we've invested in it purely for quality purposes. Not everyone can afford to do that, especially not someone just getting into the business. So for the smaller aspiring entrepreneur in the wine business looking to make a high-end, quality wine, the buy-in may be a lot more expensive than it used to be. That's just an unfortunate byproduct of all the technology changes.

The internet and the fact that we can apply technology to almost any process today are clearly changing our world. Dramatically. Those changes aren't just impacting how we've done business in the past. The internet, artificial intelligence, robotics, and biotech are creating opportunities for entrepreneurs to create new applications for these technological advances, which has created increasing numbers of new opportunities.

That can be a plus or minus for entrepreneurs. These days, you clearly can't rely on yesterday's market, especially if you're a traditional or nontechnology entrepreneur and happen to be interested in going into the retail business. Technology has sent a whole lot of that online, and Amazon is growing a lot faster than you can grow on Main Street. On the other hand, new opportunities are springing up as old ones are getting destroyed. And while they absolutely rely on today's trailblazing technology, they don't necessarily have to be cutting edge conceptually to work. They just have to fill a need faster, cheaper, and better.

Creative Destruction

While technology has helped big companies get bigger and driven a lot of smaller ones out of business by bringing about change and consolidation at warp speed, it has also created niches for startups to create products and/or services that apply technology to old-school industries.

That's called creative destruction. Take the buggy whip. You didn't need buggy whips when cars began to replace carriages. So the advent of the car made the buggy whip business go bust. That was the last kind of business you wanted to be in, let alone start up, because there weren't a lot of people buying buggy whips. But think of all the automotive-related manufacturing and sales companies that have sprung up since then.

Today we're seeing a number of innovations cause other businesses to go out of business. Thanks to Amazon, starting up a bookstore on Main Street is not the smartest idea today. That ship has sailed, at least for now. On the other hand, from big ideas that add convenience to our lives to big ideas that will change marketplaces, web-based applications are now springing up for every need imaginable.

In June 2015, for example, former winemaker Ashley Dubois Leonard launched InnoVint, a cloud-based wine production software that allows winemakers to enter data in real time using mobile devices in order to streamline the production process and quickly gather analytics and insights. In the past, winemakers have just jotted down notes on whatever paper they had handy. Excel spreadsheets were about as sophisticated as it got. But Ashley's InnoVint software helps them track every bit of information—from how the grapes in a specific vineyard block were grown to how the wine from those exact grapes was produced. Ashley is now working on a vineyard program to cover the entire season, from when the grapes start to grow through to the harvest. That program will tie in to the winery production software she has already created. This will take out a lot of the guesswork involved in making high-quality wine.

InnoVint, along with a host of other tools designed to help control vineyards and winemaking, is typical of what's happening in a lot of industries today. There are all kinds of similar processes being developed for any kind of factory-type operation. The same documentation and systems integration that InnoVint provides for wineries will be developed for craft beer and hundreds of other industries. Whether InnoVint or any given company is going to be the winner in that area is not the point. The point is that across the board, entrepreneurs are going to create the answers to streamline workflow and production processes.

That's exactly what Frank Mycroft did when he used a computer app to help service an old-fashioned industry, something I found out about through a phone call toward the end of 2015.

"Craig, it's Ross," the voice on the other end of the phone announced. Ross Perot Jr. is a friend of mine and a great entrepreneur and investor. As usual, he got right to the point.

"There's this Seattle rocket scientist I know who has created an on-demand fuel service called Booster. It could be great for your Frisco office park. I'm investing, and I thought you might want to as well."

Ross is really smart when it comes to investments, so I immediately checked out the opportunity. I discovered that Frank Mycroft had designed cool-looking gasoline trucks that fill up at the same place that the big tankers fill up. Then they come to you. When you need gas, you just leave your gas tank unlocked and use the app on your phone to let them know what you want. GPS tells them where you are. When they reach your parked car, they not only fill your tank for the same amount you would spend at a regular gas station without your having to pump the gas, but they'll even wash your windows. Talk about a new convenience that improves quality of life!

Booster couldn't have existed even ten years ago. Still, the technology that the business relies on isn't exactly groundbreaking, since we all use phones to order products and services, and GPS to get to and from locations. Booster is also modeled on not one but two very traditional businesses—gas stations and trucking. And yet, as Booster has demonstrated, there's a lot of money to be made by meeting a need or solving a problem in a new way.

Similarly, Patrick Brandt, along with cofounder Aakash Kumar, has built a company called Shiftsmart, which essentially helps connect workers with the new economy of the part-time job. Every thinkable variety of employer, from hospitals to attorneys' offices to factories to transportation, is looking to hire people for a partial shift on a certain day, at a certain time. Shiftsmart matches those employers with workers looking for job opportunities. It seems simple and logical, and yet before Patrick and Aakash, this service didn't exist.

Shiftsmart's idea of connecting company needs and worker needs clearly depends on the use of technology. Interestingly, the company's customer base originally consisted of large technology companies like HP, Google, DoorDash, and Postmates. As it turns out, Booster's early adopters are also large technology companies. The tech giants get it. They understand that the world is changing and that there are a lot of new ways to meet old demands, and they're willing to experiment.

Revolutionary Times

In the age of technology, everything is changing so quickly that it's hard to keep up. Even simple signs for businesses are poised for a total metamorphosis. After I gave a recent speech on entrepreneurship, one of the people in the audience came up and introduced himself. I quickly realized that Daniel Black is a very smart young man, so I made a date to meet with him at my office. I really liked his idea. Daniel had taken an old business—signage—and turned it on its head by using technology in a whole new way.

"Think about a restaurant," he told me, as I recall. "They write down the morning specials on a blackboard, then erase it and put the lunch menu dishes, then turn around and do it all over again for dinner. Day after day after day. What if you had a projection-powered display sign that you could change by computer whenever you needed to?"

After he met with me, I introduced Daniel to Bryan Tolbert, one of HALL Group's executives, who, among other things, handles our limited number of angel-round investments. Eventually, even though Daniel hadn't come looking for backing, we ended up investing in his company, Glass-Media.

As a side note, when Daniel and I first met, we talked a bit about entrepreneurship and his experience. He actually knew a lot about the Silicon Valley area, where he had worked at one point. He said there was no question that had he stayed there, it would have been much easier to get funding for his business. As it turns out, it had been really difficult to get funding in Dallas, which is a lot better on that front than other parts of the country.

Daniel is one of the exceptions when it comes to the average aspiring entrepreneur. He had enough grit, knowledge, and heart to work and hang on until he was well along the curve to making it. So I was only too happy to get involved and fund him. But as he and I both discussed, the funding circumstances made getting his business off the ground exceedingly difficult.

I'm happy to report that Daniel's Glass-Media is taking off. As you might imagine, the ability to change a sign at a moment's notice works for a lot more businesses than just restaurants. Not only will it improve their marketing, it will save a lot of them a significant amount of money. Of course, the more Daniel's idea takes hold, the worse sign-making businesses will fare.

In the big picture, we may be entering a time when more and more technology ends an increasing number of today's job needs. There's no question that driverless trucks, for example, will hurt the three and a half million truck drivers.[6] On the other hand, the fact that we can apply technology to almost any process today and improve it means that as a society, we have the potential for a rising tide that will lift us all.

Startup Promise and Reality

We've barely scratched the surface when it comes to using recently invented technologies to create small niche opportunities. If one has ideas to make the world a little more productive or a better place to live, there are always people who will appreciate them, just as they appreciate the services of Booster, or the filling of very important needs such as connecting workers and employers like Shiftsmart does.

Considering that we're just beginning to identify niches for applying technology, thousands of business ideas will come into being that were either never out there at all or that were out there but weren't as good. Out of those should come many, many small businesses, especially as a lot of technology is now available at virtually no cost. So opening the businesses themselves is a whole lot easier than it used to be.

In most business startups, not only is the cost of entry lower compared to years ago, but the cost of failure is lower as well. While that may sound negative, it's not. Many entrepreneurs start out with one sense of direction and end up changing several times before they find a formula or an idea that turns out to be successful. That's just a reality. Silicon Valley's mantra, for example, isn't "Don't fail." It's "Fail fast"—so you can quickly move on to the big idea that will really hit. Luckily, for a smaller amount of money these days, you can try an idea and, if it doesn't quite work out as planned, have more latitude to pivot and change to another.

With all of these technological opportunities and cost-effective improvements, you would think that entrepreneurship would be booming. Instead, it is not. In fact, the number of startups in 2018 is substantially lower than before the start of the Great Recession more than ten years ago. Despite the ability to do things faster, cheaper, and better, the system remains stacked against Main Street startups in favor of unicorns. Despite the excitement and interest in *Shark Tank* and the numerous nonprofits and educational programs in existence today, we are still facing a significant shortage of new startups.

Technology could and should be applied to help startups save money and reduce risk. We need to make it easier for the Daniels of the world to start their businesses because there is so much need and there are so many great ideas and talented folks to get them done.

The Kauffman Foundation, a charitable organization dedicated to promoting economic independence through entrepreneurship, does a great deal to help encourage startup activity in 170 countries, including the United States. Ewing Marion Kauffman believed in education and entrepreneurship, and that having the ability to turn a big idea into a business was a fundamental right. When he sold his generic pharmaceutical business for $6 billion, he sunk $2 billion into the Kauffman Foundation. As the leading research source on entrepreneurship, the Kauffman Foundation addresses the subject through three initiatives:

- Individual learning and how the foundation can help individual entrepreneurs
- Communities and ecosystems for entrepreneurship
- "Bridging gaps" (sound familiar?) by funding entrepreneurship grants

In 2012, the organization launched its 1 Million Cup program in Kansas City, Missouri. It's "based on the notion that entrepreneurs discover solutions and engage with their communities over a million cups of coffee.... 1 Million Cups works with entrepreneurs, empowering them with the tools and resources to break down barriers that stand in the way of starting and growing their businesses."[7] Now, only six years later, 180 communities feature the free program that's designed to educate, engage, and inspire entrepreneurs around the country. When I visited the organization in 2018, Vice President of Entrepreneurship Victor W. Hwang explained that during the meetings, entrepreneurs talk about what they're doing, and other entrepreneurs give them feedback.

"We call it 'Shark Tank without the edge,'" he said.

Other programs include an online, self-paced FastTrac curriculum, which provides "multiple tools to help you think about your business, including a Canvas tool, a planning template and a financial forecasting workbook,"[8] and a free online playbook for building, nurturing, and growing entrepreneurial ecosystems.[9]

I recently visited the Kauffman Foundation's headquarters in Kansas City. After Victor Hwang described its robust research program (the largest for entrepreneurship in the country) to the group I was part of, he noted that Kauffman's research shows that positive growth in entrepreneurship is directly correlated with the reduction in inequality in our country.

After Victor's comments, I had only a little time before another meeting to corner him privately for more detail.

"What does your research show regarding why entrepreneurship is declining?" I asked.

His answer?

"That's the million-dollar question we can't answer yet."

You would think that the news about the decline of U.S. entrepreneurship impacting jobs would make national headlines. Instead, as Victor pointed out, you hardly ever hear about entrepreneurship in terms of these realities. No wonder so many people react with disbelief when I ask their thoughts about the decline in startups. Most are under the impression that the U.S. is doing great in terms of entrepreneurship. To Albert Einstein's point, we need to spend much more time and effort defining the problem before we'll be able to solve it.

I've spent the past seven years trying to understand the problems we are facing in the U.S. in terms of entrepreneurship and to come up with possible solutions. The latter starts with defining our terms and being clear that micro-entrepreneurship and entrepreneurship are not the same thing.

Micro-Entrepreneurship

Whether by choice or financial necessity, many people are participating in a variety of part-time micro-entrepreneurial activities today. To make ends meet or for a little extra cushion, people sell things on eBay. People rent their homes on Airbnb. People drive for Uber and/or Lyft. There is an explosion of part-time, 1099 work going on that is arguably entrepreneurial.

These self-employed go-getters are not whom I'm talking about in this book. Clearly, despite decades of declining startup growth, the spirit of Americans to be entrepreneurial is alive and well. That doesn't mean, however, that we don't have serious problems when it comes to U.S. entrepreneurship. Those problems are varied, nuanced, and anything but simple. Look beyond the myriad of details, however, and you'll find two key deficiencies: first, the capital for traditional non-tech startups, and second, the confidence to jump in and take risks.

As you will read, I have a lot of thoughts as to why, despite many positives in the entrepreneurial environment, we have not yet reached the tipping point to turn around the decline we're seeing in startups. In the next chapters, I'll offer some analyses of the two key deficiencies and other challenges facing American startups.

CHAPTER 3

Entrepreneurs Make the World Go Round

Why should we care about all of this? Entrepreneurship is the backbone of not just our free-enterprise system but of the U.S. as a whole. The impact of entrepreneurship on our country's way of life and economic well-being helps explain why we should care about how U.S. startups and small businesses are faring. Especially since, as we've already seen, the picture isn't pretty.

So again, why does that matter?

For starters, consider that many of the innovations that have improved and simplified our daily lives have come from entrepreneurs starting small businesses that grew.

Our Changing World: Computers, Phones, and Electric Cars

To get a better idea of how this directly impacts our lives, let's look at three household-name entrepreneurs who have overhauled how we live and do business.

Microsoft's Bill Gates, one of three kids in an upper-middle-class Washington family, discovered computers when his parents, concerned about his apparent boredom and withdrawn behavior, enrolled him in private school at the age of thirteen. There he was introduced to the endless possibilities inherent in computers. He also met fellow computer enthusiast Paul Allen, a student two years his senior. Those two events would change his life and ours.

Gates and Allen, who both dropped out of college, wound up founding Microsoft after contacting a small computer company to gauge its interest in a BASIC software program they were developing. The call had been intended as a trial balloon to find out if the company might bite at the idea in the future. Instead, the company bit then and there, requesting a demonstration. The two friends, then in their mid-twenties, scrambled to come up with the program. It worked. Soon after, in 1975, they founded a company that a year later would be known as Microsoft. Having dreamed of a time when every desk and every home could have a personal computer, they created a myriad of programs that have become critical components of how life is led and business is done. [1]

Apple's Steve Jobs didn't make it through college either. Adopted by a blue-collar San Francisco couple shortly after his birth, he grew up in Mountain View, a future hub of the area that would become known as Silicon Valley. His birth mother had made Jobs' adoptive parents promise that he would go to college, but higher education proved less than gratifying for a boy who was a self-admitted terror in school as a child. Four years after dropping out of Reed College, where he completed just one quarter, he cofounded Apple with Steve Wozniak. The resulting user-friendly products, like the iPad and the iPhone, turned computing into on-the-go technology for work and play.

You can't talk about revolutionary on-the-go products without mentioning Tesla's Elon Musk, whose companies focus on things as wide-ranging as electric vehicles, aerospace manufacture, space-transport services, artificial intelligence research, and brain-computer interfaces. Future endeavors already being tested include rocket-propelled cars that can fly, friction- and air-resistance-free pods to speed up passenger and freight travel, and supersonic jet electric aircraft that can take off and land vertically. The stated goal of this visionary—who, after graduating college with a double major in economics and physics, dropped out of Stanford grad school after just two days—is nothing less than changing the world as we know it.

Sometimes it's hard to remember that these tech giants all started out as small entrepreneurs. But, like other entrepreneurs who have come before them and who have followed them, their innovations have and will continue to massively improve the way we live. Let's face it. Without entrepreneurs, we wouldn't have a lot of the modern inventions and technological breakthroughs we have all come to depend on. Not that long ego, industrial manufacturing breakthroughs led to our replacing horse-drawn carriages with cars made on assembly lines. Pretty soon, thanks to technological developments in the works, those cars will drive themselves and we won't even have to get behind the wheel. The cars will just come and pick us up when we need them.

Restricting entrepreneurship means fewer innovations like these that can enhance our quality of life. So does the weakening and/or disappearance of small businesses. According to the SBA, "Of high patenting firms (fifteen or more patents in a four-year period), small businesses produced 16 times more patents per employee than large patenting firms."[2]

But innovation is far from the only benefit associated with entrepreneurship.

Jobs, Jobs, and More Jobs

In 2014, according to U.S. Census Bureau data, there were 5.83 million employer firms in the United States.[3]

- Firms with fewer than five hundred workers accounted for 99.7 percent of those businesses.[4]

- Firms with fewer than twenty workers made up 89.4 percent of businesses.[5]

"New businesses are disproportionately responsible for the innovation that drives productivity and economic growth," stated John Dearie, president of the Center for American Entrepreneurship (CAE), a nonpartisan research, policy, and advocacy organization, a few years back when he was executive vice president for policy at the Financial Services Forum.

We will need 11.5 million new jobs by 2026, according to the U.S. Bureau of Labor Statistics.[6] As we already know, research by the Kauffman Foundation found that from 1980 to 2005, firms less than five years old accounted for all net job growth.[7] That means that productivity and job growth are singularly dependent on new entrepreneurs.

A 2010 U.S. Census Bureau Center for Economic Studies paper titled "Who Creates Jobs? Small vs. Large vs. Young" confirms the key role that business startups and young businesses play when it comes to generating jobs in our country.

In a way, that's nothing particularly new. When Henry Ford launched the mass production of cars in 1914, offering workers five dollars a day (double the average factory wage in those days), he put fourteen thousand men to work and America on the road. In the process, he also set the groundwork for what would become the middle class.

Ford Motor Company would go on to become a giant, employing more than two hundred thousand people at some ninety plants and facilities worldwide, one hundred years after its inception. That's a lot of jobs.

Would Ford have gotten his company off the ground in today's environment? I'm not so sure, which is exactly why I'm so distressed about what's happening with U.S. entrepreneurship. Dearie's latest message rings that alarm bell loud and clear when he states, "If new businesses are the engine of net new job creation, and if new businesses are the engine of innovation, and new business creation is at 30-year lows, that's a national emergency."[8]

Tax Base

The bad news related to the decline of entrepreneurship doesn't stop there. Not only is entrepreneurship a job creator, it's a tax-base creator. The public gets a piece of any and all business. An individual making a salary pays taxes. A company making a profit pays taxes. If you build a building on raw land, the new building will be assessed at a much higher tax rate than the land, which means greater property tax revenue for various taxing authorities.

In one way or another, all those entrepreneurial startup ventures that employ people create new assets and make profits that increase the tax base. That allows us to have safety services, education, and many other amenities—including art—that enhance the quality of life, along with other basic services that we're all used to. Obviously, the more people who work and pay taxes, and the more companies that exist and pay taxes, the larger a community's tax base will be. So the government is essentially a partner in—and profits from—the success of new ventures, which means the public gets a piece of any business's success. Less entrepreneurship equals less tax revenue, which negatively impacts the quality of life for all of us.

Buying Local

The loss of local startups and small businesses impacts our communities even more directly. When a consumer buys locally, significantly more of that money stays in the community. A study conducted in Chicago by a firm called Civic Economics found that only $43 of every $100 spent at a chain stayed in the city, as opposed to $68 when that $100 was spent at a local establishment.[9] In addition, local business owners often have an incentive to support other local businesses, patronizing them for both business and personal reasons. On the flip side, chain businesses tend to get their supplies from corporate. Less money in the community means less money for improvements.

Community Well-Being

The buck actually doesn't stop there. Entrepreneurs strengthen local and regional economies for one simple reason. Instead of redistributing wealth, they create new companies and new revenue, which helps combat poverty. In addition, entrepreneurs give back. They reinvest in the community through charitable giving, community support, leadership, and in many other ways, supporting a virtuous cycle that creates and or enhances vibrant communities. Unfortunately, that's not happening as much as it used to.

A Cure to Our Growing Income Divide

When my parents got out of the Navy, they had no nest egg of money. They were enlisted sailors without a college education. Although my father's family had money before the war, their business depended on German imported materials. During the war, they lost their business and all of their money, and his parents divorced. So he couldn't exactly depend on them for financial support.

In short order after the war, my folks got married, got jobs, and had my brother and, later, me. Despite many challenges and the postwar rebuilding of society, I was brought up like many to believe that my generation, the baby boomers, would live better lives than our very hard-working parents, and that my children's generation would do even better.

Hope and opportunity are the currency of a growing middle class and the foundation of the American dream. Entrepreneurship can help cultivate this. And yet, as our economy and society have drifted into a greater divide between haves and have-nots, we have seen our middle class shrink. We have seen our politics become divisive as we look for easy answers and all go to our own corners and reinforce our own views.

The truth is, there is no silver bullet to eliminate America's income divide and its implications. But a broader base and the renewal of opportunities for people to become entrepreneurs and start businesses would be a huge step in the right direction.

Life, Liberty, and the Pursuit of Entrepreneurship

Healthy, brand-based entrepreneurship is a question not just of community well-being but of our country's well-being and the protection of our founding principles. There is an inextricable tie between freedom and opportunity in our society. The ability to own one's own home, the ability to own property, and the ability to start one's own business are all critical to the American experience and to the whole idea of liberty and the pursuit of happiness.

Entrepreneurship is all about having dreams and not taking no for an answer. For me, it was also about doing things in those early days that I wouldn't think of doing today, in large measure because I didn't know any better.

Take Knob on the Lake, a property in Belleville, Michigan, that I noticed in 1974 when I was twenty-four years old on my way to catch a plane and go on vacation. It was probably the biggest property I had ever seen. It had marinas on the lake, a golf course going through the property and, I would later learn, 1,145 apartment units—a huge number of which were clearly vacant. At the airport, I called my top managers of the company I had created six years earlier using a pay phone, since cell phones then were just a science fiction dream.

"This is going to be our next acquisition," I announced, even though it wasn't for sale.

They thought I was crazy. They were probably right. We certainly had no money for a down payment.

Had I known then what I know now, I would have realized how stupid it was for me to go out and try to buy a $25 million building with nothing down.

Instead, as soon as I got back from vacation, I began the quest to purchase Knob on the Lake. After finding out who the owner was, I tried to set up a meeting with him. No luck. So I tried again, and again, and again. Ultimately, I got an appointment to see the elusive Frank Volk. He was seventy-nine years old and I was twenty-four years old, so we didn't exactly have a lot in common.

The first meeting didn't go well. To be more precise, he threw me out. The second, third, and fourth meetings weren't a whole lot better. By the time I got a fifth meeting, I had done my homework. I knew that Volk was in great financial distress over the property. His long building career was in trouble, and this property could have put him into bankruptcy.

"You have six mortgages that are all in default, and the lenders are about to foreclose," I told him. "On top of that, you owe more than $1.6 million to trade creditors." Then I convinced him that I had a plan to save him, and that if it succeeded, I would pay him a bunch of money. He had to trust me, because I was his only hope. So he sold me the property, which I renamed Lemon Tree (since everyone said I had bought a lemon) for $25 million with nothing down except a $300,000 note that would become valid only if I worked out all the loans.

That's when my great team and I really went to work. By the end of 1975, we had raised $3.3 million in equity, negotiated resolutions to all six mortgages, and come to a resolution with each of the trade creditors, all without filing bankruptcy. It sounds a lot easier now than it actually was. In reality, the process entailed months of agony and a lot of sleepless nights. But by working with the various lenders and creditors in a reasonable manner using reason, logic, and facts—while trying to understand their positions—we managed to come up with workable solutions.

Once I took over Knob on the Lake, other challenges popped up. The first weekend after I bought it, we got hit with a big snowstorm. Of course, I didn't have any money, but the snow had to be removed from this enormous property. When the guy with the plow presented me with his bill for $5,000, I almost choked to death.

"Thank you for removing the snow," I said. "I'll get back to you on that bill."

Somehow, our team made it work. We had to. And we turned a dilapidated property into a viable one.

The risks I've taken over the past five decades have put me in a position to start numerous businesses and create more than ten thousand jobs. Those businesses that I've been honored to be part of have, for the most part, made a big difference in individuals' lives and in the communities my company and I have served. That's what a lot of entrepreneurs do.

Talk About Impact!

Some of us are born knowing that we want to make a positive and meaningful impact on our world as entrepreneurs. In hindsight, that may have been the case for me. While it took me well into my mid-twenties to realize that being an entrepreneur could also be a positive for society, for me—and likely for some others—becoming an entrepreneur was initially a way to overcome my lack of success as a student, as an athlete, and at other "normal" things. It provided a sense of freedom to control my own destiny and succeed or fail on my own efforts. In hindsight, I realize I took that opportunity for granted. Today, I realize how lucky I was to feel a sense of hope.

Roberto Rivera[10] didn't grow up with much of that. His father was an alcoholic who was abusive when he drank. As a second grader, Roberto was diagnosed as learning disabled, due to his language acquisition, which was determined to be "somewhat delayed." No one had bothered to find out if English was actually the primary language spoken at home. The label meant one thing to the Madison, Wisconsin, native: He was dumb and would never amount to anything.

"I internalized the LD label so profoundly that even when we moved from Madison to Texas and my transcripts were delayed, faced with the opportunity of being in regular classes, I self-selected to be in the remedial classes, because I thought I was truly slow," says Roberto.

Eventually, some older kids in the neighborhood told him he had good people skills and asked if he wanted to start "hustling" for them. His marijuana-selling career ended in eighth grade when his parents found out and had him arrested.

Roberto was on a dead-end path, but his grandfather saw promise in him, which eventually prompted Roberto to change his ways. Hip-hop culture helped him detox from the poisonous institutional racism he had ingested. Deciding to "hustle something legitimate," he began to design his own hip-hop-inspired line of clothing, drawing on the talents of a visual artist he knew, as well as the skills of someone who made clothing. While selling his T-shirts and hoodies at a concert, he met a man who was working with kids who wanted to learn about the hip-hop movement. Roberto became their guide, an involvement that morphed into concerts, festivals, and hip-hop theatrical productions.

That was just the start. Roberto decided that he wanted to use hip-hop to transform kids' educational experiences, hopefully turning at-risk kids into at-promise students. By then he had married a woman who was in graduate school to obtain her master's degree in public affairs. Together the two wrote a sixty-seven-page business plan for an innovative hip-hop-based curriculum, and a business was born. Their trial run involved students for whom nothing else had worked. "We've tried everything else under the sun," the school superintendent said. "Might as well try this hip-hoppity stuff."

"We worked with these students over the course of ten weeks to think critically about their role in the community through the lens of hip-hop and embrace their different types of intelligences," says Roberto. "Their project was to lead a schoolwide talent show and to emcee the event. We opened it up to the community. The students performed poems and raps and dances and monologues, created a plat-form for their peers. They got standing ovations for that, and the data showed that students' GPAs in all four classes we worked with went up half a percentile point, so 0.5 on a 4.0 GPA scale. The kids who were the most disengaged, their GPAs went up a full point, and attendance improved. Behavior issues in the school went down."

Over the years, Roberto continued to work with kids labeled unreachable, and as of this writing is wrapping up a PhD in educational psychology, focusing on post-traumatic growth in his work with youth. His words about that show the power of entrepreneurship to change our communities:

> With young people engaged in this way, we've seen young people go from attending school 50 percent of the time to 96 percent of the time. We've seen these students go on and become community leaders. They're engaged as being these agents of change in solutions instead of the problem.

What it does is it allows us to reach these young people, not as these objects that need to be changed, but to engage them as agents of change themselves. If the trauma and the pain can be converted into propane, then they can be empowered to provide solutions to different problems going on in their schools and their communities and in the nation.

My dream now is to transform public education in my lifetime. I sold my business on March 1, 2017, and now I'm an executive with the company, an equity partner, and I'm digitizing the curriculum. Now we're moving towards reaching millions of kids.

Clearly, being able to live one's dream doesn't just launch the kind of career I've had. It can turn around the lives of people who are decidedly less fortunate. Access to entrepreneurship and startup opportunities has allowed people to become better citizens as they have delivered goods and services, which in turn helps create better stability in our society. For every entrepreneur who succeeds despite the odds, however, there are a lot more who don't.

This is not a problem just for would-be entrepreneurs. It's a problem we all need to care about, and not just because the financial health of our country hangs in the balance. At its core, this issue involves questions of what is important and what we want in our society.

Until now, there has not been a real, meaningful dialogue about the opportunities versus roadblocks for entrepreneurship today, which ultimately explains in part why this crisis exists. We can and should proactively talk about what our values are in terms of entrepreneurship and fostering an environment in which people have a better chance of starting successful businesses. The alternative is to continue on our current path of being a very strong country when it comes to unicorns but faltering otherwise, with a declining number of startups per capita and a worse environment for Main Street entrepreneurs.

Carrie Kelleher Stein knows better than most how tough it can be to start up a small business. After being forced to drop out of high school and experiencing homelessness in her teenage years, she remained determined to succeed. She decided to go to the Dallas County Community

College District.[11] There, her own grit, combined with an inspirational teacher impacted her life and set her on a course of improving her learning skills. The community college made such a huge difference that she went on, first to the University of Texas at Austin, which she found to be too large for her, and then to night school at the University of Texas at Dallas. There she was exceptional at math, financial concepts, and research. Upon her graduation, the dean at the school made some introductions, and she was interviewed by Bank of America and then the Federal Reserve. The Federal Reserve of Dallas typically hires Harvard, Yale, Wharton, and Princeton types but made an exception for Carrie. For a local non-high school graduate to end up at the Federal Reserve in the research department was a big coup.

"I had to work extra hard every night and then call my old professors for advice to keep up with the others," Carrie recalls. "There were a lot of wicked-smart people there, but I made up for any deficit by working harder and finding the resources necessary to support the economists I had the privilege to work with and for."

Although she loved her time at the Federal Reserve, the job ultimately didn't satisfy her soul. So she switched to working in nonprofit and then to the corporate world to support her family.

When she turned forty, she decided that if she was ever going to realize her long-held dream of opening an eatery, she had to jump. So she dug up a business plan she had been noodling since she was nineteen, finished it, bought an abandoned building in her neighborhood, and fixed it up to make a community café.

Unlike so many entrepreneurs, Carrie didn't have an issue with capital. Like me, she's a supersaver. Not spending the money I made allowed me to buy my first apartment building. By living as frugally as possible, Carrie managed to pay off her house—her goal before launching a new venture—and bootstrap her way into her new business.

She finally made the leap in 2010, taking advantage of Section 179 of the tax code to help her get started.[12] That tax break alone saved Carrie about 40 percent of her startup costs. You'll also find buried in the tax code's seventy-four thousand pages[13] that in the year you launch your business, you can deduct $5,000 of your startup-related costs, including office supplies, legal fees, and fees for human resources and market research.[14] Too bad more aspiring entrepreneurs don't know about these breaks!

Still, it wasn't easy. As a single mother, Carrie had not only herself to consider but her young son and daughter as well. She worried about whether she could cope with being both a business owner and a mom. Luckily, she found out how resilient kids are. "I dragged my kids around, and they helped as we refinished the restaurant," she recalls. Even so, the lack of affordable childcare available to female entrepreneurs made it extremely difficult to balance the time and monetary investment needed to start a business with being a full-time parent.

"My children were in cots in the side room of the café during my early years, and the angst and stress I had with everything from transportation to homework help was crisis level for me as a single parent when I started my business," Carrie says. "I survived on tenacity more than anything else."

In 2010, Carrie opened Coffee House Café in Dallas. She couldn't pay herself for stretches that lasted months at a time, but she's still there today, serving three meals a day.

Of all the challenges that have arisen since, some of which you'll read about in the section about regulations, the challenges that come with starting a business as a mother are what she remembers most. Since Carrie and the man she subsequently married now have four children, the childcare issue remains top of mind. Regardless, as I write this she is planning her next move.

During a recent meeting with Carrie, she recalled my telling her a couple of years ago that she wasn't taking enough risk, an idea that a couple of other important mentors echoed. As you'll really understand by the end of this book, risk aversion is not my problem.

On the other hand, research shows that women appear to have less confidence in themselves when it comes to entrepreneurship, in great measure because they, along with people of color, aren't supported to gamble and fail the way white males are. As a result, Carrie hypothesized during our get-together, women like herself don't think big enough and don't take risks like they could or should.

Doyenne's Amy Gannon concurs. "It's not that women don't want to scale. It's not that they don't want to take risks. But they want to be in control, and they want to be clear about what's happening. Part of the reason for that is cultural training. Women are being held to a different standard culturally. When a white male fails, it's 'Yep, he's building his chops. He's getting practice.' When a woman or person of color fails, it's 'I told you they would.' Women feel they have far less latitude to fail, so they are hypervigilant about that. The ecosystem is less forgiving for them, and they internalize that pressure."

That's a problem, since risk-taking is a critical part of being an entrepreneur. Of course there are a lot of levels of risk tolerance. Still, it's hard to really have a big success without taking a significant risk.

The Immigrant Model

We would do well to model ourselves after immigrant entrepreneurs. Not only do immigrants tend to be bigger risk takers—witness the fact that they're willing to leave their homes behind and build a life in a completely new country—but they're often driven by the need to succeed.

Daniel Lubetzky—entrepreneur, philanthropist, and author of the *New York Times* bestseller *Do the KIND Thing*—launched his entrepreneurial career even earlier than I did. By the time he moved to the U.S. from Mexico at age sixteen, he had already started several businesses. He would go on to start several more, including KIND, among the fastest-growing snack companies in the country. Inspired by his father—who wound up in Mexico as a teenager after being rescued from the Dachau concentration camp—and his mother, *Lubetzky* believes that "you don't wait until you are old to help others; you do it all along." Accordingly, his business ventures all include a component for social good. "With so many challenges that we're facing and with business permeating our lives, it behooves us to find more ways to have an impact," the social entrepreneur told *AARP The Magazine*.

While stories about the acts of kindness that allowed his father to survive in a concentration camp helped forge Lubetzky's "not only for profit" approach to entrepreneurship, relocating to the U.S. helped fuel his business drive. "People immigrating to this country have an appreciation of all of the opportunities and the greatness that America brings, and so they fight hard for it," says *Lubetzky*, who in 2015 was named a presidential ambassador for global entrepreneurship by President Barack Obama and Commerce Secretary Penny Pritzker. "Immigrants don't really have a can-do attitude; it's a must-do attitude. You don't have another option. You have to survive."[15]

In entrepreneurship, I often say success is all about surviving until you thrive, something immigrants really understand. Maybe that explains why a 2017 study conducted by the Center for American Entrepreneurship found that "43 percent of the 2017 Fortune 500 were founded or co-founded by an immigrant or the child of an immigrant. The analysis also found that the occurrence of first- or second-generation immigrant founders is significantly higher among the largest Fortune 500 companies—accounting for 52 percent of the top twenty-five firms and 57 percent of the top 35 firms."[16]

The press release regarding the study goes on to point out that these striking results "should be carefully considered by policymakers as they continue to deliberate the fate of 800,000 so-called DREAMers—undocumented immigrants brought to the United States illegally as children—and U.S. immigration policy more generally. In particular, the analysis provides compelling support for the creation of an entrepreneur visa, an important aspect of the Startup Act, bipartisan legislation reintroduced by Senators Jerry Moran (R-KS) and Mark Warner (D-VA) on September 28, 2017."[17]

"The findings of our analysis, along with a vast research literature, demonstrate the remarkable and persistent importance of immigrants to the creation and growth of America's largest and most valuable companies," states Ian Hathaway, CAE's director of research, who led the analysis underlying the report. "Our work also shows that many of America's most iconic entrepreneurs migrated here from a wide range of geographic and socio-economic backgrounds—it is questionable whether some of them would have been allowed to come here under current policy."[18]

"Our nation's universities and startup ecosystem attract the best and brightest innovators from all over the world," says Blake Patton, founder of Tech Square Ventures in Atlanta, Georgia, and chairman of CAE's board of directors in the same media release. "We need immigration policies that enable us to keep that talent here to launch and grow startups that are the drivers of innovation, growth, and job creation in America."[19]

Meet Fernando De Leon, one of the most remarkable people I have ever encountered and a great contributor to society. Today, he directly employs more than two hundred people and, indirectly through his numerous other ventures, thousands more. In 2018, his company began construction on three thousand apartments. He has made a lot of money for a lot of other people throughout his career, while doing very well for himself. At age forty, he has accomplished far more than most people ever dream of. He is a highly successful entrepreneur. He is also a philanthropist who supports several local Dallas nonprofits. Put simply, he is the epitome of the American Dream.

Now let me tell you the story of how Fernando got to where he is today. One night over a long dinner, he explained to me that he was what we now call an "anchor baby." After having had six children before him, his mother, at the urging of many, crossed the border and gave birth to Fernando in the United States. They lived in Matamoros, Mexico, a town just across the border from Brownsville, Texas, where Fernando was born.

So, here was a young child who was a U.S. citizen by birth. His parents had since become citizens, as well as a number of his brothers and sisters. Fernando grew up dually in Brownsville, Texas—then the poorest county in the United States—and Matamoros, Mexico. His family worked hard in both cities. As Fernando grew up, he attended school twice a day in both the United States and Mexico—due to his parents' encouragement as well as his own desire. In short, he worked very hard to get a great education. When it came time for Fernando to take the SAT exams in high school, he got a perfect score. Coming from a city that normally does not produce college-bound students, this was a big shock for many.

As a result of his SAT scores and geographic location, virtually every big university came calling. Who was this wunderkind from a school system in the poorest county in the U.S. who had achieved a perfect score? When they found out that Fernando did not have the resources to attend these kinds of prestigious universities, he was offered a number of full scholarships. He ended up at Harvard.

If there is a singular example of how education can change someone's life, giving them the ability to rise up out of poverty, and become a successful contributor to society, it's Fernando De Leon. He's an incredible person.

After Harvard, he became a partner in a business that grew. When the majority owner eventually bought him out, he went on to form his own company. The rest, as they say, is history. He has had an extraordinarily successful career. He has also contributed greatly to society in many ways. By bridging the opportunity gap through his academic pursuits, Fernando was able to create his own business and inspire others to do the same. In his case, the full scholarship to Harvard was a game-changer. While a unique one to be sure, the principle of bridging opportunity gaps and helping people to help themselves has guided Fernando to where he is today.

Restoring Opportunity and Hope

America's diversity, our emphasis on individual liberty, our sense of responsibility for giving back to society, our unique brand of entrepreneurship—all these ideas are connected to the American dream. We have all heard, perhaps too often, the phrases "only in America" and "America is the land of opportunity." But in every cliché, there is some truth. Rags-to-riches Horatio Alger stories are American legends known around the world. I want to get back to an environment in which more people have the opportunities and sense of hope I had. It is in America's interest to ensure a growing middle and upper class by providing opportunities to people to earn their way into having dreams become true. The right to aspire to be anything should be an ingrained philosophy communicated to each American from childhood. I know because that's my story.

CHAPTER 4

A Crusader as an Accidental Entrepreneur

Bernice was right on time as always. Her ten-year-old, four-door boat of a car seemed an odd choice, directly contrasting her diminutive stature. She had suffered some difficulties along the way—severe arthritis and a stroke—but she was not going to let any of that get in her way. Bernice probably didn't know what she was getting into when she took on a pimply-faced teenager as a client. She may not have been the top real estate agent in town, and I was certainly not a dream client, but in the end we made a great team.

I hopped in the passenger-side seat, and we left my parents' Ann Arbor, Michigan, house to look at a 97th investment property together. In hindsight, I wonder how many agents would show 97 properties to a prospective client. At this rate, she'd be lucky to get back all the money she'd spent on gas driving me around. But Bernice was undeterred. Nothing was going to stop her from helping me make my first deal.

I was seventeen when we first started looking for properties. Bernice and I quickly realized that no bank would loan me the money for a real estate mortgage. A lot of commercial properties, however, were sold with land contracts, which was the legal equivalent of the seller's providing the financing. But what seller would finance me? In those days in Michigan, any contract entered into before age twenty-one was voidable, and I sure didn't look twenty-one. That didn't help. One look at me and we'd get turned down before we could even make an offer.

So we came up with a new plan. If at all possible, I wouldn't meet the seller, and we would do everything through written offers. The paperwork would pass from broker to broker, then to the seller or his or her lawyer. Meanwhile, we would keep our fingers crossed that no one would realize they were dealing with someone who, after a year of looking at properties, was happy to be eighteen.

As we turned onto Hamilton Place, I realized that we were in the heart of the University of Michigan. The location, fairly close to the student union and pretty much walking distance to all the important places on the main campus, could not have been better.

The same could not be said for 427 Hamilton Place, a dirty three-story rooming house whose large porch's greenish paint was either chipping or peeling. We walked up the stairs and into a hallway. Off to one side was a door into the first-floor apartment and a flight of stairs. The second floor had a long hallway with five rooms, a common kitchen, a bathroom, and a door that opened into a stairway leading up to the third floor. The third floor, which was basically the attic, had only three rooms, but they were larger and really quite nice.

The students who inhabited the eight rooms on the second and third floor, which rented by the week, loved the fact that they had a shared kitchen. I was less enchanted. While the smell of Indian and Chinese food made the place seem fairly international, the leftover dishes in the sink negated that United Nations vibe, making the place seem trashy at best. The unpleasantness was compounded by the fact that there was a single bathroom for all the tenants and their friends. That said, the rooming house was for sale and available. I was excited.

Bernice and I made our way back downstairs and went into the large apartment that took up the entire first floor, where we found a huge living room, a separate dining room, a kitchen, and two bedrooms. A stairway into the basement revealed two additional bedrooms and a storeroom. The four-bedroom apartment housed a part-time minister/part-time barber, along with his wife and their seventeen-year-old daughter, in addition to some hippie male students to whom they sublet the basement rooms.

As we left, Bernice and I discussed how much more money I could make with the rooming house. For starters, the apartment was going for only $70 a month, because the minister/barber was also the manager of the house. Since I'd be taking over all property management, we could raise the rent to market value. That meant at least $450 a month. In addition, if we cleaned up the place and put in some nicer furniture, we could charge more for each of the lower-priced rooms, which would really improve the rent roll.

We made an offer of $25,000. I would put down the $4,000 I had saved up from years of paper routes, stocking doctors' offices with instant coffee and soup, selling Cutco knives, and more. Since I knew I'd never get a bank loan, Bernice and I asked the seller to carry the land contract for $21,000.

Ultimately, we reached a negotiated deal of $27,250, with $4,000 as a down payment and the rest at 7 percent interest. I was so excited. We had finally found a deal! Here I was, an eighteen-year-old college freshman and now the proud owner of a rooming house.

I saw this as my big chance, but not to launch a long-term career as an entrepreneur. Despite my childhood startups, I had planned to be in business for only two years, as at the time I considered it boring and not terribly noble. This was my big chance to make a difference. I was definitely influenced by the community I had grown up in. Ann Arbor was a place that valued academics and people with causes over business. At the time, headline after headline in *The Ann Arbor News* talked about how student tenants were waging rent strikes against their landlords, alleging that they didn't maintain their properties and overcharged for them. The landlords' typical retort was that they were just trying to make a decent living, and nobody was forcing the students to live in their particular building. Now I could be the good-guy landlord. I would do all the maintenance, keep the place in A-1 shape while making a reasonable profit, everyone would love me, and everything would be wonderful.

The Best-Laid Plans

The building at 427 Hamilton Place proved to be an education in many ways. First, the idealism that drove me to buy the property completely bombed. Everything I had hoped for and planned worked out exactly the opposite. Instead of proving that it was possible to be a good-guy landlord, which was my main objective in buying the property, I was perceived by the tenant union at the University of Michigan as a turncoat and bad-guy, capitalist kid. One of the union's goals was to financially break landlords and force them into a collective bargaining agreement to set rents and building-owner requirements. Perceiving me as vulnerable because I was so young, the union made me a target.

Beyond my shattered ideals there were new realities. The seller had misled me by telling me that the apartment on the first floor and basement did not have a lease. I was counting on getting $450 per month for that apartment, but the tenant who lived there with his family claimed they had a lease contract I couldn't break. After getting all the facts, my lawyer sided with the tenant and told me that my only recourse was to sue the seller. This would become my first lawsuit and, unfortunately, far from my last. More about that later.

Entrepreneurship Is Addicting

My ideas had proven ill-founded—the rooming house was a disaster that wasn't making any money, and cleaning the bathroom and kitchen daily was awful. Even so, I loved being an entrepreneur. Despite my initial misgivings about business as a career, having my own business proved to be fun. I loved the autonomy and empowerment. It was life changing for me. During most of my childhood, I hadn't excelled at school, sports, or much of anything else. I'd be down and out, and I'd think, "I'm going to show everyone. I'm going to have a successful life." Now, I was suddenly able to control aspects of my life I never thought I could.

I was hooked.

As I've mentioned before, by most objective views I would have been the least likely to succeed as an adult at anything, especially considering the fact that when I was two years old, I was diagnosed as having a form of childhood epilepsy. I remember waking up in the hospital after having seizures. By the time I was four or five, my seizures were fewer and more controlled by phenobarbital, a barbiturate I took until I was thirteen. The drug's depressant effect was profound, impeding me mentally and physically and, indirectly, emotionally.

Even so, like most American children, I spent a lot of time thinking about what I wanted to be when I grew up. At five, I wanted to be a social worker. Later, despite being a mediocre student at best, I decided I wanted to be president of the United States. I got over that idea but continued to want to do something big with my life, to be stronger and more successful than I had been as a child. I wanted to change the hand that life had dealt me and always believed that was possible. I held on to the vision that if I worked hard enough, I could do more. I could be better. I could be whatever I wanted to be. That credo kept me going.

None of this basic ambition came as a result of pushing by my family or any one person around me. In fact, the focus of my entrepreneurial activities, which started when I was eight, was to make money so I could avoid the worry I saw my parents experience when it was time to pay the bills. This financial fixation concerned my parents so much that they sent me to a therapist.

In those days, people in Ann Arbor highly regarded university professors and auto executives. Entrepreneurs, on the other hand, were generally looked down upon and definitely did not fall in the category of the important citizens. Even so, people believed that Americans could start their own businesses if they wanted to. It was a simple given. Most everyone was entitled to take a risk and start a business. So I took advantage of the opportunity that the times provided, got lucky, and found out I enjoyed it.

Between the ages of eighteen and twenty-one, I continued to buy, manage, and operate more and more rooming houses and finally smaller apartment buildings. I expanded my portfolio from the University of

Michigan to a second school twenty-five miles away, Eastern Michigan University. Within three years of my initial real estate purchase, and despite not having money for a down payment, I wound up purchasing my first multimillion-dollar property.

This was just one of many acquisitions during that period.

From my second property on, I had no money of my own for down payments. To solve that problem, I started putting together investment partnerships and raised money first from fellow students at $200 per share and later from rich individuals at over $150,000 per share.

At the age of nineteen, I got married and became a full-time liberal arts student in addition to being the owner, operator, and janitor of a growing real estate business. I also washed pots and pans at a cafeteria to pay for it all.

Two years later, I had already made $1 million on paper, but my cash flow was highly negative. I certainly wasn't living like it, but I was somewhere between a paper tiger and a cash-desperate broke person.

By the time I was in my mid-thirties, I had purchased a few billion dollars' worth of property and raised over $1 billion in equity through hundreds of limited partnerships. My companies owned more than seventy-two thousand apartments and millions of square feet of commercial properties at this time. I was well on my way to proving to myself and others that I wasn't the childhood clown and failure that I had been labeled.

Lots of Fingers, Lots of Pies

Property acquisition was far from my only focus as I was starting out. Then, like now, I had to have my fingers in a lot of different pies. As a result, in the fifty years since buying that initial rooming house, I've been involved in many different industries, which has given me a unique window into the entrepreneurship landscape.

In addition to acquiring properties over the years, I've owned, operated, and sold hotels in the U.S. and abroad. Even though I've always had a love-hate relationship with hotels, these days I first build a model room so that everything from the placement of the reading lights to the location of the windows can be vetted.

I also started developing properties early on. Those initial apartments and condominiums in Michigan, constructed in wood, have since given way to sophisticated high-rises. Handwritten progress notes, thankfully, have also gone by the wayside. Construction is risky, and a lot can go wrong, including soaring costs. While my team and I can't always control that piece of it, we control what we can. These days that includes, as mentioned previously, monitoring the entire process with a time-lapse construction camera way up in the air that documents what's happening 24/7. We can even return and see what any given worker was doing and what any given process was being done at any point during the build, no matter how high off the ground they are.

Speaking of being up in the air, after moving to Dallas I invested in American Airlines. My theory was that the airline industry is really a real estate play, and that if you have legal routes, you gain a quasi-monopoly and can make money. I didn't understand that airlines are mostly about two cost factors: labor and fuel. Between labor unions and the volatility of fuel costs, historically the airlines have had good times and then they get clobbered. Live and learn! Too bad you can't just read a book and figure out the smart thing to do based on somebody else's mistakes; sometimes you just have to learn the hard way.

That was certainly the case in my early twenties, when my closest friend and I jumped into the oil business and drilled our first well. Even though we knew that states like Texas and Arkansas had tons of oil, a whole bunch of guys, ourselves included, decided that Michigan just might become the new hotbed for natural gas. I still have a photograph of that Upper Michigan well. And that's about all I have, because of course we drilled a dry hole. After that, I did wildcat drilling for oil and natural gas off and on for forty years or so. But that's all over.

During the time that I did drill for oil, I had some big wins and some big losses as well. Thankfully, I have had big wins in other fields at the right times.

As I've already discussed, with others I built and sold various software companies to large firms such as Oracle and EMC, and also cofounded a health maintenance organization that we grew from scratch. I've also been in and out of the lending business since 1975. My involvement began when I was in my early twenties and a wide-ranging group of local folks decided to start a financial institution called Michigan Savings & Loan. They populated the board with people from all walks of life. The chairman of the S&L board was a pharmacist. Other directors represented a sample cross section of the community. I was the token young entrepreneur. We each invested some money and some time, and together we created a financial institution that successfully made loans to regular people, most of whom would never have gotten off the ground without the kind of funding we were able to supply.

After that, I bought and owned a number of banks and savings and loans. In 2017, HALL Group's lending business was the third-largest hotel construction lender in the United States.

Of course, Kathryn and I also have our wine business. Kathryn's plan was to have a top-quality vineyard and produce some wine. But I have a bad habit of putting things on steroids. You could drop me on Mars, and I'd be starting businesses. So we now own several hundred acres of prime vineyard property, along with HALL, WALT, and BACA wine brands and wineries. As we continue to grow our business, remaining committed to producing artisan, high-quality wine vintages and customer experiences, we are earning an ever-increasing number of accolades and perfect scores.

Finally, while I'm not a substantial startup investor, I do take part in some angel-round early venture capital investing when I'm not swamped with this admittedly crazy array of business ventures.

American Dream or Pipe Dream?

Yes, I have lived the American dream—the ups and downs (and ups again) of it. Barring a few fairly significant hiccups (if that's what you call losing a few billion dollars and being forced to file for bankruptcy),

I've been fortunate, even during the early days when I was so green, I didn't know what I did not know.

I've learned a lot since then. Enough to know that the American ideal I benefited from is under attack. During my time in such a broad spectrum of industries, I've witnessed a troubling change of attitude between when I started as an entrepreneur and now, and I've bumped up against a lot of the issues that now threaten U.S. entrepreneurship, including "not in my backyard" activists (NIMBYs), who in various forms are growing in number and intensity.

In the next chapter, I'll tell you the story of how Kathryn and I tried to develop a vineyard on a piece of agriculturally zoned property that we bought in 2005. Hopefully you'll get a sense of what it's like for entrepreneurs to be hit year after year with roadblocks ranging from overregulation to extremists. It's quite a ride. Had we been a startup, we never would have survived.

CHAPTER 5

Extreme Positions

Entrepreneurship has never been—nor should it be—easy. These days, however, increasingly persistent extremists entrenched in their positions—usually opposition to new, productive ventures—make doing business almost impossible for those without the deep pockets to fight the ensuing legal challenges.

If the events in this chapter seem crazy to you, I understand. They seem crazy to me, and I was involved in most of them. But these kinds of obstacles are not unique. In an era of political extremes, they and their unintended consequences have become all too common and have helped contribute to the decline of U.S. entrepreneurship.

Negotiating Napa

When we purchased our winery in St. Helena, a city in Napa Valley, we couldn't wait to improve the ramshackle property. Even though we had struggled with a handful of long-fought objections from our neighbors at our Rutherford winery, we didn't anticipate problems at St. Helena. We simply figured that our new St. Helena winery neighbors, to say nothing of the county itself, would be just as excited as we were to see the historical aspects of the facility restored and all the nasty outdoor fermentation tanks on the property replaced by something beautiful. To our surprise, we quickly realized that some of the people whose homes bordered the winery were decidedly displeased. Moreover, they were organizing others to protest.

So we pulled back and reached out to neighbors and the community. That fall, we traveled the length of the valley, meeting with people in community centers and church basements. In more than thirty meetings, we spoke about our plans and goals for the winery.

"We want to work with anyone and everyone," I had told the *St. Helena Star.* "Call us."

We meant it.

We listened and learned. One group emerged that appeared to speak on behalf of the neighborhood. To meet the group's concerns, we significantly redesigned the winery.

Then the county stepped in with different requirements, saying they wouldn't recognize the agreement we had made with the neighbors. More meetings. More negotiations. More architectural drawings. More design changes. More time—our winery was delayed three years. And more money.

While the conflicts related to our Rutherford and St. Helena wineries eventually were resolved, others have proven to be more virulent. Developing a winery creates jobs, but it also encourages tourism, which is seen as a negative by some. Many of the people who protested our hiring legendary architect Frank Gehry, for example, did so because they feared that the winery he designed would attract too many tourists. When things didn't work out with Frank, that issue became moot. But the tourist controversy remains a hot topic.

People who talk about the risk of too many tourists point to the growing traffic in Napa Valley. They also note that more and more wineries are deciding to sell wine directly to the public, and blame the wineries for encouraging visitors and further burdening the roads. Add increasing traffic to this congestion that's simply due to a rise in the number of people who live here. Napa's population has grown from 79,000 in 1970 to 137,000 in 2015. In addition, as property values rise, fewer and fewer of the people who work in the valley can afford to live here. The need for low, affordable, and even "normal" housing is high, and the supply continues to decline. So workers commute to and from the valley every morning and every night.

The reality is that there are simply many more people living and/ or working in the area and on the road, and the infrastructure hasn't kept up.

Everybody is here for quality of life, but how we all define our own quality of life differs. For some people that quality means no change. For some, change is okay, but "not in my backyard." Most people want to preserve open space and to save trees, yet how to balance these ideals against a wine industry that increasingly wants to encourage winery visitors and plant more vineyards? We need to address the growing traffic problems, and that means creating new affordable housing for the local workforce, but in whose backyard? We need to allow some change, but if we lose the pristine beauty of the valley, we will have lost many of our tourists who are as attracted to Napa's natural beauty as to our wines. The key is to find the balance, but how?

All of this said, our St. Helena winery situation ultimately worked out. The neighbors negotiated a deal we both could live with. The key to resolving people's concerns was a dialogue and ultimately compromise. The delays and added costs would have ended the efforts of less financially able entrepreneurs, but fortunately, that wasn't the case for us. So we all won in a sense, and we moved on.

Years Later—Negotiating Napa, Round Two

Fast-forward to 2014. One hundred and eighty people jammed into the temporary Napa County building to discuss concerns over the property we had bought nine years prior.

The 2,300-acre property, located on Highway 121 and priced at $8 million, had views from the top parts that actually extended to the Golden Gate Bridge in San Francisco. It was a beautiful and unusual piece of land. We hoped we could do it justice. When we bought it, we certainly had no idea that we were about to become enmeshed in a complex web of tensions that pit development against environmentalists. Before this moment, we thought we were the environmentalists. In fact, we still think we're responsible environmentalists, a fact that's reflected in everything from our certified sustainable and largely organic vineyards to our winery itself, which earned Gold certification from LEED (Leadership in Energy and Environmental Design)—the first in California.

Part of the reason we never saw problems coming is that we were not planning to "develop" the property—that is, add buildings. We were just going to plant a vineyard.

In our due diligence before the sale, we verified that, as we had expected, the property was zoned as agricultural watershed (AW). This AW zoning encourages agricultural uses, and the guidelines state that "agriculture is the highest and best use of the land." Our goal was to plant a vineyard on about 14 percent of the land that we had purchased. Over time, we reduced that to just 8.5 percent of our land.

We assumed that planting a vineyard would not be a problem once we complied with any environmental requirements. After all, the land had been designated for agriculture, which in Napa means vineyards. Neighbors wound up protesting so vociferously against Walt Ranch, the county held public hearings never before conducted for a vineyard development. That would be the beginning of rules being changed to accommodate an extremely vocal minority of Napa Valley residents.

Kathryn and I believe in talking with neighbors and trying to come to compromises. So we were prepared to listen to their concerns. The neighborhood organization next door, after delaying for weeks on end, refused to meet. Finally, just three weeks prior to the county's public hearing, on November 6, 2014, we hosted a public meeting at the Meritage hotel. The meeting was beneficial, as we were able to discuss the community's concerns, and we made changes to our plans to accommodate those concerns.

Unfortunately, the solid start to the dialogue in that first meeting went nowhere once the formal Napa County public hearings began. Unlike the give-and-take discussion at the prior meeting, the residents who had come to this public hearing had no intention of listening. Their "HALT WALT" placards and buttons made that clear. But that wasn't enough for one attendee, who bent down close to where Kathryn was sitting and said, "You're the devil. You're the devil."

In Napa County, proposed vineyards on slopes greater than 5 percent require an erosion control plan. Large vineyard projects also require Environmental Impact Reports, or EIRs. EIRs, it turns out, are complex documents designed to ascertain that the overall project will not adversely affect the environment in an unacceptable manner. In order to execute them, a local government agency on behalf of the State of California hires and oversees competent experts who analyze the property. At the time, the State of California guidelines specified that EIRs, which are paid for by the property owner, on average should take one year and be three hundred pages long. Naively, we didn't think that would be a big deal, as most EIRs involve complicated controversial development or redevelopment—like building a winery, hotel, or shopping center—and this was simply a vineyard on agriculturally zoned land.

In 2008, we filed our first Notice of Intent with Napa County for our EIR. When the public was notified, we did receive some adverse comments, but at least our intent regarding the planting of a vineyard on agriculturally zoned land was on record.

The EIR process can be very difficult or relatively easy, depending on the agency running it. In our case, Napa County was in charge, and to its credit was very detailed. The ultimate result of those efforts, while costly and time consuming, was an approved EIR that could stand up to court scrutiny. As of this writing, that has proven to be the case with two appeals that have been filed.

All Good On the Environmental Front

We knew from the start that water would be an important issue. That didn't seem like it would be a problem when a water study the county had commissioned at our cost showed that our property was located on an abundant natural aquifer. The data suggested that 1.4 billion gallons of water on our property—and much more likely 3.6 billion gallons—was accessible for vineyard use. A second water expert reviewed the first expert's report and confirmed those conclusions.

The erosion control plans were similarly very positive for the project. By improving the twenty-one miles of roads that already existed on the property, our project would actually lower erosion rather than increase it. Better roads would prevent soil from washing down into the watershed. This would be favorable, as a portion of Walt Ranch was located in the Milliken Creek watershed, one of the City of Napa's municipal watersheds. According to the experts, our development would actually reduce the amount of sediment washing into Milliken Creek.

Mounting Opposition and Misinformation

Our Draft Environmental Impact Report (DEIR), which wound up being more than fifteen hundred pages, came out in July 2014. Almost immediately, groups started to organize against our project. This ultimately led to five thousand more pages of studies and reports.

Despite our best efforts to develop the vineyard responsibly, and the county's efforts to be thorough, opposition mounted. When we tried to meet with the neighbors spearheading the fight in order to discuss the issues, they declined yet again.

By the following public Planning Commission meeting on November 24, tensions had rocketed to an all-time high. The property's many neighbors had become increasingly contentious. The ones who had come to the meeting were determined to have their say, and 1,500 pages of draft EIR provided plenty for them to pick at.

The county tried to encourage comments, which turned out to be good and bad. Everyone has a right to assemble and a right to complain, but it seems to me that leadership should also put that in perspective and retain a sense of order to encourage real discussion. Instead, the county allowed a loud minority of residents to set the agenda. In our case, that meant that instead of making any kind of real progress in terms of resolving differences, a handful of individuals heatedly repeated concerns based on fabrications rather than facts.

The next evening, a dead rabbit appeared in the entrance of our St. Helena winery, which is known by many for its rabbit sculpture visible from Highway 29. Mike Reynolds, who is the president of our wine businesses, found the carcass when he was leaving work one evening and quickly got it off the road.

"Rabbits are killed on the highway all of the time," he wrote in a memo to us. "But its placement and timing does not seem like a coincidence."

The possibility that someone had deliberately left a dead rabbit on our doorstep wasn't just ugly, it was threatening.

There Are Two Sides to Most Stories

Don't get me wrong. Having a point of view and fighting for it are important parts of our democracy. Citizen advocacy is a vital and important check to stop extreme abuses by large companies, or government leaders bowing to lobbyists over the needs of the local communities. There are ways of combining a well-preserved environment with an economically viable and physically livable environment. That middle ground, however, is frequently lost to the extremists on either side. Too often, the loudest voices wind up winning the battles, albeit perhaps losing the war.

My wife and I absolutely believe in protesting and fighting for causes we're passionate about. Those include corporate and government abuses that need to be challenged and stopped. It's not okay for developers to pave over wetlands, mow down protected forests, or dump chemicals into our waterways. It's not okay for renters to have to put up with hazardous property conditions. It's not okay for companies to implement unsafe working conditions, to bilk customers, or to discriminate. But these things happen, which makes oversight and, yes, activism absolutely necessary.

What concerns me is people who hurt the chances for new businesses to have a fair, level playing field just because they want to maintain their sense of an appropriate status quo. If you don't want vineyards next to your home, go get the land rezoned from agriculture to another use. Instead of playing games and dealing with untruthful extremes, let's try to face things in fair and transparent ways.

Most important, let's try to work together for the greater good. Too often these days, it seems that we all reinforce our biases and watch the news stations we agree with rather than branching out. Wouldn't it work better to deal with our differences with transparency and honesty, and try to solve problems through understanding and compromise?

Organized Opposition

Of course, that's not what happened with Walt Ranch, in part because the opposition was heavily influenced by out-of-the-area nonprofits. At the end of the day, we received unanimous approval by the five-member Board of Supervisors in an appeal to move our project forward. From there, the nonprofits appealed to a superior court and lost again. As of this writing, thirteen years after buying our agriculturally zoned piece of property, the proposed vineyard is facing yet another legal appeal. These are well-funded organizations. How could any startups fight these kinds of deep-pocketed opponents trying to prevent new vineyards from being established on agricultural land?

That's not a problem just in wine country. Across the country, groups of dissenting citizens determined not to allow development in their backyards have managed to hold development hostage.

In 2016, an eight-story condo development at 603 Jefferson Avenue in Redwood City, California, was proposed as part of the city's new wave of development. However, when local NIMBYs got involved, the project's trajectory dramatically shifted.

The San Francisco Bay Area has been facing a regional housing crisis for years, yet despite the lack of supply and surplus of demand, residents near the proposed complex files a California Environmental Quality Act (CEQA) lawsuit that shrank the size of the development by a quarter, causing the owner to sell the space to another developer, who decided to maintain the building as office space.

The Redwood City Residents for Responsible Development, the group that brought the suit against 603 Jefferson Avenue, has blocked four other local projects and vocally opposed several more. Apparently, preserving the character and history of the community trumps the housing crisis as well as the city's downtown master plan.

An article in the *San Francisco Business Times*[1] sums up the issue:

> The anti-development barrage overrides the will of other residents who elected the council, resident Isabelle Chu previously told the Business Times. Chu founded the pro-development group Redwood City Forward. Others have questioned whether [opposition attorney Geoff] Carr's suits constitute abuse of CEQA standards, which are meant to protect the community from environmental harm. "The city did not think the 603 Jefferson Ave. suit had any environmental merit," said Community Development Director Aaron Aknin.
>
> "Essentially what's happening is that a couple of people are determining what does or doesn't get built in Redwood City," Chu said. "These people can deny housing for 50 or 60 people with a couple hundred bucks and an afternoon."[2]

If established multifamily development companies can rarely combat this opposition unscathed, how are fledgling startups supposed to survive?

Mom-and-Pop Abuse

Think this kind of organized opposition is relegated to big developers?

Think again.

In Wilmington, Delaware, a mom-and-pop Italian restaurant called Scalessa's "My Way" Old School Italian Kitchen was targeted by local NIMBY group Forty Acres Civic Association for attempting to get a liquor license. The NIMBYs did not stop there. Soon they attacked the restaurant for painting its exterior, adding a sign, and installing a fan. They even dug into the owner's tax records to find out if he was delinquent (which, unfortunately, he was). So the group delivered a ninety-page presentation to city officials, prompting owner Frank Scalessa to withdraw his liquor license application. Even that, however, has not appeased his opponents.[3]

The battle has taken its toll.

"I'm exhausted by it," says Scalessa, who, despite trying to be cooperative, feels beaten down by the neighbors. "They've taken my passion out of this.... I'm worn out."[4]

This kind of opposition effort is perhaps understandable when deploying a political campaign, but to decimate a quaint red-sauce Italian joint? I don't see it.

NIMBY-ism is pandemic in Delaware, according to Delaware Online.

> This neighborhood has seen its share of these brouhahas. Last year, nearby NIMBYs besieged Southeast Kitchen, another delicious small business, when it wanted to allow patrons to bring their own alcohol. And in case you think it's just restaurants, local NIMBYs quashed plans to demolish four homes and make a parking lot for a nursing home—the public hearing on that issue lasted six hours.
>
> NIMBYs have harangued a church's plan to build tiny houses for Dover's growing homeless population. NIMBYs tried to stop the Constitution Yards beer garden on the Wilmington Riverfront, which has turned out to be a hugely successful attraction in a city that desperately needs more cool things to do.[5]

Bureaucratic Overreach

Certain trends seem common today, whether in Dallas, Frisco, or Napa—all places where I have worked extensively in recent years— or among any number of local governments across the country. The NIMBY movement in particular is impacting elected officials and raising fears of negative reactions, leading to the rise of greater levels of NIMBY control.

Where rules historically deal with heights, setbacks, and uses, over time local planning studies suggest that more "controls" are better. They ask:

- What types of materials?
- Where will your future buildings be located?

They request landscape details and open-space plans.

On long-term projects, governments want to know workable unrealistic specifics on what a developer will be doing twenty to thirty years in the future.

This belief that greater controls on businesses result in a better consumer or citizen result is simply wrong. Instead, the oversight of minutia adds unnecessary cost, which is ultimately passed on to consumers.

Getting through local government staff that feel a great sense of power and often an anti-business bias is completely counterproductive for communities, but nevertheless all too frequent. Ironically, these overly stringent controls don't curb bad actions or eliminate problems with projects or businesses. Instead, the added complications and cost just hurt new and smaller businesses.

Startups Do Not Have a Chance

This contentiousness, which is representative of the uncompromising perspectives that are so much more common today than in years past, affects aspiring entrepreneurs and startups more than other businesses for one simple reason. Fighting to get the necessary approvals now takes longer and costs more. Established businesses can afford both the time and expense. Aspiring entrepreneurs and budding businesses cannot.

Our legal and political systems are aiding and abetting the hijacking of our decision-making process by a small number of people with extreme positions. While there are many great leaders in elected office, there are unfortunately too many others who value reelection over leadership. These officials, however unintentionally, empower the loud minority while encouraging and furthering the extremism that's occurring throughout the regulatory and approval processes.

Too often these same politicians, whether influenced by big business or a vocal minority of constituents, pass so many regulations for new businesses that they make it impossibly expensive for a startup or small business to compete. As challenging as Walt Ranch has been for us, the barrage of regulations is worse—and utterly unfair—for smaller vineyard owners and farmers who don't have the deep, deep pockets now required to buy their way in.

If the "not in my backyard" folks, combined with certain nonprofits that have their own extreme visions of right and wrong, use the powers of our political and legal systems to delay and add costs to projects, the only business groups that can sustain fighting them are big corporations and well-to-do entrepreneurs who have already made it. That means that the aspiring startups and the small businesses are toast.

A National Problem

This trend of small, vocal opposition groups sandbagging beneficial—more often than not—developments is not isolated to any one state or community and has caused local government representatives to get involved in the most pedestrian disputes, simply because they cannot afford to upset their constituents and risk losing reelection. Moreover, there seems to be little concern about—or accountability for—group representatives lying to the media to play on people's fears. As a result, NIMBYs have local governments by the throats, along with many of those in the private sector who hope to develop in these NIMBY-heavy neighborhoods.

So how can we create accountability for both opposition groups as well as corporate entities? And how can we make sure that popular as well as political decisions are guided by truthfulness rather than deceit?

This is a complicated area that we have yet to figure out on a federal level, let alone a state- or citywide level. For elected officials, who are often well intentioned, these loud extreme voices make governing difficult. We have seen how vocal far-right and far-left groups have influenced federal elections by polarizing the country and leaving the middle without representation. The toll that this can take on startups at all levels of the process—from local zoning ordinances to federal public policy—could be catastrophic.

"Before I leave, I'd like to see our politics begin to return to the purposes and practices that distinguish our history from the history of other nations. I would like to see us recover our sense that we are more alike than different," said the late and great senator John McCain.

Until that happens, the growth of "not in my backyard," "I've got mine; I don't want you" attitudes—coupled with a lack of respect for truth and increasingly radical positioning on everything from politics to business—is hurting the very communities that people are trying too hard to protect. Who is going to invest in these areas that are so divided?

Speaking of two sides and compromise, let me be clear that to this day our issues in Napa over Walt Ranch bring me sadness rather than anger. I have asked myself, *How could we all have worked better together?* There is no question that the local political leadership did a good job both publicly and privately seeking compromise. And aside from the out-of-town extremists, I don't doubt the goodwill of those on the other side. I also don't doubt that we all love and value the beauty and history of Napa. Despite the other side's goodwill, however, the process was made regrettably unproductive for all involved.

That's just not smart. It's also not what was intended when the legislation was drawn up.

CHAPTER 6

Unintended Consequences

It seems like every time there's a problem, large citizen groups push bureaucrats and legislators to try to solve it by creating new regulations, which often happens fast and results in consequences no one ever anticipated. As much as I believe in protections for consumers and the environment, I think we need to examine whether we've overly controlled a lot of industries in ways that bring marginal benefits and massive complications—especially as sometimes the remedy winds up being more harmful than what it was created to fix.

Take those California Environmental Impact Reports mandated by CEQA that helped prolong our Walt Ranch battle. Even though the guidelines stipulate that the report should be three hundred pages and take a year, ours now exceeds fifteen hundred pages and has taken eleven years. And that's just to plant a vineyard in an agriculturally zoned area.

Of course, we're far from the only business impacted by this statute, which was passed in 1970.

"The worst problem in California is the California Environmental Quality Act," one of the panelists announced at the Urban Land Institute in 2016, shortly before I was to speak.

I about fell out of my chair. *This guy is singing my song*, I thought. In the decade-plus that the CEQA had been used against Walt Ranch, it had never crossed my mind that this was a statewide issue. I assumed the ranch was an exception, not part of a bigger problem.

Wow! I thought when the panelist proceeded to talk at length about how the CEQA laws were too broad and too subject to interpretation. *We're not the only ones.*

Far from it, as it turns out.

Despite the best of intentions, California has a problem with CEQA. It's not like there's any one entity or any one person who made these laws, and in and of themselves, they aren't unfair. No one with any sense, for example, could quibble about the intention of California's environmental law to protect our environment. But it's been loosely written with no deadlines, time limits, or cost limits specified, a fact you have to live with (assuming it doesn't kill your business first) if you're setting up shop in California. The idea of a local agency with a blank check to charge the applicant by the hour may sound like a fair way to pay for costs, but the truth is that it encourages a longer, more burdensome process.

There obviously has to be a reasonable way for legitimate environmental causes to be protected while still allowing for viable business. But by constantly allowing extremists to dominate the conversation, we have ended up with the unintended consequence of making it very difficult for people to come in and be players in Napa Valley, even though everybody wants to be there because it's such a uniquely great grape-growing valley.

Limiting new vineyards makes Napa's existing vineyards more valuable, but it's not good for Napa overall. From an economic point of view, it discourages investors (myself now included) who would rather invest their money in a place with fewer headaches. So at a time when Napa's—and for that matter, the state's—infrastructure needs help, the tax base is being compromised, with businesses on the move—right out of California and into more business-friendly states like Texas.

Gavin Newsom and Texas One

That's something that Lieutenant Governor Gavin Newsom is all too aware of. Rarely am I impressed by elected officials' stump speeches, but when Gavin was running for governor in 2018 he spoke eloquently at a fundraiser about entrepreneurship and the need for California to be more competitive.

"Entrepreneurship is critical to jobs and innovation, and California needs to do more on that front," he said—or at least words to that effect.

Gavin is a bit unusual because he has been both an entrepreneur and a politician. At a large dinner party directly following the fundraiser, he brought up how competitive Texas had been when Rick Perry was governor.

The story Gavin told that really stuck with me was about a CEO from Silicon Valley who had recently called him.

"I just got off the phone with the governor," she said.

"What did Jerry [Brown] say?" Gavin asked.

"No, not that governor. Rick Perry called to find out if I had gotten the package he FedExed to me."

Included in that package was an iPhone with a single phone number programmed in it—Governor Perry's personal cell phone number for the CEO to call when she was ready to talk about moving her company's headquarters to Texas.

At the fundraiser, Gavin went on to say that having the public sector appreciate the importance of business to communities is more important now than ever. Part of that involves the kind of personal attention Rick Perry excelled in as governor, as well as programs focused on bringing companies and jobs to the state. Another part involves making sure that the laws and programs related to issues like environmental safety and standards are handled in an efficient manner that balances reasonable business interest with reasonable protection. There is no question in my mind that the two can work together.

As an important side note, despite these issues, California under Governor Jerry Brown has flourished, going from being in severe trouble and debt to having a booming economy that excels in innovation. Still, like so much on this topic, this is a mixed picture. For starters, just consider the state's convoluted infrastructure and insane housing prices. So yes, there are reasons why, despite such great progress, California is losing business to Texas. The point Gavin was making, and that I agree with, is that California, as great as it is, can do better, especially in its efforts to help entrepreneurs outside Silicon Valley, San Francisco, and Los Angeles. The bigger point here is that state and local governments can and should take actions to encourage entrepreneurship. Part of that includes balancing regulations and business.

Regulations: Finding the Balance

I'm not arguing for complete deregulation. Far from it. Monopolies sure don't serve us. Neither, for the most part, did banking deregulation. Speaking of monopolies, airline deregulation hasn't exactly helped to make air travel more widely available.[1] And the elimination of net neutrality, which prevented internet providers from slowing speeds to certain websites, certainly won't help small businesses.

In addition, deregulations, especially recently, have helped big companies crush entrepreneurs and small companies, a sentiment the Center for American Entrepreneurship echoes:

> Regulation is essential to market economies. It establishes the rules of competition, ensures a level playing field, governs participants' behavior, and protects consumers, public health and safety, private property, and environmental resources. In this important sense, economic growth and wealth creation depend on the promulgation and enforcement of sound regulation.[2]

On the other hand, regulations not carefully thought out have wound up benefiting established companies at the expense of smaller ones and startups. As the Center for American Entrepreneurship further points out:

> Regulation isn't free, or without consequence. Regulation imposes costs—costs by businesses. A wave of new regulations, inconsistent or outdated regulations, or complex and confusing regulations can distract business owners' focus and time away from their product line and the marketplace, and impose costs

that consume resources that could otherwise be invested back into businesses.[3]

In the early days, regulation was so much less intrusive than today that I did not realize how good things were, because they simply weren't bad. Over time, however, regulation has become more and more burdensome. The numbers don't lie. The pages in the federal registry have been going way up in the past thirty years—the same time period when startups have been going down. Coincidence? I don't think so.

This transition to overregulation may have been a reaction to the greed of the '80s. The private sector certainly needs oversight after that decade's excesses, but it has gone overboard. Napa, where business development is admittedly much more regulated than in many other places, is far from the only locale dealing with the fallout of overregulation. I may have a great relationship with local government officials in Dallas and Frisco, Texas, for example, but that doesn't mean I'm spared from dealing with a rash of overregulation in either of those places.

Here's just one example: It took several years of problem solving to build our five-hundred-thousand-square-foot office building in Dallas's famous Arts District, which is the largest contiguous arts district in the United States. HALL Arts is a mixed-use, multiphase destination development that, in addition to the office building completed in 2015, features an adjacent half acre HALL Texas Sculpture Walk. The second phase of the development, now underway, includes a luxury residential high-rise and a full-service boutique hotel.

Needless to say, I have a lot of experience dealing with building challenges in the Arts District, most of which are due to something called the Sasaki Plan, which controls every detail related to the outside of every single building and every bit of landscape in that district. These rigid regulations developed some twenty-five years ago[4] mandate, among other things, that there be two rows of trees on all streets in the district and three rows on Flora Street, all to be bald cypress trees.[5] Even though over time these trees have caused the sidewalks to buckle, that doesn't matter. The regulations still have to be adhered to—or challenged.

In 2014, I was engaged in yet another Sasaki Plan–related battle, so I was looking over architectural plans during a flight.

"Are you an architect?" asked the individual sitting next to me.

"No, I'm a professional client. But I feel like I should be an architect."

It turned out that my seatmate *was* an architect.

"What firm are you with?" I asked.

"Sasaki," he replied.

"Oh my God. I know Sasaki," I blurted out. "It's the bane of my existence. You're my worst nightmare at times."

"What do you mean?"

So I told him about the Sasaki Plan, which it turned out he had worked on as a junior architect.

"You're not still using that, are you?" he asked.

"That's so out of date," he added when I answered in the affirmative. "We've learned a lot since then. I would suggest a whole different approach now. That plan should be changed."

Easier said than done. As of 2018, the city, through the Arts District stakeholders, has been working on doing just that for the past year-plus. While that's in process, we're stuck following a plan we know isn't working. Needless to say, that can complicate and delay the development of new properties, especially when those at the plan's helm have the discretion to make what can only be called unreasonable demands.

After months of numerous and expensive compromises on our end related to that five-hundred-thousand-square-foot office building near the Arts District, for example, the woman managing the Sasaki Plan essentially coldcocked us.

"Sign this deed restriction or I will not give you the building permit," she demanded. A deed restriction is an agreement that encumbers or ties up the property based on whatever you're agreeing to do. In this case, the deed restriction that had been requested required us to include two floors in the front of the property with certain dimensions that were overly burdensome.

What to do? I needed to get my building going, because I already had tenants lined up and leases in place.

In Dallas, you generally wait until you absolutely can't handle the bureaucrats' mandates, and then you go over their heads to the elected officials. That's what the system has become. I could have gone to the mayor, but I hate to bother him too often. So I called John Crawford, then the head of Downtown Dallas Inc., an organization that works to help bridge public and private interests related to the downtown area.

"Hold your nose and sign it," he advised. "You can get the city council to overturn it later."

Once we were up and running, we needed to get approval for a sign—one measly sign—wanted by a potential tenant in our Dallas Arts District building. The process should have been easy, especially since the Dallas Arts District committee, as well as the planning and zoning committee, had both unanimously approved the request. But we hadn't factored in how dysfunctional or how expensive local politics could be. Our legal bill wound up being $100,000, and the tenant never did come on board, since the sign that was approved was deemed unacceptable.

What a waste of time. And talk about something that saps productive energy!

Overall Dallas is good to work with. It's just that today versus decades ago, roadblocks for real estate developers and entrepreneurs are seemingly put up everywhere. These are the times we work in. While we clearly need protections for society and consumers, we also need to protect people's right to start a business and not get creamed before they get a chance.

Legislative Side Effects

It's hard to change legislation, especially when it's supported by a large, organizational constituency or when its unintended consequences aren't all that obvious. I remember unloading on a number of state senators about the CEQA and Walt Ranch over a private, nice dinner.

"Yeah, you're right," they all said in one way or another. "We know there's a problem. We're going to fix it."

And that was the end of the conversation. It's not fixed.

I would imagine that a lot of people in California think environmental acts should be as tough as possible, because we want a good environment. I agree that we should have a good environment, but maybe we're doing it the wrong way. Maybe we should look at more practical ways to do things. But it's hard for legislators, even in the face of an undeniable problem, to reform. And it's even harder to anticipate the full impact of legislation, no matter how well intentioned.

Take the Dodd-Frank Wall Street Reform and Consumer Protection Act—legislation passed by Congress that was meant to correct the financial abuses related to the Great Recession. It turns out that limiting financial markets, which in the short run may seem protective, limits liquidity, which ultimately can complicate the ability of markets to protect against normal economic forces. So it turns out that when we make major changes to what banks can and can't do, we can unwittingly cause problems. While the Dodd-Frank and Sarbanes-Oxley acts did a lot of needed good for consumers and helped ensure the safety and solvency of banks, they have made things particularly more difficult for small businesses and startups that already have a hard time obtaining credit.[67]

While preventing the kinds of actions that almost toppled our country's economy and trying to protect citizens from other misdeeds make total sense, it's not uncommon for that sort of legislation to trigger these unintended consequences. It's a bit like taking medication. You hope it helps your condition, but the prescription often has side effects—and sometimes those side effects can kill you, especially if you're taking other medications for other issues.

That's exactly what has happened on the business front. Over the past five decades that I've been an entrepreneur, the best intentions have led to an increasingly complicated system replete with sometimes conflicting laws and a large number of people who are hell bent on enforcing without question whatever agenda they are responsible for.

As a result, today's regulatory environment is beating small business to a pulp. According to *The State of Small Business in America*, a 2016 report from Babson College in which more than 1,800 small-business respondents across the country participated, nearly 60 percent of entrepreneurs either don't understand or have trouble managing government regulations and laws. That's more than half! On average, the report states that business owners—the people who generally handle all the compliance work in small firms—spend half a day a week and more than two hundred hours a year dealing with regulatory issues.

I'm not surprised. At HALL Group, we have a lot of staff dedicated to keeping up with all the rules and regulations that different businesses we own face. Now think about what it's like to deal with all these regulations when you're trying to get a company off the ground. It's like birth control for business.

Consider New York. Even though it's one of the places that gets the most investment capital and is one of the most successful places for entrepreneurship, New York City is a prime example of this kind of overregulation. It will take you six procedures to start a new business there.[8] Compare that to New Zealand or Canada, where a business can be launched with a single procedure.

New York is certainly not alone when it comes to encumbering the business formation application process. And as the chart below shows, there seems to be a direct correlation between the increasing length of time necessary to start a business and the slump in business applications.

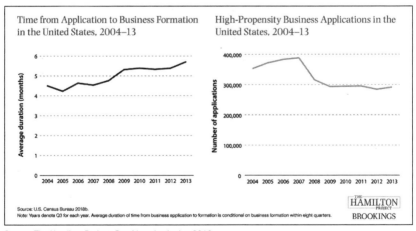

Source: The Hamilton Project–Brookings Institution 2018

No wonder the World Bank ranks the U.S. forty-ninth in the world when it comes to the ease of starting a new business. It's actually easier to launch a new business in France or Korea, or even Russia, than in the U.S.[9]

Maybe that's why the U.S. has the second-lowest self-employment rate among any of the developed nations. In fact, according to the World Bank, in 2015 the U.S. ranked forty-first in terms of entrepreneurship per capita. Countries like Mexico, Greece, Chile, Italy, and South Korea all rate higher than we do on this front.

Part of business today is constantly running the gauntlet while trying to figure out how to get to the other end of the process, oftentimes dealing with little bureaucratic obstacles, one after the other. So those new ventures frequently don't happen, because the regulatory environment makes it too difficult.

Talk about unintended consequences!

Now I'm not suggesting that we throw out all regulation or roll back significant protections. Regulations clearly serve a number of laudable purposes, from protecting individuals to safeguarding the environment. Under President Obama, for example, the Consumer Financial Protection Bureau (CFPB) did great work when it came to controlling payday lender abuses. As of June 2018, the CFPB had provided $12.4 billion in relief to more than thirty-one million consumers by taking action against, in their words, "predatory companies and practices that violate the law." That includes everything from challenging discrimination[10] to taking banks to task for their overdraft fee policies.[11]

Those are the kinds of regulations we need to keep everyone safe. But that doesn't mean that regulations are the answer to every problem. Unfortunately, that seems to be the approach these days. As a result, the regulatory system has ballooned like one of those expandable toys made of a superabsorbent polymer that quintuple in size once placed in water. Lack of transparency, approval process delays, outdated laws, and agencies that don't communicate with one another or coordinate their efforts are just some of the problems we businesspeople face on a daily basis. Then there's all the red tape, as well as all the licensing, ranging from occupational licensing standards that constrain new small businesses to national regulatory boards like the Federal Communications Committee (FCC) and Environmental Protection Agency (EPA) that impose undue fees on what could be groundbreaking new ventures.

The Money Squeeze

Overregulation doesn't just make life tougher and more expensive for startups. It has helped to dry up funding, which helps explain why so many startups fail before they ever get off the ground.

What's behind his?

In the wake of the Great Recession, regulators understandably have clamped down on banks to ensure their safety and soundness. Ultimately, this is making it harder and harder for all but the most creditworthy borrowers to get loans. Regulators are particularly tough on new ventures such as constructing buildings. And community banks that tend to be more interested in smaller customers are shrinking in number all the time.

Since 1990, the number of new banks forming per year has fallen from one hundred to three,[12] due in large measure to this vast increase in regulatory restrictions. In the meantime, eight hundred U.S. commercial banks shut their doors—a 14 percent decline. Most of those were small community banks, the one type of financial institution that entrepreneurs and small businesses could rely on.

Many banks that remain in business are learning to make money from areas other than lending, such as wealth management services. As a result, a lot of banks now proudly boast about how little of their revenue comes from interest income and how much of their income comes from fees. That's not helping revitalize our country, which is still trying to recover from 2008.

It's ironic when you listen to Federal Reserve Bank presidents give speeches and interviews in which they talk about how we need to get the banking system to make more loans. Even if the banks wanted to, today's financial regulations have tied their hands. Of course, this whole conversation is far worse if you need money to open a business, as banks generally don't loan to startups.

There actually was a time when you could go into a bank and borrow based on your integrity and associations. Those days are long gone. While that's an oversimplification, the legislation to stop bad bankers is having unintended consequences and making things substantially tougher on the little guy.

Whereas historically we've had cycles of overbuilding in Dallas, now the equity and credit requirements have resulted in only a handful of developers, like my company, being financially strong enough to get any kind of loan to construct new buildings. Sure, whereas HALL Group used to be able to get loans from any number of banks that would finance 80 percent of construction, we're getting only 60 percent loans these days. But that has not been a huge problem. In fact, it's arguably an opportunity, as other companies don't have the financial wherewithal that we do to put up more equity. So this whole scenario works in our favor.

Is that good for our country? Yes and no. The answer is not simple. We do need banks to be risk averse and avoid bad loans. However, figuring out ways to allow and even encourage banks, if they so choose, to take some risk on people who don't have quite the pedigree would boost competition and the availability of office space. Sure, at times there would be some losses. Still, I think for the greater good, that would be a better direction, especially if coupled with the banks being encouraged to have enough capital to remain solvent in the face of some problems. Instead, since the 2008 crisis, we have at least in part overreacted when it comes to banking, unintentionally creating business barriers that ultimately favor established, successful companies at the expense of startups and small businesses. Of course, that's great for big business, which does whatever it can to try to ensure that it can operate in an environment that's as close as possible to having a monopoly or an oligopoly, and as far away as possible from having a fair, level playing field.

SBA Push-Pull

The United States Small Business Administration (SBA) is supposed to, among other things, encourage startups that have problems. Part of how it helps with the money squeeze is through something called a small business investment company (SBIC). Established by Congress in 1958 as a way of giving entrepreneurs more access to startup capital, SBICs are privately owned investment companies licensed by the SBA that use their own capital, along with SBA-guaranteed funds, to loan money to qualifying small businesses.[13]

After the Great Recession, one would think the SBA should have wanted more private sector applications for SBICs. Right?

Consider what happened to HALL Structured Finance, our lending company that provides construction loans for new properties and bridge financing to renovate or reposition existing properties. Not only do we lend to businesses that traditional banks often don't have the inclination to deal with because of the headaches and complexity inherent in construction lending, but we understand real estate, we understand construction, and we understand entrepreneurs. So we can help them succeed. And that helps *us* to succeed.

The loan terms we offer are based on what we pay to borrow. We would lower our rate and save entrepreneurs money if our source of funds expanded and *we* received more favorable terms.

Sounds good, right? We thought so. So in October 2014 we applied to have HALL Structured Finance become an SBIC. We did this without talking to any elected officials we knew, as I felt it would be inappropriate to seek help in that way. Moreover, we should not have needed it.

The whole idea behind SBICs is to help small business, but SBA senior bureaucrats want to show Congress that they never lose money. So when you apply to have your company become an SBIC, the SBA vets you like crazy. As it should. But that can get expensive.

After double-checking to make sure that hotels were in their purview, we spent more than $100,000 on legal fees and a year filling out forms. Despite our being greenlighted at every step of the way, the final SBA committee decided that hotel construction was too risky. So, our track record notwithstanding, they turned us down. Being able to say to Congress, "We continue with our unblemished record of never having a loss" was more important than enabling us to make more loans at a lower interest rate, thereby helping more entrepreneurs start up hotels, which are a great source of jobs. I felt bad for us, of course. But I also felt bad just because the whole thing seemed misguided. Still, I let it go and moved on.

The SBA's risk-averse approach is good in a fiscal sense. On the other hand, if properly structured, it could carry out the dual mandate of helping more startups while remaining fiscally prudent. There are many ways our SBIC application could have been approved, but unfortunately someone high up decided that the risk outweighed the benefit. The current administrator has focused on getting more people into SBICs, a move I heartily agree with. Ironically, this comes right at the moment when President Trump, having convinced Congress to pass the largest spending bill in the history of the United States, has proposed reducing the agency's federal funding by 25 percent,[14] effectively compromising rather than strengthening the agency responsible for the health and well-being of small business in this country. This shows a real lack of commitment to small businesses and startups.

Those cuts are bound to negatively impact entrepreneurs as well, especially since, as *The Washington Post* points out, "the agency is considering increasing the fees it charges to back small business loans larger than $1 million, something that could deter lenders from offering small business loans."[15]

Clearly, supporting startups hasn't been a priority from a national policy standpoint. Even though a lot of people give speeches and say nice things about entrepreneurship, in a broad sense this has not been given the attention it merits.

The Big Picture

Priorities come with real support, not lip service. And real support requires that we look at the big picture when it comes to entrepreneurship.

The more difficult the environment is regulatory-wise or capital-wise, the more it favors big, established players over startups. All these actions taken to prevent the 1930s' deflationary depression and stabilize the economy have ended up helping rich folks—especially in real estate and in the stock market. No wonder there are growing feelings of injustice, confusion, and anger throughout the country. The Great Recession made the growing schism between the 1 percent and the other 99 percent much worse, since it's now almost impossible to get a bank to lend you money if you're not a heavy hitter.

The money squeeze doesn't stop there. Before the recession, a lot of broker-dealers did what's called private placements; that is, they raised money for little businesses. These days the Financial Industry Regulatory Authority (FINRA), which oversees broker-dealers, has basically put unregistered, or private, placements in a very difficult position. Fewer are being done because of regulatory fears. And while it's true that there were abuses, the solutions have caused overregulation and ultimately resulted in hurting commerce and contributing to a system that, once again, is stacked against most startups. These types of all too frequently problematic solutions designed to deal with the lowest common denominator of abuse can cost society by sacrificing the greater good.

It's not as if the government doesn't recognize that we have a problem on the financial front. To help encourage the funding of small businesses and startups, the Jumpstart Our Business Startups (JOBS Act) was passed by Congress, with bipartisan support no less, and signed into law by President Obama on April 5, 2012. The idea was to ease related federal regulations and allow individuals to become investors. Under Title III of the JOBS Act, the U.S. Securities and Exchange Commission (SEC) was required to enact regulations permitting companies to offer and sell securities through

crowdfunding offerings within 270 days of the date of the legislation—that is, on January 5, 2013.

For whatever reasons, the SEC did not act as Congress had
required. Instead, it didn't even propose its initial set of rules until
October 2013, with its final set of rules not going into effect until
May 16, 2016.[16] Almost any lawyer would have advised clients not
to use the law that Congress had passed until the rules that the SEC
was supposed to prepare were final. That's exactly the advice my attorney gave me. So any benefits that could stem from the JOBS Act were
delayed for four years. Any way you slice it, in my world that's shocking
and unacceptable.

A Change in Attitude

While overregulation is proving just as harmful as overmedication, few
seem to be paying attention to the resulting unintended consequences.
Instead, despite entrepreneurship's new popularity, government officials are seemingly determined to nail people for infractions no matter
what the situation.

That's not how it used to be.

Like a lot of entrepreneurs, I jumped in without knowing what I
was doing. You may remember that as a college freshman, having sunk
all my own money into buying my first rooming house, I coaxed a
number of my University of Michigan classmates into putting up $200
each and co-investing in a second one. I would go on to put together
some thirty-five or forty partnerships before I was twenty-one years
old. I had probably raised over $50 million in partnership investments
before I knew there were laws regulating that sort of thing. Then I got
a phone call from a guy who identified himself as Hugh Makens, the
director at the Michigan Corporation & Securities Bureau for the Michigan Department of Commerce.

"What's that?" I asked.

Makens explained that limited partnership interests were securities,
which entailed various legal requirements.

"I hear rumors that you're selling these partnership interests illegally," he said.

Ouch! That did not sound good.

Today a regulator would look at that as a great opportunity to make an example of someone, but in those days, Makens just wanted to get me to do the right thing. He requested that I, accompanied by a lawyer, come up to the Securities Bureau in Lansing and meet with him and his team. Since my original attorney clearly wasn't the man for the job, I quickly stepped up my game. At that meeting, Makens helped me understand how to put together these partnerships legally. In short, instead of locking me up, he told me how to do things the right way. I later became a model on how to legally offer securities and became good friends with the Securities Bureau team.

While some of the decline in entrepreneurship can be or should be blamed on the maturity of the economy and big getting bigger, a change in attitude over the years has also contributed to the current entrepreneurial deficit.

Instead of creating legally binding mandates for every minor detail, it just might make more sense for us to step back, take a deep breath, and start from an attitude of respect for ethics and the rule of law, along with an agreement to work towards viable compromises or solutions on a case-by-case basis when problems arise. By taking a different approach and looking at the bigger picture instead of getting stuck in the minutiae, we can better avoid the unintended consequences that are hurting small businesses. Ultimately, there would be more opportunities for startups if we didn't create so many small hoops (many engulfed in flames) for them to jump through.

Instead, however, too many of us are a part of a very broken system of money and influence, where the dialogue isn't about how can we work together or what is a good balance. It isn't about what is just or equitable. Instead, it's all about how to minimize potential damage from would-be competitors by grandfathering in businesses already in existence—that is, making it tougher on the new guy but leaving established businesses alone.

This us-versus-them attitude extends to local government. In many, though clearly not all, areas of the country, ethics and caring about others have been sacrificed in the name of winning at all costs. The concept of integrity seems about as American as apple pie. But somehow, it's not what it once was.

The attitude and ethics of a country have everything to do with whether or not we provide a fair, level playing field, which is what we must strive for if we want to encourage startups and widespread entrepreneurship. But that's clearly not happening. Too many entrepreneurs across the country have opted for financial success over supporting fairness and a system in which anyone with a viable business can thrive.

Businesses basically succeed by having barriers to entry, which come from being the only one on an island surrounded by water even though everybody else wants to be on the island as well. Let's face it. Barriers to entry in general are a great way to make money. If you have a monopoly, meaning you control an industry or a business with no competition, your company generally has a much higher profit margin than if you were in a very competitive business.

Some barriers to entry occur because of totally legitimate circumstances. For instance, if you've developed a great new technology, getting patents on it will protect you from people trying to knock you off. That's fair. The same thing is true with drugs. Pharmaceutical companies spend a lot of money to create a drug, so having a barrier to entry for a period of time seems like a reasonable concept. In fact, in the name of success, every business should look to establish barriers to entry. But that's different from trying to eliminate competition in order to dominate the market.

Does the latter happen?

You bet.

Potential competitors can be discouraged by making it expensive for customers to switch service providers or by making it expensive to start a business in that field. And newcomers can be denied entry—or forced out—through legislation and industry regulation, which is why corporate America spends a lot of money to influence and entrench itself at the expense of a fairer playing field. The relationship between money and politics is a huge problem for small startups, especially since the large, established companies can buy influence and steer policy toward a monopoly.

These sorts of bad barriers—which also include overregulation, limits on new businesses, and the tightening of money—simply help companies like mine get bigger at the expense of smaller entrepreneur developers who need getting started to be as easy as possible and who definitely need the ability to secure funding. Oh, and let's not forget our legal system, which has been twisted into a bad barrier of entry that limits competition at the expense of our country's entrepreneurship.

Justice for All

Beyond finding capital and the impact of too much or too little regulation when it comes to entrepreneurship, we also have problems with our legal system. That's a double whammy for startups and small businesses.

Regulatory protections, which are necessary, by their nature inherently involve paperwork, restrictions, accountant services (not exactly inexpensive), and legal services (definitely not inexpensive). For a large company, the costs can likely be passed on to the consumer. That's not something a startup can do, assuming it even has the funds to lay out for such services in the first place. In this way, we have geared the economy to favor big over small.

Nowhere does that show up more than with the legal system. Barriers to entry that rig the system in favor of big companies often involve intellectual property that's protected under legal standards, or interpretation of contracts enforced by litigation.

It's simply getting tougher and more expensive to get justice under the law, and this is only getting worse. The all-too-frequent ploy of delaying cases and driving up costs so that people are forced to settle instead of getting their day in court is just plain wrong. But that's a reality for any startup or small business. Litigation for smaller amounts of money is virtually impossible, because of the costs and complexities of lawsuits today.

Legal Brawling

In my world, I try to get along with people. When there's a dispute, I find resolution through communication and negotiation. In other words, I like talking about mutual grounds and facts to make sure differences are real and to find compromise. But all too often these days, that approach proves impossible.

Seeing the world as black and white instead of shades of gray is a dangerous thing. Our legal system allows and even encourages extreme fights to go on for years and years at enormous costs. That simply tells small aspiring entrepreneurs that they can't play in this arena.

Our courts, however, aren't being used just to prevent people from doing business. In an increasingly litigious society, the legal system is used and abused by people looking to profit at the expense of others.

Carrie, the café owner you read about in Chapter 3, recently told me about five lawsuits she had survived over the course of just one year.

"One of my employees who was mad at another one claimed sexual harassment. Another employee claimed to have been hit by the refrigerator door two years prior—just one day before the statute of limitations had expired. A third employee found a lawyer who filed a class action suit over wage and hour laws that I didn't really understand or know about. Once I looked into it and discovered what was right, I aggressively went out and found every employee I owed any money to and paid them. The lawyer sued me anyway," she said. "It's amazing how many twists and turns can almost put you out of business and get you thinking, *Why am I doing this*? I had to go for most of last year [seven years after opening the coffee shop] without a salary, so I could afford to pay legal bills. But I'm still here."

As Carrie was telling me about her legal issues, I was reminded of a lawsuit years ago against our Senza hotel in Napa Valley. The lawyer, we later found out, had sued hundreds of properties by having one

American with Disabilities Act client as the plaintiff, using Google Earth to find hotel properties that were older and then filing complaints about accessibility issues. In our case, the lawyer had some out-of-date information about a condition we had already rectified, as we are always very sensitive to accessibility. Ultimately after months—and significant time, effort, and money—the case was fully dismissed.

That said, there are a lot of lawyers today who, as Carrie and I have found out the hard way, make entrepreneurship a lot more complicated and difficult, especially when they file lawsuits not so much to solve a real problem or multiple problems, but just to shake people down for money. In most cases, those lawsuits require a serious outlay of funds even when the defendant is in the right.

If you're an entrepreneur who isn't a billionaire and who doesn't have a high-tech unicorn idea, you're not only going to find it harder to fund your project or your business today than a few decades ago, but you'll find it almost impossible to defend it. All too often, small startups and businesses don't have the money to sue or can't last long enough to find justice through the legal system. They're screwed. If they have to protect intellectual property, a growing problem for today's businesses, they're really screwed. No wonder startups are going under. The moment you start to succeed and are seen as a competitive threat, all the big guy has to do is eat you.

There's something seriously wrong with a court system that encourages and supports that kind of unscrupulous lack of ethics, but by virtue of high costs and long delays, that's often the practical result. While I would love to tackle this issue in more detail, it would require another book entirely. The point is that this is one more area that during my fifty years as an entrepreneur has become increasingly problematic.

In an era of overregulation that threatens businesses from inception, it's critical that small entrepreneurs and startups have some form of real justice that occurs in an efficient economic way and on a fairer basis than it does today. "Justice for all" shouldn't be for sale to the highest bidder or to the person who can most afford to contend with the court system.

It sure didn't used to be this way.

"As previously mentioned, when I bought that very first rooming house at age eighteen, I asked my real estate agent, Bernice, to check with the seller about the length of the ground-floor lease. I knew that apartment was worth $450 per month and that the current tenants were paying only $70 because they were managing the property, something I planned to handle. After the sale went through, I discovered that instead of the month-to-month lease we'd been told they had, they actually had a verbally enforceable lease with just under a year to go. So I sued the seller for misrepresenting the property, using the real estate attorney who had closed the sale to handle the court case. I think he worked for $50 an hour.

The lawsuit went on for a year or so, and I was under financial stress the entire time. Even working full-time jobs at the University of Michigan hospital, I was barely making my payments. Ultimately, we prevailed; the lawyer's fee was a whopping $350. Even adjusted for inflation, that sum is a pittance compared to the industry average for a lawsuit today; legal fees on a small case can run several hundred thousand dollars. The fees on bigger cases are considerably more. I sued an ex-partner for fraud and won. When he appealed, I won again. In total I collected $30 million. That's rare. Oh, by the way, my lawyers collected $18 million over the course of the eight-year grind. Yes, I netted $12 million. Even though I wasn't made whole, it could have been worse. But really, when it takes eight years and a huge financial risk in terms of paying out exorbitant legal fees to fight for your rights in court, that's anything but real justice.

Reality Check

I may be naive, but from the time I was a teenager and started working, I have always believed that being fair generally works to your advantage. Most people like to do repeat business with people who are fair and just in their dealings.

However, as I look back over the past fifty years being in business, it seems that people today are much more polarized than they used to be, and a lot more specialist lawyers are all too primed for combat. As a result, too much of business today involves fighting over regulations or polarized perspectives on issues. And an awful lot of that happens in court. These are in part unintended consequences of trying to build a system to protect, regulate, and resolve conflicts.

Overall our U.S. rule of law is a great system, particularly if you have a big budget. Don't get me wrong. I'm grateful we have the system we have, particularly when it comes to preserving our freedom along with some sense of boundaries and right and wrong. I just wish we could find solutions that would help judges speed things along, hold lawyers accountable to ethics rules, and create effective small claims courts at high levels of, say, $1 million. Regrettably, these days some people seem to harbor more of a legalistic "get away with what you can" attitude instead of taking pride in the "my handshake is my bond" idea. That's too bad, as ethics and how one approaches business can be a good way to stay out of court.

In years past, taking a case to court was seen more as a last resort. Business legal disputes occurred less frequently than they do today, and when they did occur, they were usually worked out. That has clearly changed. Today's combative world is toughest on new and small businesses, largely due to expensive lawsuits they can't afford even when their survival depends on it.

There has to be a better way.

CHAPTER 7

Corporate Darwinism, Technology, and Greed

Just as our whole country has been impacted by otherwise well-intended overregulation, it's been hijacked by the consolidation of every sector of our economy. Nowhere is this more obvious than in retail. The term "Walmartization" describes the increasing phenomenon of Americans' turning to big businesses and chains. Not only do the big stores usually have what consumers are searching for, but they can often offer deals that smaller businesses can't begin to match. That's because big-box stores and other mega-chains have the resources and the systems to offer consumers discounted pricing while maintaining their own profit margins.[1] Costco is a notable exception to this, since it actually has lower margins, which it makes up for with volume and efficiency. Either way, entrepreneurs with small businesses can't begin to compete in this kind of marketplace, which explains why so many have had to fold.[2]

Now even those big businesses are being crowded out by the internet and online shopping. Let's face it. If it's tough for a gigantic entity like Walmart to compete with the likes of Facebook, Google, Amazon, and Apple, which combined have a value of almost $2.5 trillion, what's a simple startup supposed to do?

"Greed is good," Gordon Gekko says in the movie *Wall Street*. Like a lot of subjects in this book, that's a two-sided coin as far as I'm concerned. Growing a business is certainly good. There's no way that going from small to bigger is a bad thing, unless you do it by making it impossible for the other guy, whomever the other guy may be, to do business. Facebook, for example, has shown little compunction when it comes to buying out potential competitors, making it clear that the target companies can either sell out to Facebook or have the features that made them so popular copied.[3] Talk about the big getting bigger!

While on the one hand we have Warren Buffet, Bill Gates, and a number of other generous souls doing a lot of good in the world, we also have rising greed and selfishness among many entrenched businesses. As the rich have gotten richer over the past few decades, every industry I've been involved with has experienced dramatic consolidation. This corporate Darwinism (survival of the biggest) has created a political constituency of bigger players, which has decimated any kind of level playing field for startups.

In 2016, President Obama's White House issued the following statement:

> Across our economy, too many consumers are dealing with inferior or overpriced products, too many workers aren't getting the wage increases they deserve, too many entrepreneurs and small businesses are getting squeezed out unfairly by their bigger competitors, and overall we are not seeing the level of innovative growth we would like to see. And a big piece of why that happens is anti-competitive behavior—companies stacking the deck against their competitors and their workers.[4]

That takes a toll on all of us and points to yet another contributing factor to greater challenges and lessening opportunities for startups. As a result, as the Brookings Institution chart in Chapter 1 shows, startups are down dramatically in *every* industry group.

Corporate Darwinism for the purposes of my book is about economic cycles' being Darwinian. In other words, it's about picking off weak companies and leaving stronger survivors. In the case of corporations, this often involves corporate consolidation as well. In looking up "corporate Darwinism" online, I found that some definitions are inconsistent with "survival of the biggest." In my intended use of the words, I'm really referring to survival of the biggest and corporate consolidation, which in my view is a product of the evolution occurring in the business community. It sure didn't used to be this way.

Big Is Triumphing Over Small (and New)

Looking back over my years as an entrepreneur, I see that a lot has changed in the United States. Some of the changes have made it easier and better for entrepreneurship; I'll cover those in Part II when I talk about how we can build on good movements to help increase the number of business startups. Before we consider that, however, we need to look at one clear trend that has dominated the past few decades—massive consolidation driven by technology, globalization, political policies, and just plain greed—and decreased opportunity for new businesses.

The theory of corporate Darwinism stipulates that big conquers little and that most businesses want to escalate in size and profitability. That kind of success is a good thing in my book. But with a longer, slower burn, this natural desire of companies to get bigger coupled with the creativity of capital formation, which these days is happening in the stock market and all kinds of different financial vehicles, encourages acquisitions and growth on the one side, and the failure of those who can no longer compete on the other.

We have all observed the death of a number of small businesses on Main Streets that have been crowded out by bigger businesses selling the same goods for less money. Just as Wilds and Walt Drugs disappeared, so have most bookstores. Even RadioShack and Toys "R" Us have bitten the dust.

Businesses come and go. There are always plenty of businesses that go out of business as new startups come in. That's the nature of entrepreneurial evolution. In addition, the past few decades have seen a continual decline in startups of small businesses. Welcome to the dark sides of consolidation, globalization, and technology that have simply wiped out the need for many small businesses. As globalization has shipped lower-priced labor jobs outside of the U.S., entrepreneurs have lost the ability to start or own textile mills, along with many other manufacturing businesses. Similarly, technology has made many things so much faster, cheaper, and better that a lot of smaller service businesses, including management systems and accounting firms, for example, are no longer needed.

Arguably, some of this shift away from small business is in the interest of efficiency and boils down to an evolutionary survival of the fittest. Globalization and technology have driven a revolution of innovation and new frontiers in business that have benefited the U.S. and the world. But a lot of the shift away from Main Street startups has happened because of the overregulation and restriction of capital for new entrepreneurs to start a business, both of which we talked about in the last chapter.

This corporate Darwinism has created a political constituency of bigger players who want to keep expanding. As we've seen, one way to do that is by having fewer competitors, and one way you have fewer competitors is by making it more difficult for people to start a new business and to come into your space. Another is to eliminate existing competition through dramatic consolidation.

This trend is damaging the entrepreneurial opportunity that has been—and should be—such an integral part of the American experience. And it's happening in every industry. Let's look at just four of the ones I'm involved with, starting with software.

Less Is Not More These Days

In 2000, I bought most of the stock of a small software company that we called Skywire Software. The company went along for a number of years growing very modestly until we came to a turning point. We had to become a bigger fish or we were going to get eaten.

"We need to do some acquisitions and grow or get out," I told our CEO, Patrick Brandt.

Patrick made a list of companies to buy. We decided to make a run at acquiring a small public company called DocuCorp, which was in the business of insurance document software. The chairman, it turned out, was a friend of mine. When I inquired as to whether or not the board would sell, we discovered that our timing was good. Very good. For a variety of reasons, the board actually did want to sell, and we were able to negotiate a deal. So we bought DocuCorp, took it private, and folded it into Skywire. We then bought a number of other insurance document software companies. Patrick did a great job cutting overhead and combining these companies.

By 2007, Skywire just might have been the largest software company in the insurance document space (even though by software standards we were still pretty small). Despite its being dominant in a sliver of the field, I came to the realization that a great consolidation was occurring in software that has continued to this day, with customers wanting to buy their software from as few suppliers as possible so that everything would be compatible, the purchase process streamlined, and any service needed down the line facilitated. I figured that we had to get out before we got run over. So in 2007 and 2008, we sold part of our business to Oracle for $240 million, and later another part of our business to EMC, and finally a third piece to a Canadian company. In each sale we tried to give bigger companies pieces they needed for their consolidation. While that helped us command the kinds of prices we were looking for, in hindsight we were part of helping the big get bigger.

It was corporate Darwinism in action. We were going to benefit by being bought by a bigger player or risk the consequences of bigger players taking over our competition and squeezing us out. In the long run, I'm pretty sure we would not have made it on our own. Fortunately, that's not the same extreme case with real estate, at least for now.

Real Estate Then and Now

The same consolidation we've seen with software has occurred with real estate, but not to the same extent.

When I started in the 1960s, a complex with fifty apartments was considered large. A big-time owner of apartments had maybe five thousand or ten thousand apartments. That helps explain why by the time I was thirty-four, my company was the second-largest owner in the world with seventy-two thousand apartments.

As my budding company grew over a fifteen-year period starting in the 1970s, we raised more than a billion dollars in equity capital one investor at a time. While raising more than a billion dollars wasn't easy, that's small compared to today's 225 real estate investment trusts with approximately $1.1 trillion in total capital[5] and companies that have multibillions in capital with which to buy real estate. These capital markets are one of the drivers involved in the real estate big players getting ever larger.

Part of what enables capital markets and real estate to consolidate and grow is technology. The ability to control and manage operations of this size is a whole lot easier today than it used to be. Fifty years ago, before the internet and without even the most basic software, everything was much more expensive and difficult to do. That said, a lot of smaller accounting firms had plenty of business in those days, and many more people were employed doing accounting and trying to build software. Machines have clearly displaced a lot of people in real estate, as in many other industries. So the resulting increase in productivity carries with it the negatives of eliminating jobs and some small businesses. That's the bad news.

The positive side of that coin is that technology hasn't just facilitated real estate operations and management; it has transformed the availability of information. We all used to be seat-of-the-pants developers who had very little in the way of market data upon which to base decisions. We would go into any given area and guess at how much demand there would be if we built fifty or one hundred apartments. So if I wanted to go build an apartment building, I'd have to walk around the city and put my finger up in the air and wonder, *Is there demand or not?*

The problem in Dallas in the old days was that there were always so many talented real estate companies that if one hundred apartments were needed, several companies would each build one hundred apartments and we would all lose.

Today I don't even have to walk outside or visit another city if I'm looking outside of Dallas. I can just go on the internet and start pulling reports for free that give me a vast amount of information. If my preliminary research looks good, I can keep digging or I can do what a lender is going to force me to do anyway and hire somebody who does this for a living, and that person will write a report with so many numbers it'll make my head spin. And that will tell me if building the apartments is a good or bad idea.

As a rule, industries are becoming much more efficient, much more scientific, and less fly-by-the-seat-of-the-pants. We just have much more information to collect, synthesize, and understand. Developers and lenders all have access to these huge amounts of real-time data, which substantially lessens their risk and contributes to making real estate more corporate and less entrepreneurial.

For starters, the investment money chases larger and larger real estate portfolios—public real estate investment trusts—which can then turn around and finance the construction of a new building by using their public stock market equity and their borrowing capacity. That all comes in at a fraction of the cost of a competitor who has to go out and raise money from individual investors and put together a limited partnership like I did.

Generally, the bigger you are, the more efficiently you can purchase and borrow, which automatically puts startups at a disadvantage. The company with the several-hundred-million-dollar market capitalization also has several hundred million dollars of debt at a very, very low interest rate.

If your company is a private, small, growing, or aspiring competitor, the game is further stacked against you. Not only will you have to pay more for the business capital you need, but you're also going to pay more for janitorial supplies, toilet paper, computer paper, notepads, and any other supplies simply because you're not buying in bulk like large companies are.

Strike one for startups.

The Wine Business

Just as with real estate, consolidation is going on like crazy in the wine business. There's still a massive number of small wine producers, just as there are plenty of people who still own one or two apartment buildings. But increasingly the three main groups involved with making and selling wine—the producers who make it, the distributors that sell it, and the stores and restaurants that buy it—are merging into larger and larger entities. That's especially true on the distribution side of things.

While my wine business experience goes back only twenty-five years, even in that short time my company has seen dramatic changes in the distribution network. Where we used to have some thirty distributors in California, you can now count them all on one hand, thanks to mergers and acquisitions. So, of course, they've become huge. While there are some new small distributors coming up, the few with any real clout have divided up the United States among themselves.

Similarly, in the production area, a lot of wineries are selling out to corporate ownership. The economies of scale of companies' having multiple brands and selling them through the same channels are enormous. The large corporations that are acquiring these wineries aren't folding them under a single, generic umbrella. Mondavi, for example, is still marketed as Mondavi, even though it was purchased by Constellation Brands in 2004.[6] A lot of this is driven by the advantage bigger companies have in capital markets. Like real estate, wine is a capital-intensive business, and having more capital at lower costs benefits the big instead of the small.

In the end, not only do these large companies wind up with more and more control over the wine industry, but they can increase their bottom lines using their efficiencies while maintaining the little guy's uniqueness. So theoretically they wind up with the best of both worlds, along with the ability to market these wineries as if they're still a family business.

That's not happening just in the wine business. Large companies interested in craft beer, iced tea, and more are realizing that it's easier and more profitable to buy an existing company than to create a new one. As they expand, so does their competitive edge.

Strike two for startups.

Banking and Lending

Is the deck really stacked against entrepreneurs and aspiring entrepreneurs? You bet, starting with finances. As we've seen, capital availability has been greatly restricted to big companies and big ideas with a heavy emphasis on tech and California.

Yes, there are disadvantages inherent in being a small fish in a pond of large ones. That certainly holds true on the lending front, where banks are definitely getting bigger and fewer. In 2013, there were six thousand commercial banks[7] licensed and 936 savings and loans.[8] Today, there are no savings and loans and fewer than five thousand banks.[9] The small community banks occasionally get public policy support and can stage a resurgence of sorts, but in general it's all about the big ones. And they're not just big these days, they're huge. As of July 2018, JPMorgan Chase & Co. had $2.59 trillion in assets,[10] Wells Fargo had $1.88 trillion,[11] and Citigroup had $1.92 trillion.[12] There are a couple of other giants, but you get the idea.

These monster numbers and some significant competition from a growing number of other robust financial institutions mean that these banks need to focus on big, strong customers whose growth they can facilitate and support. Where does that leave the average entrepreneur? Nowhere. Big banks don't really have the time or ability to deal with small growing businesses, let alone startups, in their traditional lending roles. Despite the reality that startups are not their customers, to their credit some of the big banks, including JPMorgan, Goldman Sachs, and others, have created social programs to try to help startup entrepreneurs. I'll describe these in future chapters. But that doesn't always help the aspiring entrepreneur or small-business owner who needs a loan— and, as we've seen, many of the smaller banks that might have helped in the past have gone by the wayside. No wonder our HALL Structured Finance company is doing so well.

We're proud of helping entrepreneurs turn their visions into reality by making loans to build hotels and other properties. I have the greatest respect for those who borrow from HALL Structured Finance. To see how hard entrepreneurs work to put together the complex financial and business structures required to build a hotel is truly amazing. Even before my company looks at doing a construction loan, in many cases years of work related to the potential hotel has already taken place. People's motivation to engage in that level of risk taking is just incredible. When it pays off and the hotel goes from a dream to reality, our society winds up with new jobs, new hotel rooms, and a great uplift to a local economy. That's really what America is all about. We need these types of entrepreneurs.

The fact that these entrepreneurs are ending up with private lenders such as HALL Structured Finance because they lack more economical bank financing has been beneficial for our business, but there needs to be a bigger solution. Banks are less expensive because their funds come from deposits insured by the government. As we'll discuss later in the book, if the federal government helped private lenders, we would be able to lower rates. But to date our efforts to become an SBIC so we could lower our rates and increase our lending have been turned down by the SBA. I'm sure we're far from the only one, which is definitely not helpful for the rest of the country and is a deterrent to aspiring businesspeople.

Strike three for entrepreneurs.

The U.S. needs to make sure that startups and growing businesses have capital support just like stronger companies do, but consolidation within banking makes this an increasing challenge. It doesn't have to be this way. In Part II, we'll look at the many options we can employ to help level the playing field. But before we can rectify the situation, we need to acknowledge and talk about the problem.

Is Big Always Better?

In the United States, we have had very little public dialogue about whether bigger is better and whether corporate Darwinism, technology, and basic structural changes in our economy are fostering a situation that inadvertently rigs the system against the little guy. In the absence of conversation about the situation and governors to control it, greed will win out. But it doesn't have to. Just as our federal government controls mergers of companies that have reached certain levels to make sure we avoid monopolies and maintain a reasonably competitive landscape, we can use public policy to impact the state of entrepreneurship.

This is a problem that we all should care about. We can and should talk about what our values are in terms of entrepreneurship and fostering an environment in which people have a fairer, level playing field to start businesses. If we don't, the U.S. will continue on the path it's on, being a very strong, innovative billionaire entrepreneurship country with a declining number of startups per capita, a decline in the jobs and productivity gains those startups create, and a worse business environment.

Just as our country's main industry went from farming to factories, a certain amount of business evolution is inevitable. Today's trend toward consolidation means that big guys are going to squish little guys who don't have the platform to fight back. The answer isn't to try to turn back the clock by penalizing corporate Darwinian growth, but to figure out how to help new businesses compete against the efficiencies of bigger companies, as well as how to incubate new industries like app development, for example, as those will provide jobs, a tax base, and communities we want to live in.

Being big may allow companies to produce and distribute goods and services faster and more cheaply, but it negates other benefits inherent for traditional nontechnology startups. So we have to ask ourselves whether we want this kind of big dominance to continue, or whether we want to take action at the federal level to also have more opportunities for startups. I would argue strongly for the latter.

PART II

SOLUTIONS

Building Bridges to Level the Playing Field

Now we are ready for what Einstein suggested should be the five minutes of our hour. As we have described in Part I, defining why entrepreneurial startups are down in the U.S. today is complex and nuanced. While there are no simple solutions, there are some potentially game-changing strategies I will propose. Moreover, as we touched on in Part I, there are a lot of positive efforts being made in connection with entrepreneurship. They should be applauded and continued because ultimately, with much-needed federal support, we may hit a tipping point where things get materially better.

The first chapter of this part of the book focuses on policies at the federal level that can make a huge difference. These are not perfect ideas. Rather, they're intended to be a launching pad to create a discussion and ultimately lead to legislation that can make a difference.

The final two chapters describe and recognize the activities of local governments, nonprofits, and educational programs working to address the challenges facing entrepreneurs and startups today. Following the conclusion are appendixes that will lead you to more resources related to both the local government efforts and the nonprofit activities.

At the risk of repeating myself, I remind you that as commendable as all these endeavors are, on their own they are not yet enough to change the current trajectory. For real progress to be made, we need federal policies to step in.

CHAPTER 8

Game-Changing Public Policies

When I was growing up, almost everybody assumed that those in my generation were going to be more successful than our parents. Indeed, our parents told us that. Today, however, many kids as well as their parents have abandoned that notion. Many people today are simply concerned with making ends meet and getting by.

Why does this matter?

Because if we don't provide hope and opportunity, we'll ultimately create the kinds of dangerous outcomes brought about by hopelessness, and a country that does not embody the heritage and greatness of America.

We don't have to settle for that scenario. But that's exactly what will happen if we don't start addressing the issues surrounding the need for broader-based opportunities.

While being an entrepreneur is not for everyone, the ability to start and own a business of one's own is an integral part of being an American. From 1997 until the fall of 2001, under President Clinton and President Bush, my wife was the U.S. ambassador to Austria. During that period, I learned firsthand what the former Soviet countries bordering Austria were like from a business perspective, as I bought and started companies there. The experiences taught me to appreciate even more the freedoms I had growing up, including the opportunity to be an entrepreneur. You don't get that in a communist country, and I can't imagine that we want to lose that opportunity in this country.

However, entrepreneurship in the U.S., despite its popularity, has become much more of a challenge, because we haven't really made it a priority in terms of public policy. If we as a country decide that we value startups and small businesses over simply chasing unicorn ideas, then we need public debate that shines a light on the problems facing U.S. entrepreneurship.

Either way, as a society we need to restructure our country's policies so they reflect our ongoing need to improve efficiency and advance technologically, while recognizing the toll that consolidation, globalization, and technology are taking on retail and other industries. In short, we have to figure out how to encourage new types of small businesses and startups. We should be asking:

- What kind of environment do we want for startups in our country?
- Do we care if only the big and strong survive?
- Does it matter that, according to the World Bank, when it comes to the ease of starting a business, we are forty-ninth in the world and slipping?[1]
- Do we want a society in which everyone is trying to get an edge on everyone else at the expense of integrity and ethics?
- Do we care more about greed and self-interest than a level playing field?

Finally, if we really do want a society that encourages the American ideal of owning one's own business, which seems to be going by the wayside, then the next question we have to ask is what we're going to do about that.

The Critical Role of Federal Policy

There is no question that we have some state and local practices that are working. The nonprofit support for entrepreneurship is great.

Educational institutions are helpful. However, all of that, which we'll talk about in subsequent chapters, has not solved the problem. The single most needed addition is the help of federal public policy.

For its 2018 *State of Entrepreneurship* report, the Kauffman Foundation partnered with two research firms, Public Opinion Strategies and Global Strategy Group, to conduct a nationwide representative survey of 2,165 entrepreneurs. They found that, by a strong margin, entrepreneurs feel that the federal government favors big companies over startups and small businesses. More than half perceive that businesses larger than theirs are doing better than they are in part because of government incentives not available to smaller companies.

Their perceptions are absolutely correct.

What a sad irony that the entrepreneurs who most need support get it least! Simple logic will tell you that young startup businesses need help more than established or growing companies that have been in business for more than five years.

In this chapter, we will explore the types of federal actions that could be taken to improve the state of U.S. entrepreneurship. These include game-changing policies designed to help the flow of capital into traditional startups, policies designed to help provide more banking support once startups begin to grow and get going, policies that would bolster women- and minority-led startups, and policies designed to provide more of a cushion and debt relief for millennial entrepreneurs to take risks.

We need a national agenda that recognizes and prioritizes the need for solutions and policy changes at all levels of government. Many politicians claim to be pro business and pro entrepreneurs, yet they are most likely not aware of the problems I have described in this book.

It's time we changed that and started leveling the playing field. Substantive federal policy changes to encourage capital for traditional startups—and other policies to improve the environment for startups—are desperately needed.

The Hamilton Project

One of the key voices behind this sentiment is the Hamilton Project, which launched in 2006 as a public policy initiative of the Brookings Institution. The Hamilton Project has spearheaded and disseminated research related to, among other things, problems stemming from the decline of entrepreneurship. It has also offered specific solutions, some of which I will share later in this chapter when I address the state of women and people of color in entrepreneurship.

I'm fascinated by the Hamilton Project's work in part because it's inspired by Alexander Hamilton, the nation's first secretary of the treasury, who symbolized the American values of opportunity and upward mobility. Hamilton believed in enhancing market forces with "prudent aids and encouragements on the part of government."[2] Clearly, as I have said throughout this book, I believe this kind of public policy is a fundamental part of our economic system and is critical to helping bridge the opportunity gap that exists for most entrepreneurs.

As David R. Burton, senior fellow in economic policy at The Heritage Foundation, pointed out in his 2015 testimony before the U.S. House of Representatives' Committee on Small Business, "There is not any one policy change—or even a few—that will lead to a sudden renaissance in entrepreneurship. Since the decline is caused by the combined weight of many poor public policies, the solution requires systematically improving public policy in a wide variety of areas."[3] While I agree with Burton, there are some new policies that could really make a difference.

The Politics of Big vs. Small

Public policy does not happen in a vacuum, nor do we elect policymakers who bring vast knowledge on every subject. Instead, policy is heavily influenced by the politics of the day, including the critical money that helps elected officials gain and retain their positions. Campaign monies flow to both parties from big companies looking to gain and maintain influence.

Part of the way members of Congress get their information is from lobbyists hired by big businesses to further the causes of those businesses. The considerable influence of highly successful entrepreneurs who have grown large businesses is, by its nature, often contrary to the needs of people wanting to start a new business. And it's not like start-ups have lobbyists of their own. You can't exactly hire influencers if your company doesn't exist or is struggling to make it and you don't have the time or money to invest in swaying the political process. So even if you could create a constituency of wannabe entrepreneurs, by definition they wouldn't have any clout.

As a result, entrepreneurs and startups have virtually no seat at the table when it comes to influencing legislation, even though when it comes to the greater good of the country, they are probably the most important business constituency. Fortunately, there are a growing number of individuals, as well as organizations like the Kauffman Foundation and Center for American Progress, that care about the greater good. But make no mistake, politically the money and lobbyists remain devoted to the status quo.

At the risk of repeating myself, no wonder the gap between the haves and have-nots is getting bigger and bigger.

Let's look at how that actually plays out by reviewing the Tax Cuts and Jobs Act of 2017 that was passed. The new tax law—which was clearly designed to lower corporate taxes, as they went from 35 percent to 21 percent—had a couple of provisions that were very good for small businesses; specifically, incentives for companies to invest in otherwise difficult geographic areas and exemptions for smaller-revenue companies from the bill's interest limitation, both of which I'll talk about at greater length. But the provision to limit interest deductions for highly leveraged businesses, which seems to be designed to help make up the deficit created by slashing corporate taxes, discourages budding private companies from borrowing money to grow. Leverage—that is, debt financing—is a key part of many growing entrepreneurial businesses, and the new tax law's interest limitations will hurt these businesses and encourage acquisitions by bigger companies.

In the past, tax law in the United States has always encouraged debt through interest deductions for businesses. If you think about it, debt is one way to obtain capital to build assets that businesses use to produce goods and services. Accordingly, it provides the needed fuel for job creation and for innovation, much of which comes from small and growing businesses. Particularly in the areas of real estate and farming, a lot of businesses operate with huge amounts of debt. And while a complicated measure provides a way to opt out of the interest limitation, those businesses will suffer certain penalties in terms of an alternative depreciation system, making them less competitive than bigger real estate or farming companies that are public and generally have less debt.

Ironically, the new bill was marketed to the public as a tax simplification. This would be laughable if it weren't so bad for entrepreneurship. Not only did the tax laws get more complicated, but the growing businesses that create jobs are receiving little, if any, benefit while big corporations are receiving a huge windfall. In other words, once again we are seeing policies that favor the big and established over smaller startups that desperately need tax incentives.

Fiscal Protection

It's clear from the groundswell of support in the private sector, as the final two chapters will explain, that Americans deeply care about entrepreneurship. It is critical that public policies catch up to public sentiment and help bridge the gaps in opportunity.

As we've seen, the country has used fiscal policies—along with regulatory policies and various tools that the government has at all levels—to protect consumers by controlling monopolies; to assist people of color, including black Americans and Hispanics; and to help women compete on what we know isn't a level playing field. Giving that helping hand here and there has helped equalize opportunity. It's time to do that again on a larger scale.

Other countries are doing that and more. Countries like Israel.

Israel—a tiny country the size of Lake Michigan with 8.5 million people, a lot of political parties, widely divergent opinions, and a political system in which everybody fights over everything—is on fire entrepreneurially and has the world's highest density of startup companies. More than two hundred accelerators undoubtedly contribute to this unparalleled success, but that's just part of the story. I'll let Apolitical—a self-described "global network for government helping public servants find the ideas, people, and partners they need to solve the hardest challenges facing our societies"[4] explain:

> In a period when Israel's economy was disproportionately reliant on government funds, a venture capital initiative called Yozma leveraged public money to attract private investment, transforming the country into a global research and development hub. Between 1993 and 1998, the government offered to provide 40% of the money offered by private investors in combined funds, supporting more than 40 companies. The value of Yozma increased from $100 million in 1993 to $250 million by 1996, and the project is regarded as a rare example of government venture capital success.[5]

For another non-U.S. example, the government in France is far from the socialist entity I imagined it was prior to spending time there and better understanding it. It may surprise you to learn that France—which, according to *Forbes* "is home to the world's largest startup incubator,"[6]—outpaces the U.S., Germany, Italy, and the U.K. when it comes to the number of businesses per inhabitants. One explanation may lie in the fact that France's startups can take advantage of generous tax deductions, including a larger one for R&D than is offered in the U.S, Japan, the U.K., and Germany. Another lies in the changes that have come with the country's new, young president. I'll let *Forbes* explain:

> Using executive orders, [French president Emmanuel Macron has] quickly pushed through a raft of new employment laws, making it easier to hire—and fire. To add some honey to the medicine, he's also put $18 billion into professional retraining over the next

five years, including a controversial extension of unemployment insurance for France's growing number of self-employed and small business owners. He's slashing at taxes on wealth, capital gains and worker compensation, and "simplifying everything."

How far is Macron willing to go? He reveals to *Forbes* that next year he intends to permanently end France's notorious 30% "exit tax" on entrepreneurs who try to take money out of France—a tremendous disincentive for foreigners to start a business there and a strong incentive for French citizens to launch elsewhere. In doing so, he's moving in the opposite direction of President Trump, who has gleefully threatened American companies who expand abroad and promised subsidies for those who stay.[7]

The U.K. has also jet-propelled its entrepreneurship with its Seed Enterprise Investment Scheme (SEIS) program, which gives startups access to capital in exchange for equity and sizable tax breaks for investing in small and early-stage startup businesses. Introduced in 2011 as a way to boost economic growth in the U.K., the now wildly popular program was implemented the following year. SEIS investors may place a maximum of one hundred thousand British pounds (which can be spread over a number of companies) during a single tax year in return for up to a 50 percent reduction in their taxes for the particular year in which the investment was made. To qualify for the program, companies seeking this vital funding must be based in the U.K., have fewer than twenty-five employees, be no more than two years old, and have assets of less than two hundred thousand British pounds.

The results speak for themselves. By 2016, just four years after its inception, the SEIS provided 410 million pounds in capital to more than five thousand startups,[8] with the investment amount almost doubling from year to year.[9,10] Not bad for a country that's a third of the size of Texas. The fact that the U.K. offers working parents of preschoolers thirty hours of free childcare a week sure doesn't hurt either.[11]

It's time for U.S. federal policies to come to the aid of their country's entrepreneurship. And that starts with tax policies.

Tax Policy

Over my fifty-year career, understanding the practical impact of tax laws and how they likely will impact investing is something I have focused on a great deal. That probably wouldn't have happened with quite the same intensity or results had I not met Arthur Klearstien—a short guy with curly hair and big glasses—in 1974. At the time, I was six years into my real estate business, and Arthur was a brilliant lawyer with a master's in tax from New York University.

"You're stupid and doing everything wrong," he announced after looking at my recent deals. Then he bet me that he could structure the deal I had in process to raise over $3 million in a way that would be much more lucrative. He told me I could make a big profit, a first for me, plus raise way more to fix up the property than I thought possible. For a $60,000 fee, he would tell me how to do it. "And I'll wait to get paid until my ideas work," he concluded.

How could I say no?

Well, he got his fee and I learned a lot from him. One of the things I've never forgotten is that for decades before that deal was done and up until this very moment, Congress has used tax legislation to encourage or discourage investment activities. Sometimes it works well, and sometimes there are unintended consequences. Most big tax law changes have portions that are aimed at encouraging investment capital. In the Tax Cuts and Jobs Act of 2017, there are special tax write-offs that benefit investors in small-budget films or productions under $15 million. It's time we were intentional when it comes to using tax policy to help turn around U.S. entrepreneurship.

A lot of the big money going into Silicon Valley, New York, and Boston is for deals that consist of pension funds or similar pools of capital that are invested through professional venture capital companies. New Enterprise Associates (NEA), Sequoia Capital, and others now manage billions of dollars. Similarly, in real estate, big professional fund managers have gotten into the game. At the same time, all over the country, a lot of individuals are investing in real estate partnerships in part because of tax benefits.

We need to create the same interest when it comes to entrepreneurship. Today there's a lot of individual taxpayer money out there that is simply not being invested in startups—but that with some incentives could be. Fiscal policy has been used to incentivize capital for real estate and to encourage conservation easements to protect the environment. Tax benefits are offered to reward private companies for their investment in research and development.[12] So implementing tax policies to encourage capital formation for traditional startups seems obvious to me. This is a huge potential game changer. It is the single most effective way to catapult U.S. entrepreneurship, as it would increase funding, thereby solving the number-one problem inherent in starting up a new business. Moreover, it would encourage the private sector to allocate capital, and in turn oversight and help, to many startups, which ultimately would benefit the treasury. Finally, policies could and should be structured to help deals that likely would not otherwise get funded, rather than technology deals that have a lot of funding.

While the details—such as what areas of the country and what industries would qualify—are critical, the actual policy direction is not that complicated. Individual U.S. taxpayers could receive incentives to invest up to some per-person maximum amount in qualifying startups. For example, any individual taxpayer investing up to $250,000 in a startup business that's less than five years old with less than $10 million of total equity capital could write off for tax purposes the initial investment against active income while receiving a tax basis equal to 50 percent of the investment. (Limiting the amount that can be invested in a single startup will encourage investments in multiple startups rather than a concentration of investors' capital.) Similar to what the 2017 tax law did with many depreciable capital items, these investments would receive an immediate tax write-off instead of being written off only when a deal fails. To incentivize further investments, capital gains on successful venture investments could be deferred if investors reinvest those monies in startups within a one-year period.

The impacts of the above proposed tax incentives?

- Our country would have significantly more available capital for startups, as a lot of people would be motivated to take idle capital and put it to work (and then ideally help the startups they've invested in to succeed).

- New jobs would be created.

- This could well be a revenue-enhancing project, as more start-ups mean more business revenue and more jobs, all of which means more tax revenue that would pay for the incentive costs and then some.

For what it's worth, this is not a brand-new idea. The 2017 tax law has economic zones specified that defer capital gains, which is part of what I believe should be considered for investors who successfully profit from startups and then reinvest in the same types of startups. As I mentioned above, the idea has also been put into practice to encourage the creation of qualified films, television shows, and theatrical productions. Like I suggested for startups, the new section 181 of the 2017 Tax Cuts and Jobs Act provides for a 100 percent deduction of reinvested monies. In this case, the productions cannot exceed $15 million. That might be a better number for startups than the $10 million I proposed.

While the details of these proposals will be subject to a lot of debate and retooling, the key point remains that using tax laws to help encourage capital investment in startups is something that we desperately need. The fact that there's precedent on this front can only help.

I'm not here to get overly technical or say there is only one way to design the tax changes. But I would point out that the Center for American Entrepreneurship lists a number of interesting tax-related proposals on its website.[13] The Center for American Entrepreneurship is a very impressive advocacy group that was started in 2017. It, like the Kauffman Foundation, offers great research and great ideas. I became aware of the Center for American Entrepreneurship as I was completing this book and have enormous respect for its thoughtful and detailed ideas about taxes and more. That said, the perspective I share in this book is that of an entrepreneur who has a lot of experience with tax incentives.

The bottom line, in my experience: If Congress enacts thoughtful tax incentives, huge progress could be made towards entrepreneurship's number-one issue—the availability of capital for the nontechnology, not likely grand-slam but still very important startups.

Target Areas (and Possibly Target Businesses) for Entrepreneurship Zones

I'm not talking about equal opportunity tax relief. From the start of this book, we have looked at the dramatic opportunity gap between areas in the U.S. where entrepreneurship is flourishing—places like Silicon Valley, Boston, and New York—and the vast part of the United States where it's not. While we may never be able to eliminate this gap, we certainly need to shrink it. Put another way, taxpayers don't need to encourage a flow of money into Silicon Valley in the same way that they need to encourage a flow of money into the rural Midwest or the South.

With all of this in mind, the above tax incentives should encourage capital formation in target areas that need it the most. In addition to identifying these entrepreneurship incentive zones, we might even consider delineating industry groups that could use some federal-incentive bolstering as opposed to those that don't. Tech, for example, is doing just fine on its own. Manufacturing is another story.

The above tax incentives are a solid way to encourage investment that otherwise wouldn't occur in the areas or industries that desperately need it. But funding needs to become more readily available if we want startups and small businesses to succeed.

Boosting Female- and Minority-Led Startups

That's particularly true for female- and minority-led startups. We don't need to just level the playing field when it comes to certain types of entrepreneurs. First, we have to actually get more of them on the field.

So yes, it's time for some equal opportunity initiatives, as according to national research, women and people of color are a lot less likely than white males to start or own their own businesses.[14]

Federal programs—some of which exist and need to be expanded and others that need to be created—could address the three main obstacles preventing people of color and women from joining the entrepreneurship ranks:

- Access to capital, a problem discussed in Chapter 1

- Business networks

- Skill development

A 2015 policy brief published by the Hamilton Project spells out a proposal put forth by the University of Michigan's Michael Barr that I would love to see our government run with. The highlights (in the brief's words):

- *Access to Capital.* The federal government would expand two of its vehicles for providing financing to small businesses— the State Small Business Credit Initiative (SSBCI) and the New Markets Tax Credit. Both of these programs would have their application procedures adjusted to focus further on minority- and women-owned small businesses, and both would require rigorous data collection and evaluation as a condition for funding.

- *Access to Business Networks.* Congress would allocate an additional $500 million as a part of the SSBCI to create and expand business networks in states and local jurisdictions. These networks would link small business owners with established business leaders, providing opportunities for exchange of knowledge and information about new business opportunities. Funded networks would be subject to rigorous evaluation.

- *Access to Skill Development.* Congress would allocate an additional $500 million as a part of the SSBCI to fund locally administered skills-building programs. These training initiatives would be designed with a focus on the needs and constraints of small business owners and aspiring entrepreneurs. Funded skills-building programs would be subject to rigorous evaluation.[15]

Community development financial institutions (CDFIs) are another great way to get equity and debt capital into underserved areas. These private financial institutions, which fall into four sectors—banks, credit unions, loan funds, and venture capital (VC) funds—are "100 percent dedicated to delivering responsible, affordable lending to help low-income, low-wealth, and other disadvantaged people and communities join the economic mainstream," according to the Opportunity Finance Network. "CDFIs are profitable but not profit-maximizing. They put community first, not the shareholder. For more than thirty years, they have had a proven track record of making an impact in those areas of America that need it most."[16]

Just in case you've forgotten, let me remind you about the Kauffman statistic from Chapter 1: "If minorities started and owned companies at the same rate as whites, the U.S. would have over one million more businesses and up to an extra 9.5 million jobs."[17] And that doesn't even factor in how many extra jobs would be created if women were starting businesses as often as men. Nor does it consider the tax base that would be created.

My proposed solution is to provide stronger investment incentives for female- and minority-owned businesses than others. For qualifying startups, I would expand the tax benefits by allowing the 100 percent tax deduction while keeping the tax basis at the full investment level. That way, if the deal doesn't work, the taxpayer would get a second write-off at that time. While this would cushion the loss, investors would still have risks and potential real losses, as they should. Furthermore, if a company proves to be a success, investors wouldn't have to pay taxes if they reinvest the profits in another woman- or minority-owned business within twelve months.

However, more needs to be done to encourage growth in female-led startups. Research shows that forty-five is the age of most successful startup creators, an age when women who have elected to become mothers typically have children at home. That means they have to contend with policies—or the lack thereof—that put them seriously behind when it comes to creating a business.

Currently, for example, the U.S. is the only developed country without federally mandated maternity leave.[18] Of course, once mothers return to work, they're forced to cope with our country's childcare crisis.

Only by subsidizing childcare to eliminate the child or motherhood penalty will the numbers of female entrepreneurs seriously grow. That alone would make a huge difference. A 2015 McKinsey Global Institute (MGI) report found that if women had parity with men, the GDP among advanced countries would grow by 10 to 12 percent in just ten years.[19] That's incredible!

Not only do childcare and early childhood education benefit working mothers, allowing them to enter the workplace and start businesses if they so choose, but these programs make economic sense. The Heckman Equation, by esteemed economist James Heckman, shows a 13 percent return on investment (better than the stock market) for such programs.[20]

Of course, you have to pay to play.

Banking

Entrepreneurs need the ability to compete in an arena populated by more established players. So their lifeblood is a combination of equity and debt.

As we've seen, however, getting a business loan has never been more difficult. For starters, the number of banks in this country has shrunk dramatically. Over the past three years, the number of U.S. banks has fallen from more than eighteen thousand to fewer than 5,800. As we've discussed, instead of having a lot of smaller local banks, which can, by their nature, be less capitalized and riskier, the federal government and most states have favored stronger, bigger banks. From the perspective of safety and soundness of the banks, this makes sense. However, this trend has also encouraged mergers and organic growth of banks. Just 0.2 percent of U.S. banks now hold more than two-thirds of industry assets.[21] A 2015 Harvard Kennedy School study reports that over the past couple of decades, "community banks' share of U.S. banking assets and lending markets has fallen from over 40 percent…to around 20 percent today."[22]

That's a problem for small business as, according to *Entrepreneur* magazine, "big banks avoid extending credit to small companies because small business loans are time intensive, hard to automate, tough to securitize, and expensive to underwrite and service."[23]

No wonder small businesses tended to secure capital from community banks, especially since those lending institutions by definition foster community relationships. As the same *Entrepreneur* article points out, "Embedded in local communities, they are better able to evaluate soft factors in lending decisions, which allows them to make loans when quantitative analysis based on credit scores and financial statements alone would not suggest it. As a result, community banks provide over half of all small business loans[24] despite accounting for less than a quarter of all business lending."

Fewer community banks, however, mean fewer loans.

To make matters worse, as we've seen in the post-recession era, the government has regulated lending institutions to the point where they need to be very, very careful about what type of credit they extend. While there's a lot of low-interest-rate money sitting in many banks, it's hard to get loans if you really need the money. It doesn't matter how great interest rates are if you can't actually borrow the money.

Banks used to work with people, ideas, and a different approach to collateral than they do today. Today, it's all about cash flow and ironclad repayment plans. On average, the small faction of entrepreneurs who do manage to secure loans despite today's stricter lending standards and capital reserve requirements get only 40 percent of what they asked for.

This overreaction to the 2008 crisis isn't going to help right the entrepreneurial ship. If we don't want it to keep sinking, if we don't want an economy composed of—and driven by—only big players, we need to find active ways of facilitating money for regular people.

What can be done? For starters, figuring out ways to encourage banks to take some risks on people who don't fit today's rigid constraints will encourage more competition—and yes, at times some losses. Banks get their deposits because of federal guarantees, and we want them safe and sound. And at the same time, having banks provide a limited amount of needed community-support lending by helping startups is reasonable.

We need to bring back community banks (or their modern equivalent) and create more privately owned small business investment companies (SBICs). As mentioned, an SBIC is a type of privately owned investment company licensed by the SBA that supplies small businesses with financing in both the equity and debt arenas.

In addition, there are numerous legislative public policy methods that can help create new incentives for these specialized financial institutions to make loans to startups and small businesses that are not unicorns. Historically, the federal government has used the banking system as a tool to encourage certain types of action. The Community Reinvestment Act, for example, promotes economic growth and prosperity in lower-income and moderate-income communities by awarding banks brownie points for giving back to community-based organizations. Earning a certain number of Community Reinvestment Act points positively impacts how banking regulators evaluate a bank's ability to do mergers and grow.

I like the Center for American Entrepreneurship's idea that "Congress and financial regulators should consider allowing banks to count losses incurred through lending to start-ups as part of their annual Community Reinvestment Act obligations. Doing so would be consistent with the CRA's goal of economic revitalization by helping to unlock bank credit for the new businesses that drive growth and job creation."[25]

Developing similar programs in which startups (defined as companies less than five years old with $10 million or less in total capitalization) could qualify for special consideration and receive expedited and more readily available loans would encourage lending as well as equity capital for small and growing businesses. Some of these loans would be SBA-guaranteed loans, and some would provide credits similar to CRA credits that would be part of their banking licenses.

U.S. entrepreneurs need this kind of help. During the past several decades, more and more sophisticated financial markets have developed that have driven growth in all industries. This, along with the different ways today's capital markets can finance that growth, has accelerated much faster than any sophistication related to how we can capitalize starting businesses. We have legislation that enables raising money in stock markets. We have market makers and liquidity. We have all kinds of really smart people who do nothing but figure out how to get more and more money to potential superstar ideas or how to help big businesses grow even larger. But our best brains, the investment bankers and the rest, gravitate toward working on bigger deals because that's where the money is. While that makes perfect sense, we need to step back and ask, "How do we help start more small businesses?" This is especially needed as the big venture capital companies that could fund them don't want to bother with these kinds of seed rounds or angel investing. Ironically, the success of Silicon Valley has meant that companies that used to deal with relatively smaller startups are now looking for second- or third-stage companies.

The bottom line is that if we want more startups, we're going to need to find a way to finance them. And we're going to need to find a way to encourage more individuals, especially younger generations, to become entrepreneurs.

Specific Policies to Encourage Millennial Entrepreneurs

Just as we must reduce regulatory obstacles and target certain parts of the country and certain industries when it comes to strengthening U.S. entrepreneurship, we need to focus on bringing the millennial generation on board. Trust me, millennials want to come. A study conducted by America's Small Business Development Centers (America's SBDC) reveals that 49 percent of millennials want to start a new business. They just can't afford to.[26]

It doesn't help that millennials were crushed by the Great Recession. Data gathered by the Federal Reserve Bank of St. Louis's Center for Household Financial Stability shows that in 2016, "the median family headed by someone born in the 1980s remained 34 percent below the level we predicted based on the experience of earlier generations at the same age. ... Alone among the six decadal cohorts we studied, the typical 1980s family lost ground between 2010 and 2016, falling even further behind the typical wealth life cycle."[27]

If millennials are going to start companies in their thirties and forties at the same rate their baby boomer parents did, the overwhelming financial problems facing them need to be addressed. But that's not the only challenge. As we've seen, whereas baby boomers had little or no student debt and many owned homes that allowed them to take out second mortgages, millennials are saddled with tons of debt, and far fewer own homes with equity that could be used to start a business. Public policies could and should mitigate these problems, since that would help encourage millennials to risk becoming entrepreneurs.

Let's tackle the student debt issue first. If someone is actively involved in starting a new business, student loans should not hamper his or her ability to otherwise survive. So specific programs should be put in place that allow payments on student debt to be suspended or subsidized by a government program during the period in which a business is being started. Further, for each year of active entrepreneurial efforts to get that business off the ground, a portion of the student debt should be written off.

Win or lose in terms of the entrepreneurial business, entrepreneurs with student debt should receive credits against their debt that make it worthwhile to try to start a business, and help carry their student debt during the business's formative years.

In addition to student debt relief, other support and benefits, such as buying homes with no down payment (a program that veterans can currently take advantage of), could be put together to encourage the millennial generation to create startups rather than opting for the safe route of a job. That's the kind of incentive we need.

Finally, we need a program to provide health insurance to *all* entrepreneurs and startup employees on a reasonable basis. Health insurance—perhaps the number-one issue that discourages entrepreneurship[28]—needs to be removed as an obstacle for entrepreneurs.

Increasing Immigration

Research shows that immigrants (skilled and unskilled) tend to start companies at a much higher rate than residents with a similar degree of education.[29] In the wake of the Trump administration's "America First" anti-immigration and antitrade stance, which is counterproductive to new business formation, I would like to suggest that we need more immigration, not less. I may be a big dreamer, but we really do need a new immigration policy in this country that could hopefully be embraced on a bipartisan basis.

Immigrants have built and shaped our country. Similarly, the history of U.S. entrepreneurship has clearly benefited from the vast numbers of immigrants, who in many cases started from nothing and went on to grow big businesses that have not only made money but have made a difference in many people's lives.

The Center for American Entrepreneurship notes that:

> More than 40 percent of Fortune 500 companies were founded by foreign-born entrepreneurs or a child of immigrants. A recent study by the National Foundation for American Policy found that of the top 50 venture capital-backed companies in the United States in 2012, half had at least one foreign-born founder, while 37 have at least one immigrant in a major management position. Similarly, The Washington Post recently pointed out that "in the decade ending in 2005, the founders of half of the firms in Silicon Valley were born overseas. Intel, Google, Yahoo, eBay, Tesla, YouTube, and PayPal are just a few examples of American

companies—employing and creating wealth for millions of Americans—founded by foreign-born entrepreneurs."

With these realities in mind, a special visa should be created for foreign-born entrepreneurs meeting national security requirements who want to start a business in the United States and who have secured at least $100,000 in initial funding (some funding requirement is necessary to demonstrate seriousness, but it should not be a significant obstacle).

I love the Center for American Entrepreneurship's unabashed conclusion:

The United States is the only industrialized nation that does not have a visa category explicitly for foreign-born entrepreneurs who want to start their businesses in the United States. "It's the single stupidest policy the U.S. government has around high-tech immigration," Eric Schmidt, executive chairman and former CEO of Google, told the Wall Street Journal in 2012. "These people will create billions of dollars in investment in the economy and provide us with the ability to be world class in every industry."[30]

It further points out that we need our foreign-born entrepreneurs to make sure the U.S. stays competitive on the world stage. "With global competition for innovation and growth increasingly fierce, ensuring that the next generation of great companies are launched here in America requires an explicit legal pathway to attract and retain the world's best entrepreneurial talent," asserted John Dearie, founder and president of the Center for American Entrepreneurship.

Securities Laws

Immigrant and native-born aspiring entrepreneurs alike need the finances to get their startups off the ground. Securities laws should be revised to help capital formation in concert with the new tax provisions to encourage partnerships of aspiring entrepreneurs and individual taxpayers. Similar to some of the securities legislation passed in 2012 that helped create a new type of public security, regulation A+, and promoting greater flexibility, securities laws should be examined with the goal of transparency and investor protection while encouraging capital formation for startups.

Crowdfunding on the internet has become an interesting new funding methodology that the securities laws regulate. As discussed in Chapter 6, new rules related to crowdfunding, which were finally established in 2016, allow everyone the opportunity to be an investor, even without a net worth of $1 million. Still, many feel that the rules remain overly restrictive, thereby undercutting the chance for startups to tap into the crowdfunding opportunity.

We need to change that. Several JOBS Act reforms designed to enhance crowdfunding are currently making their way through the Senate.[31] Hopefully, those will become law. In addition, specifically upping all the structures of startup funds from a security law perspective should be considered in concert with tax law changes.

Regulatory Revamp

Once we find a way to fund startups, we have to help them with the paperwork and the ability to stay alive. Part of that entails easing and streamlining the overregulation that makes starting and running a business so much more difficult and expensive for new and small businesses. In Babson College's *The State of Small Business in America 2016* survey, which was administered to participants of Goldman Sachs's 10,000 Small Businesses program, almost 60 percent of the small-business owners responding said they had trouble understanding and managing government regulations and laws.[32] Perhaps that's why entrepreneurs like these end up spending on average four hours a week—or two hundred hours a year—on regulatory issues.[33] Or maybe it's because, as the National League of Cities' *Supporting Entrepreneurs and Small Business* "tool kit" publication states, "Unclear regulations with confusing steps are especially burdensome on new and small business. Successful review and improvement of permitting and regulatory functions hinges on communication with internal and external stakeholders and committed political leadership."

We need to find ways to address just how much regulation is needed. All too often, the bigger a city gets, the more bureaucratic it gets. Thankfully, some areas have found ways to facilitate dealing with all that red tape, balancing the needs of fire safety and other various requirements with the needs inherent in starting new projects. For example, South Carolina's Rock Hill has created an Open for Business program that includes a special business assistance team to help guide businesses through the regulatory process, from obtaining a business license to making sure the company is in a location that's properly zoned, to identifying modifications that might be needed to make sure the startup complies with existing codes.

The Center for American Entrepreneurship has some hard-hitting suggestions that I agree with related to regulations. The proposals (in its words):

- **Create a Regulatory "On-Ramp" for Startups**
  The Congressional Budget Office (CBO) and Office of Management and Budget (OMB) should be directed to co-develop a preferential regulatory framework to which new businesses would be subject for the critical first five years after formation. The framework should be comprised of only the most essential product safety, environmental, and worker protection regulations.

- **Require Third-Party Review of All New Regulations**
  CBO and OMB should be directed to co-conduct third-party analysis of the economic costs and benefits of all proposed new regulations with an economic impact deemed greater than $100 million.

- **Create a Regulatory Improvement Commission**
  The federal government has a large, multi-faceted, and effective apparatus for crafting and promulgating new regulations, but no regular mechanism for systematically addressing outdated, duplicative, ineffective, or unnecessarily burdensome regulations.

*In January of 2011, President Barack Obama announced an
executive order launching a government-wide review of "rules
already on the books to remove outdated regulations that stifle
job creation and make our economy less competitive." Eight
months later, on August 22, 2011, the Administration released
the final plans of 26 regulatory agencies to implement more
than 500 reforms the Administration said would save businesses $10 billion over five years.*

*Regulatory streamlining that saves American businesses
$10 billion over five years is a step in the right direction—but
only a very, very small step. Total costs to businesses of federal
regulations amount to nearly $2 trillion annually. A more
impactful and productive approach to regulatory reform is
clearly needed beyond the occasional self-review by the very
agencies charged with promulgating and enforcing regulations.*

Congressional Entrepreneurship Caucus

As I've said before, from regulations to startup capital, fixing U.S. entrepreneurship needs to be a bipartisan effort. And really, why wouldn't it
be? So I'm delighted to report that on February 28, 2018, Congressman
John K. Delaney of Maryland's sixth district and Congressman Tom
MacArthur of New Jersey's third district formed a bipartisan effort to
focus congressional attention on the importance of entrepreneurship
and to foster a new policy discussion on how to encourage more startups.

"As a country, we've got to become more entrepreneurial, and we've
got to make it easier for more people, in more places, to start their own
business," said Congressman Delany at the caucus. "America absolutely
cannot lose its entrepreneurial edge and this caucus is all about making
sure that Capitol Hill stays focused on this topic."[34]

This is very exciting and a big step in the right direction. Both
Congressman Delaney and Congressman MacArthur have private
sector business experience, so they know, in Congressman MacArthur's
words, "that a healthy private economy depends upon the energy and
dynamism of new businesses."[35]

It's great to see that a spark of interest related to U.S. entrepreneurship exists within Congress. In my view, this has to translate into public policy changes. It remains to be seen as to what is next for this early-stage effort and its leadership, particularly as Congressman Delaney has announced plans to run for president.

Blue-Ribbon Commission

Despite this encouraging development, as this chapter clearly demonstrates, there's a long way to go, and there's a lot to be done when it comes to getting small-business formation and entrepreneurship back on track. In theory, the SBA is the voice for small business in the administration. It's also, in theory, the voice for entrepreneurship. Clearly, that's not working.

For the SBA to be an effective agency, the administration and Congress need to give it more emphasis and more authority to really make a difference in terms of startups, with its effectiveness based on the number of startups in the U.S. rather than how much money it does or doesn't lose. If the SBA continues to not carry out its mandate in these areas, its responsibilities should be shifted to a department that can actually get the job done.

Before we throw the agency out, however, we should look at how to turn it into a strong startup and entrepreneurship ally. Check out these suggestions from the Center for American Entrepreneurship for making the SBA more startup friendly:

> The mission of the Small Business Administration (SBA) is to help small businesses obtain bank credit by guaranteeing a portion of loans. But many entrepreneurs report that SBA paperwork, requirements, and restrictions simply don't work for start-ups. In particular, the SBA's physical asset-focused collateral requirements—real estate, equipment, inventory—don't work for many start-ups, especially technology companies whose only asset might be the company's intellectual property.

Given this critical disconnect, Congress should direct the
SBA to initiate a detailed and comprehensive dialogue with
lending banks and entrepreneurs with the aim of identifying ways
to make SBA-backed lending more available, less complex and
cumbersome, less physical asset-based, and more tailored to the
unique needs and characteristics of new businesses. A particular
focus of these discussions should be to identify less conventional,
more start-up appropriate metrics of creditworthiness and success
that banks and the SBA can use to increase start-ups' access to
bank credit.

To these ideas, I would add that the way the SBA is to be judged
needs reconsideration. Is its role to be making conservative, bank-like
decisions and accordingly turning down SBIC applications that otherwise fit the profile? Or should it be judged on truly facilitating help for
startups and small businesses?

In the meantime, if Congress or the Department of Commerce were
to form a blue-ribbon commission to provide a blueprint for public
policies to help encourage startups, the benefits could be immense. The
commission directive should include three distinct areas:

1. Specifying legislative policies, potentially including some of
   those mentioned in this chapter, that could enhance and encourage formation of new businesses in the United States.

2. Analyzing and producing a report on best practices for state and
   local governments (which we'll talk about in the next chapter)
   and the results those state and local governments are achieving,
   so we can figure out what's working and spread the news.

3. Reporting on best practices and available help from nonprofits
   and educational institutions for the starting up, survival, and
   growth of new and young businesses in the U.S.

The commission should have a six-month deadline to produce its
recommendations and report, as with adequate staff and an engaged
board this could (and needs to) be done in an expeditious manner.

Encourage State and Local Best Practices

If we are to successfully rebuild U.S. entrepreneurship, we need to focus on the positive changes already being made by state and local governments to encourage entrepreneurship in a way that benefits their communities. A number of state and local governments are encouraging startups and small businesses in their communities by establishing resource-heavy entrepreneurial ecosystems, assisting entrepreneurs, nurturing budding companies, teaming with university programs, and assisting with regulations. Other activities, such as recruiting existing businesses to move into a community, indirectly benefit local communities and help bolster U.S. entrepreneurship.

In Oregon, for example, Secretary of State Dennis Richardson has released a series of videos to help Oregon entrepreneurs start their small businesses. The *Start a Business* video series, which can be found through the secretary of state's website,[36] complements the "Startup Toolkit" on Oregon.gov's Business Xpress portal,[37] billed as "Oregon's one-stop shop for all things business." Information for aspiring entrepreneurs includes:

- Choosing a name and legal structure
- Registering a business name
- Getting tax numbers
- Insurance and bond information
- Business licenses based on location and trade
- Understanding employer obligations
- An overview of some of the state agencies small businesses might encounter

"Starting a business may seem overwhelming with endless details, but it's actually pretty straightforward," says Ruth Miles, small business advocate for the secretary of state. "When someone wants to start a business in Oregon, it's our job to clear the obstacles and show the way."

That approach needs to be adopted nationwide.

I've listed a number of the more exciting federal, state, and university programs in the appendixes in the back of this book, but these appendixes are far from being enough.

A comprehensive analysis of best practices should be put together that could serve as a model, or at least a springboard, for areas around the country. Obviously state and local governments will make their own decisions about what they need and what might be appropriate, but making them aware of the best practices—along with warnings about the horror stories about some things, such as our CEQA problems in California—would help. No one needs to reinvent the wheel or experience all the bumps and bruises before he or she even gets started.

In the meantime, I hope that the state and local programs in the next chapter inspire many more communities to support their local startups and small businesses.

CHAPTER 9

Can-Do Fever

Startups may be on the decline nationally, but they're not on the decline everywhere. The twenty counties—out of the country's 3,1411—that have accounted for 50 percent of our country's startups over the past few years are clearly doing things right. On my journey to understanding the challenges to U.S. entrepreneurship, I wanted to figure out not just what wasn't working, but also what was. Since three of those twenty entrepreneurially successful counties—Dallas, Collin, and Tarrant, Texas—are in my backyard, I decided to begin there.

Of course, Texas isn't exactly where I started out, and my roots provide a lot of context when looking at the American entrepreneurial picture.

Trading Detroit for Dallas

In 1980, as a young entrepreneur in Michigan, I struggled with the lack of respect accorded entrepreneurs. Throughout my time there, the auto industry dominated the state's economy. If you weren't part of that, you just didn't count. Moving from Ann Arbor to Southfield, a suburb closer to the big city of Detroit, didn't help. I still felt out of step.

That sense of being the odd man out dogged me even at YPO (which stands for Young Presidents' Organization), a global network of some twenty-five thousand chief executives. To qualify for membership, you

have to have become, before age forty-five,[2] the president or chairper-
son and chief executive officer of a corporation of significance with a
minimum revenue and minimum number of employees.

I had joined YPO when I was twenty-eight years old, which made
me one of the youngest members. My age wasn't a problem. What I
did for a living, however, was. At the time, Michigan's business community was all about the auto companies and their suppliers, all of whom
were pretty confident that they did not need to embrace new entrepreneurs and startups. Even though Michigan's economic slide had already
begun, the country's automobile industry big boys believed they would
stay big forever. Little guys like me starting a business were treated like
second-class citizens.

After a couple of years in YPO, I was confronted during one of
YPO's forums—smaller groups in which business and personal issues
are discussed—about my lack of comfort with the Detroit attitude
toward entrepreneurs. While we are sworn to secrecy on what happens
in forums, I think telling a story about myself and how the forum more
or less acted as a board of directors for me that day would be a reasonable exception to this rule.

On that day in forum when it was my turn to put forward an issue,
I complained about how I felt Michigan—be it Ann Arbor, where I
started, or Southfield, Michigan, where I was headquartered at the time
of this meeting—seemed all about the automobile industry.

"Even in this group, few people seem to really understand or care
about the difficulties and risks of starting a new business," I said. Then
I reminded those present of how I would come in with concerns about
how I was going to make my next payroll, and they would roll their eyes
and laugh, as they had huge budgets. Instead, I had growing pains.

At that point my company had swelled to the point that we owned
just under sixty thousand apartments across the country. With more
than four thousand employees, we were a national player, yet I still felt
like a disrespected small fry in auto industry-centric Detroit.

"Where do you have offices?" my friends (yes, they were friends)
asked me.

"Atlanta, Dallas, Houston, Phoenix, and Newport Beach," I replied. "Where do you feel most at home?" "Atlanta is pretty cool, but I really love Dallas," I said. The questions and answers went on and on for the entire three-hour meeting. At the end of that afternoon, they all voted to throw me out of the forum and the chapter.

"Move to Dallas," they said.

I did.

That one meeting changed the course of my company and my life. Over a two-year period, I relocated ninety families from Michigan to Dallas and officially made Dallas my company's headquarters. In hindsight, I realize that my business was just one of many leaving Detroit. This time period roughly coincides with Detroit's losing its "entrepreneurial mojo," to quote Steve Case, AOL cofounder and author of the *New York Times* bestseller *The Third Wave: An Entrepreneur's Vision of the Future*. Detroit would become a failing city for decades, finally declaring bankruptcy in 2013.[3]

Let me backtrack for a moment and say with a lot of pleasure that while for decades Detroit, and arguably Michigan in general, may have lost that economic mojo, things are really changing. Maybe the city needed to bottom out before it could really start back up. In any event, a concerted effort is being made to turn around Detroit's economic circumstances, and a lot of that effort involves embracing entrepreneurship.

At the thirty-seventh annual Detroit International Wine Auction in October 2018, our wineries were the featured vintner. So I attended not only the auction but a number of other events over a few days, just as I was finishing this book. The beneficiary of the auction is an incredible school called the College for Creative Studies (CCS). I toured their two campuses with Rick Rogers, who is about to retire after twenty-five years of growing this wonderful arts-centric college.

At one of their campuses, CCS has space they rent to help start-ups. The collaboration between creative design and entrepreneurial businesses is epitomized by Shinola from Detroit, which has its watches made and other operations carried out at CCS. I toured the area that makes leather straps for the watches as well as the area that makes the watches themselves. Shinola has extended the brand to a number of other products also being made at CCS, so they're hiring and training a lot of local workers. Their facilities are light and modern and have a real positive feel. Shinola is a great example of entrepreneurship in Detroit making a difference.

What struck me most during my visit to CCS and throughout my time in Detroit was the huge commitment the whole community has toward everything that encourages success in Detroit and, in turn, a positive attitude toward entrepreneurship. The unbelievable commitment of Dan Gilbert and his company Quicken Loans have been critical. Everyone I talked to there has a sense of pride, hope, and commitment to creating opportunities for risk-taking—in other words, entrepreneurship. This is not what Detroit was like in 1980 when I relocated our headquarters to Dallas. Local attitudes toward creating an environment that supports and encourages risk-taking entrepreneurs is a critical step towards bridging the opportunity gap.

Detroit's comeback is exciting, and I am rooting for its success. I've actually participated in the comeback by investing with Adam Lutz, the son of one of my longtime close friends Eric Lutz, in an old building in downtown Detroit to redevelop it into apartments. I'm excited to be involved in the Michigan of today. As part of this Detroit trip, I toured the building that Adam is redeveloping with Eric, along with several other buildings that are being upgraded from years of vacancy into new uses. Detroit had decades of decline and it won't be a new modern city instantly, but it's clearly in the midst of an exciting turnaround process. It's a happening place on the entrepreneurial front and a far cry from what it was when I traded Detroit for Dallas in 1980.

Can-Do Spirit

When I moved to Dallas, it had—and still has—a can-do spirit that encourages entrepreneurship and that will almost guarantee that it will never face the kind of trouble that Detroit went through. Even though the city has had its share of challenges, it's one of the most entrepreneurial places in the U.S., which explains why I originally had so much trouble believing we had a problem with U.S. entrepreneurship. Everywhere I looked, people were starting up and running businesses. I had traded a place that devalued entrepreneurship for one that lived for it. Had I been smarter, I would have also realized earlier how much better the weather was in Dallas compared to Detroit.

To say that Dallas welcomed me with open arms would be a cliché, but it would also be the truth. Within a couple of years of moving to Dallas, I was part of a small group of longtime Dallasites that bought the Dallas Cowboys football team. I was invited to a lot of social events and offered club memberships and many civic board memberships. I became active on the symphony board and helped build the beautiful I.M. Pei-designed symphony hall that exists today. That warm welcome that Dallas still extends to newcomers who are willing to contribute to our society gave me that one thing I couldn't get in Detroit—a seat at the table.

Over the past almost forty years, I have built and owned a fair amount of real estate in Dallas. My company invested a lot in Dallas, from building companies to starting other businesses, in part because Dallas is more than just a city; it's a region that includes the towns around it. In Dallas, we don't believe that we're in competition with one another or even with Chicago or Phoenix. Our goal is to be a worldwide city, a global competitor. This includes suburban cities like Frisco, which itself was recently named the fastest-growing city in the country. So we all pull together to make things happen, and the whole area benefits.

Of course, everything is not one-sided, simple, or a piece of cake. Those early years in Dallas that proved to be such great growth years very quickly turned into a huge bust. By the mid-'80s, Dallas had become the epicenter of the country's most devastating real estate downturn and the savings and loan crisis.

One could argue that making the move to Dallas was the worst thing I could have done from a lot of standpoints, not the least of which was that the fallout from these catastrophes was far worse there because all of our lenders went broke. That was true not just in Dallas but across Texas. All but one bank and more than a billion dollars were taken over by the federal government. Even at the worst of times, the community's entrepreneurial spirit and environment did not go away. Texas in general and Dallas in particular are all about risk-taking and even second chances. It is, to me, the type of place that epitomizes the heart and soul of entrepreneurship.

The Making of a City

During what was one of the region's most horrible times in financial history, I would wind up fighting for my professional life. Ironically, that time period also led to some of my best business decisions ever.

Even though I was still in severe financial trouble and mostly playing defense by the late 1980s, I managed to keep moving the business forward and seizing opportunities, one of which was buying land in Frisco, a town twenty-five miles north of Dallas. While I would eventually sell all but one of those properties, I hung on to a parcel of 175 acres with the vision of developing it into an exciting office park. My company is now evolving this vision into an all-encompassing live-work-play development.

In 1997, we built our first one-hundred-thousand-square-foot building in Frisco. The mayor at the time was Kathy Seei, a tremendous woman who really worked with us and helped us. One day she came over to my office and presented me with a large coffee table book on the history of Frisco.

"I hope you'll help build a new history for Frisco, so I want you to understand some of our past," she said.

Talk about a personal welcome!

Since then I have worked with three other mayors—Mike Simpson, Maher Maso, and Jeff Cheney—as well as a number of city councilmembers and longtime city manager George Purefoy as we've contributed to Frisco's steady growth. Today, HALL Group has completed seventeen buildings that encompass 2.5 million square feet, and Frisco has more than 170,000 residents. More than ten thousand people work in our office buildings, and our plan over the next twenty years is to build another six million square feet of office, hotel, and residential properties. This has been and remains a fun and unique project, and I encourage others to see the more than two hundred sculptures from artists all over the world that we've placed around the lakes and green space.

When I built my first building, Frisco had fewer than six thousand residents. Shortly before I got involved, George Purefoy became the city manager. If any one person deserves credit for the city growth, it's George. He is quiet, humble, brilliant, and effective. He's a behind-the-scenes guy who does not like attention and is not showy. He just works hard and gets things done.

Frisco, which, thanks to a Parks and Recreation fund, features plentiful outdoor activity, sports—professional and otherwise—and green space, is also family oriented, with a top-ranked school district (one of the fastest growing in the nation) that boasts an impressive record of 92 percent of students proficient in math and 91 percent in reading.[4] All of this helps Frisco convince companies that will eventually bring jobs to the area to move there.

Frisco focuses on quality of life to persuade companies to relocate. It also taps its economic development corporation, which will actually subsidize growing businesses there. How much it pays is based on the number of jobs the company brings or creates over a three- to five-year period, and the economic quality of those jobs—that is, how much the salaries are.

Of course, Frisco needs to convince companies not only to move but to stay. In that vein, the mayor hosts a business luncheon on a regular basis to which the CEOs of all the local companies are invited. Not only can heads of companies—no matter how small or how big—network, but the luncheon encourages dialogue. You have a problem? Bring it up at the luncheon. You may not get everything you want, but at least you'll be heard and you'll get a response.

All these efforts don't help just the big companies. By incentivizing businesses move to Frisco and subsidizing companies through
economic development corporations (EDCs), the city has turned
itself into a magnet for a variety of businesses and industries, creating
thousands of jobs. Frisco, for example, brought The Star, a development the Dallas Cowboys are building, which has received very large
public incentives. All of this was done to help make the area attractive
for corporate relations, and it has worked. CEOs like having their businesses near the Dallas Cowboys.

Neighboring city Plano has similarly attracted business relocations.
Toyota has moved its headquarters to Plano, as has Liberty Mutual, and
JPMorgan Chase & Co. has built a more than one-million-square-foot
campus for its employees. While Plano has attracted bigger companies
than Frisco, I believe Frisco will see some more big companies over
the next few years. (Nothing like having a sales tax, even just a fraction of each penny, dedicated to incentive programs designed to boost
economic development!)

From the influx of new people who are likely to buy homes in
Frisco to the increase in corporate tax revenue, all these moves positively impact the city's tax base in a huge way. That's all part of the plan
to increase the city's quality of life, allowing Frisco to maintain environmental standards, to set aside money for parkland, to focus on
education and maintain a low student-teacher ratio, and to turn itself
into a sports mecca.

Yes, it turns out that communities can change and/or develop in
ways that can make a big difference. Jamba Juice, for example, didn't
relocate from California's Bay Area to Frisco just because of a grant for
$800,000 from the Texas Enterprise Fund.[5] If you talk to Jamba Juice
CEO Dave Pace or the heads and employees of other companies that
have moved, they'll tell you that they love the Texas lifestyle as much as
its positive outlook on business and future growth.

Even while historically many cities in Texas have been aggressive with
incentives to attract businesses from around the country and beyond,
challenges and changes in attitude have started to crop up. While the

pro-entrepreneurship and pro-growth attitudes generally prevail, citizens are expressing growing frustrations about the correlated stresses on public schools. We're also seeing in Texas the kinds of growing fears evidenced in the extreme reaction to Walt Ranch in California. Yes, the "not in my backyard" attitude has hit Texas as well. Nothing is simple when it comes to entrepreneurship, or in this particular case, real estate development, near where someone lives. All too often emotions take control, and facts take a back seat. That has to change.

Attitude Rules

While local government practices are clearly a critical part of incentivizing and encouraging startups, there's no magical, all-encompassing solution. But it's equally clear that when it comes to entrepreneurship, everything starts with attitude. Creating change isn't just about adding one or two policy changes while keeping the same bad attitude. If you're begrudgingly putting up one or two policies, the odds are it won't make as much difference as we really need. On the other hand, if you really want to encourage entrepreneurship and you want a fair, level playing field and opportunities for everyone, then filling in the blanks as to how you can get there will become a lot easier than you can imagine.

Take Dallas. After receiving a number of complaints from developers about how Dallas was bureaucratic and difficult to deal with, the mayor and city manager formed a small group of insiders and outsiders to categorize the problems. They came up with eighty-three areas of difficulties and basically a lot of complaints about bureaucracy and how long it took to get permits through the city.

Clearly some kind of action was needed. So directly under the deputy city manager, they formed an elite squad headed by a very can-do person, Tommy Ludwig, who had three assistants working for him. I experienced the difference firsthand when we needed a whole bunch of infrastructure changes. In the past, this kind of regulatory obstacle course that required getting sign-offs from four departments was just part of doing business. A painful part. This time was different.

"Here's what we want to do," the guys from our company said as they unrolled our drawings.

I just laughed when I heard the squad's response.

"Take the cars out of this drawing, because for this department, you're only going to get more questions if you have those in your drawing," they said. "Those guys don't have responsibility over that, so they don't need to know about that. Don't show them things they don't need to know about."

These bureaucrats know how to speak the bureaucrats' language, cut the red tape, and get things done. We recently needed a special letter that we figured would take us six to eight weeks to get.

"No, no. no. We can do it in a different way," they said.

We had what we needed within twenty-four hours.

Supportive Entrepreneurship

Cities across the country are making similar efforts to facilitate and support entrepreneurship. The National League of Cities' *Supporting Entrepreneurs and Small Business* "tool kit" publication for local leaders highlights a handful of programs that are helping to make it easier—rather than harder—to do business.

- In South Carolina, the City of Rock Hill's Open for Business program uses feasibility studies to help new or expanding businesses understand zoning regulations and performs site inspections to determine what needs to be done to meet existing codes. Subsequent plans are reviewed in five to ten days, with help provided when it comes to setting up utility and sanitation services.[6]

- The newly created Citywide Business Advocacy Team (CBAT) in Seattle's Office of Economic Development helps local businesses figure out how to navigate the city's services and regulatory system. It also helps them connect with key political, departmental, and economic development resources through an informal monthly networking event. In addition to providing hands-on assistance to businesses, the team advocates for changes that will improve Seattle's business environment, which in the past has been plagued with a sluggish, uncoordinated and at times contradictory permitting process.[7]

- The Mayor's Office of Immigrant Affairs (MOIA) in New York, in conjunction with several other organizations, supports immigrants to launch and grow their own businesses. Assistance ranges from free courses for small-business owners in Spanish, Chinese, Korean, and Russian to a business expo that showcases locally based immigrant food manufacturing businesses and links them to consumers across the country.[8]

- Boston's thousand-acre waterfront Innovation District, the brainchild of five-consecutive-term mayor Thomas Menino, is the result of a deliberate, collaborative strategy to create jobs and housing by nurturing startups and growing research-based companies. In addition to attracting entrepreneurs, the redevelopment project, which offers networking opportunities and firm development accelerator services, has also prompted large, established businesses to move their headquarters to the industry cluster on the river.[9]

- Deciding to focus on cultivating existing local businesses rather than enticing new ones to relocate, Littleton, Colorado, assists second-stage companies that have proven themselves but are still struggling to survive and grow. Over the past twenty years, those efforts to help entrepreneurs have doubled the community's job base and tripled its retail tax base.

- Wichita, Kansas's services—ranging from training to translation and research to global credit checks—developed in partnership with the Kansas World Trade Center (KWTC) helps local businesses export their goods internationally.[10]

- Over the past ten years, events sponsored by Southern California's Valley Economic Development Center (VEDC) have brought together more than three thousand local entrepreneurs, financing institutions, and venture or angel investors. At the center's Where's the Money? events,[11] business owners and entrepreneurs can discuss lending options at loan pavilions, network over breakfasts and business luncheons, attend business workshops, and visit finance and resource expos.

Entrepreneurial Ecosystems

While the above programs may have very different emphases, they all actively support entrepreneurship in their areas and, to a lesser or greater extent, have established an entrepreneurial ecosystem. Across the country, communities like Asheville, North Carolina, and Bend, Oregon, have structured tailor-made programs to actively create a culture that will help entrepreneurs to survive and thrive.

In Asheville, startups are buoyed by an interdependence of businesses that has been encouraged. By purchasing products and services from one another, the city businesses support themselves by supporting one another. You can find that same spirit of cooperation in Bend, which the Milken Institute named the Best Performing Small City in 2016 and 2017, *Forbes* listed as number one among the Best Small Places for Business and Careers in 2016, and the U.S. Bureau of Economic Analysis (BEA) says had the number-one fastest-growing GDP (more than 8.1 percent) in the country in 2017.

Putting a premium on cooperation means helping out those who might even become your competitors. When Bend's 10 Barrel Brewing Company started to grow after opening in 2006, the small brewery asked Deschutes Brewery, the grandfather of Bend's ever-expanding craft brewing scene, for some help on an accounting issue. Deschutes not only gave advice but volunteered to help with a whole bunch of the back-office stuff behind 10 Barrel's manufacturing operations. Fast-forward to eight years later, when 10 Barrel was so successful that the "newcomer" wound up being acquired by Anheuser-Busch. While the sale price remained under wraps as of this writing, suffice it to say that the five young men who founded 10 Barrel now have plenty of capital to start other businesses. That virtuous cycle has already started—the founders have five new businesses between them.

Despite the fact that the sale of a popular homegrown brewery to "big beer" made many of those in the craft brewing scene hopping mad, Bend's beer industry has remained super collaborative. Brewers get together as a guild. They hold beer festivals together, including Bend's annual three-day Brewfest, which features more than two hundred craft beers and ciders from seventy breweries in the Pacific Northwest,[12] while raising money for local charities.

Those in the area's outdoor-gear-and-apparel industry work together in much the same way. Performance-dog-gear company Ruffwear—which, like Deschutes Brewery, was a cornerstone business, having moved to Bend from Salem in 1998, four years after being started in a garage—made a point of helping startups such as Hydro Flask. Just six years after the founder started selling his insulated stainless steel water bottles out of a truck, Hydro Flask sold for $210 million. Today, Ruffwear and Hydro Flask both share information, supplier recommendations, and the same neighborhood in west Bend. A coworking space designed specifically for the outdoor-gear-and-apparel industry, which is currently being built inside Ruffwear's headquarters, will likely be the gathering place for Bend Outdoor Worx, the country's first business accelerator dedicated to catalyzing outdoor-product companies.

Altruistically, Ruffwear and other local outdoor companies want to see the industry continue to grow and develop in the Bend area. Selfishly on their part, that growth will also grow the workforce and provide greater access to a talent pool that has expertise in their industry.

Support for local entrepreneurship isn't restricted to intra-industry cooperation. Not by a long shot. The pro-entrepreneurial resources that Bend has developed, which have helped make this town of ninety-thousand-plus the country's sixteenth largest metro area for high-tech startup density, include the Bend Venture Conference (BVC)—an annual event connecting companies in the concept and launch stages with investment opportunities—and monthly PubTalks, at which aspiring startups pitch to a friendly crowd of two hundred to three hundred investors, entrepreneurs, and business owners and hear "lessons learned" from successful founders. Both events are produced by EDCO (Economic Development for Central Oregon), which also supports local entrepreneurship by connecting young companies with funding.

"We've spent considerable time attracting local equity and early stage capital—not only via the Bend Venture Conference but through the formation of Cascade Angels Fund and recruitment of Seven Peaks Ventures as well as non-traditional lenders such as Craft3 [a nonprofit that makes loans to strengthen Oregon and Washington communities, small businesses, families, and the environment]," says EDCO CEO Roger Lee.[13]

In addition, EDCO has gathered a group of business experts who have "been there, done that" in a wide variety of industries to advise startups as well as aspiring entrepreneurs. The 135 volunteers in the Stable of Experts network not only weigh in on operations and/ or ideas but make sure that all considerations have been addressed before any funding requests are made, thereby bettering the odds of a positive result.

That certainly has helped Michelle Mitchell and Jamie Danek, founders of Humm Kombucha.

Little did they know on that day in 2008 what was in store. As the two were visiting with each other, Mitchell handed her friend a glass of home-brewed kombucha based on a recipe she had learned from her mother-in-law and spent years perfecting.

They tell their story on the Humm Kombucha website:

Jamie took her first sip and the next words out of her mouth were, "This is amazing! I can sell this to everyone!" The homebrew had a taste like nothing she'd had before, and the healthy qualities of the beverage, full of vitamin B and antioxidants, made them feel exuberant. If they could be this happy and feel this great, why not share it with the world!??

They began brewing in Michelle's kitchen and named their company Kombucha Mama. They delivered gallon glass jars of kombucha door-to-door (like the milkman used to) in a Toyota Prius. Customers would leave an empty gallon jug on the doorstep with $20 under the mat and come home to find a full one waiting. That summer, Michelle and Jamie brought their brew to the Bend Farmer's Market and started developing new flavor combinations to try alongside their original brew.

As much kombucha as they produced, people wanted more, so they moved into a tiny brewing facility and hired a small and dedicated staff. The gallon jugs were replaced by kegs, the Prius by a delivery van, and it wasn't long before demand, now extending across Oregon, necessitated another move, this time to a 5,000 square foot facility.

Though they loved being (and still are) the "Kombucha Mamas," Jamie and Michelle decided it was time to find a name to match their aspirations. Something more universal and inclusive. So with the move came a change in name, to Humm, and the hiring of dozens of 'Humm-sters' to work at this semi-large-scale brewery. They found people who shared not only their passion for brewing excellent kombucha, but also the optimism and love of life the company was founded on.[14]

The operation continued to grow. Humm Kombucha is now sold in twenty-three states as well as in Europe. With their Scandinavia facility already in operation, in 2017 Danek and Mitchell announced plans to build a one-hundred-thousand-square-foot production facility in Roanoke, Virginia, to serve a growing customer base in the eastern half of the U.S.

Humm capitalized on the collaborative business environment by bringing the CEO of Deschutes Brewery on to its board of directors, tapping into a broad range of help from EDCO and other organizations, taking advantage of tax exemptions on its ever-expanding plant and equipment, and uncovering a small army of ambassadors among its customers.

Now the Humm Kombucha founders are assisting other entrepreneurs in their industry though a new industry group called the Central Oregon Food Cluster. After all, fair's fair, at least in Bend.

Clearly, entrepreneurship is alive and well in places like Bend that have cultivated entrepreneurship. Despite the numbers of people breaking through thanks to some terrific local programs, however, the national numbers related to business formation still stink, in part because entrepreneurial ecosystems, while increasing in number, still aren't the norm in most communities. While the answer to reversing our declining entrepreneurship lies in broad-based national policy accompanied by a broad-based awareness of the problem, local programs can provide the hands-on help that aspiring entrepreneurs often need to succeed. So the more we can encourage entrepreneurial ecosystems across the country, the better.

But just how do you create a local culture that encourages startups and small businesses?

As the Bend example shows, an entrepreneurial ecosystem isn't made up just of entrepreneurs, but rather of interactive players who all positively contribute to that community. It can be as simple as having that breakfast dive where the person in the next booth has started a business and done well, and a funder on the other side of the restaurant is talking to an entrepreneur about a new deal. Put people with money and people with ideas in the same community, and you have the seed of an entrepreneurial ecosystem. Then you add the impact of universities that are educating people, particularly in technology and engineering, along with a supportive local government, and you're well on your way.

In his book *Startup Communities*, Brad Feld—an investor, entrepreneur, and a nationally recognized speaker and author on the topic of entrepreneurship—outlines the underlying principles of sustainable startup communities that can be applied when building an entrepreneurial ecosystem. He writes: "I strongly believe that startup communities can be built in any city and the future of economic progress of cities, regions, countries, and society at large is dependent on creating, building, and sustaining startup communities over a long period of time."[15]

Silicon Valley: The *Ultimate* Entrepreneurial Ecosystem

Of course, when it comes to startup communities, none comes close to rivaling Silicon Valley.

Why is Silicon Valley so successful for entrepreneurs and startups? One person theorizes that because the weather is relatively mild, people can more easily start more businesses in marginal spaces like garages.[16] Another person says the coffeehouses are so good that people sit and talk to one another more readily. Some point to business and personal amenities, including conferences and a world-class university, along with top-notch restaurants, sports teams, and entertainment options for the outdoor enthusiast as well as the couch potato. When I asked Rao Mulpuri, founder and CEO of View, the revolutionary smart-glass company I wrote about earlier in the book, he told me that he loves being in a place where he runs across brilliant fellow entrepreneurs in nearby eateries or simply walking up and down the streets.

Entrepreneurship sounds like it's in the air in Silicon Valley. But in fact, it doesn't work that way. Part of the ever-present excitement of Silicon Valley relies on people's sharing ideas and providing help as informal directors of one another's companies.

Of course, success breeds success. Having Stanford University as well as UC Berkeley, San Francisco State, and other great learning institutions close by has to be a huge contributing factor on that front. In addition, the mere fact that technological breakthroughs thrust Silicon Valley into the big league long ago cannot be minimized.

This doesn't mean that new geographic areas can't and won't become future great sources of startups. Indeed, with today's virtual reality, the internet, and increasing connectivity, the world should be enabling more startups everywhere. But it does mean that the process of creating an entrepreneurial ecosystem that really kicks into gear requires a myriad of factors—from talent to tech—to come together.

One of those factors is definitely the availability of capital. And in that game, Silicon Valley, with its concentration of wealthy investors and funding institutions, virtually runs the table. The famed Sand Hill Road venture capitalists have raised incredibly large funds, so the ability to fund a new idea in Silicon Valley is omnipresent.

Dick Kramlich's leadership at National Enterprise Associates (or NEA, as it's known today) helped build Silicon Valley. Dick was active even before he and others started NEA in 1978. Before NEA, he was a general partner at Arthur Rock and Co., and later, on his own, was a big early investor in Apple Computer. During NEA's first twenty years, under Dick's leadership as the managing general partner, NEA was the area's largest venture capital firm and created huge successes for its investors. I can only imagine how many lucky young entrepreneurs over the years have benefited from his wisdom.

My admiration for Dick and his role in Silicon Valley is huge, as he shaped the entrepreneurial hotbed into what it is today. In fact, since cofounding NEA forty years ago, he has been involved in ten companies that have grown from the startup or near-startup stage to companies with a market value in excess of $1 billion. Success breeds success.

Couple these kinds of results with the momentum factor that comes from the entrepreneurial ecosystem's having been there for a long time, and you hit pay dirt. Aspiring entrepreneurs in technology gravitate to the place where the money is, and the money gravitates to where the people are, and it just works out.

A Virtuous Cycle

Money alone certainly didn't create this mega-entrepreneurial ecosystem. World-class people's starting tech companies that have succeeded has led to world-class funding sources like NEA and the Silicon Valley ecosystem we know today. Now that's what I call a virtuous cycle!

Try as they might, not every community can duplicate Silicon Valley's recipe for success. Thankfully, they don't have to. But they do need to start stockpiling some basic ingredients.

To review, findings about successful entrepreneurial ecosystems indicate that in addition to the availability of funding, having young, highly educated, tech-savvy talent helps. Universities help. Governments that have a set of pro-entrepreneurship programs help. Local and state tax incentives help. Nonprofits that mentor and incubate entrepreneurship (we'll talk about that next) help. And success that can build on itself helps.

Compare California and Texas and it's obvious that there are different ways to create that virtuous cycle. An area can be successful because it has great universities, is a place where people want to live, and has a built-up ecosystem that's self-reinforcing. That's California. And it can be successful because of regulatory endorsement along with a pro-growth, pro-business mindset, some university support, and a technology hub, and that's Texas.

While there clearly isn't a single formula that works, to create a viable entrepreneurial ecosystem, you do need the kind of attitude that has allowed Silicon Valley to succeed so brilliantly in a state that doesn't exactly have a great pro-business agenda. Everything starts with attitude. California may not be a pro-business state, but it's sure pro-entrepreneurship and innovation, which makes all the difference.

Perhaps that explains why ten of the twenty counties responsible for half the country's startups are located in California and Texas.[17] The other ten successful counties that are spread out over an awful lot of geography point to the fact that while there is more than one way to succeed, there are countless ways to fail. Thankfully, a growing mentoring movement across the country is positioned to help counteract that.

Cautionary Note and Need for a Tipping Point

Clearly many local governments are interested and trying to learn how to attract entrepreneurs. That's exciting to see. Part of how we as a country will get to a tipping point when it comes to really leveling the playing field will be local governments engaging in changes that encourage startups.

We need to learn from the small number of local governments that are really doing things well and share those best practices so that others can learn and we all can move forward. However, what is working in Dallas, Frisco, and the other small number of urban areas experiencing relative success doesn't necessarily translate to rural areas. We also haven't explored how this really serves women or people of color in entrepreneurship. So while all of these positive-attitude pieces of the puzzle are useful and critical, we need them to combine with other solutions to help entrepreneurship in rural and other nonperforming areas pull itself out of the doldrums.

While I hate to put a damper on all the exciting developments this chapter has talked about, we also need to remember that these programs are working in a relatively small geographic part of the United States. And they are focused heavily on technology. So the deck of the broader system in the rest of the country remains stacked against entrepreneurs and small business. All the entrepreneurs I have talked to in Dallas and elsewhere, for example, complain that compared to Silicon Valley, New York, or Boston, capital is very difficult to come by in their areas. While positive attitudes and good local government support are critical components of a successful ecosystem, they aren't nearly enough when it comes to solving the problems in U.S. entrepreneurship. We've got to find ways to increase funding as well.

Opportunity Zones and Tax Credit Incentives

Under the Tax Cuts and Jobs Act of 2017, a community development initiative called the Opportunity Zones program was enacted to encourage long-term investments in rural and low-income urban communities. This new economic development tool provides for a substantial tax deferral and even an abatement of capital gains if investors reinvest their unrealized gains into the Opportunity Funds that invest in these designated communities.[18] People also have the ability to invest in commercial property or businesses in these areas.

While I originally thought the new tax law was generally ill-advised since it will create substantial debt towards the end of a long recovery, I do believe that the Opportunity Zones program has great potential. Even though I don't think the overall tax law goes far enough to address the state of startups, there are favorable tax provisions for economically depressed areas, which will hopefully result in growth in entrepreneurship in those communities. As with any new tax law, a lot of detail needs to be worked out to define the specifics, including exactly what areas qualify. But initiatives and reinvestments like these will certainly help us move in the right direction.

Moving Forward

The solution for bringing us back to where we need to be will be multifaceted. So from city and state best practices, let's look at another part of that equation—providing entrepreneurs around the country with support. Fortunately these days, unlike when I was coming up as an entrepreneur, there are an awful lot of positives in the form of nonprofits that want to help support entrepreneurship. And they're operating not just in those areas of the country that are having success but in regions that desperately need their help.

CHAPTER 10

Shark Tanks, Mentors, and More

I started out as an entrepreneur to make a difference. I wanted to help people. That has influenced how I run my business. I believe that whenever possible, it's important to give new people an opportunity, just like the American system gave me one. What they do with that is up to them.

Take Larry Harris. For years I didn't know his whole story, just that he'd had a difficult upbringing and excelled at work. I later learned that when he was hired at HALL Group, he was a homeless sixteen-year-old living on friends' sofas. His first role at the company was as a maintenance person on an apartment project we owned in Indianapolis.

By the time Larry—who, by the way, was recently promoted to vice president of HALL Group—obtained his college degree as an adult, he had already graduated from the school of hard knocks and proved himself. For me, it's all about meritocracy. If people say they can do something, we should give them a shot. If they fail but are honest about it, we learn together. If they are game players, they move on. If they succeed, it's a win-win for both sides. Larry is smart, hardworking, and fun, and has a great family. He has shared his story with local business groups and is a great role model in many ways. What he has done inspires me.

That's why I was so excited to participate in a nonprofit event recently in Dallas to encourage individuals who are as determined as Larry and who want to make their mark in the world through entrepreneurship.

The preview party came to life when Mike Rawlings—Dallas's great mayor since 2011 and a friend of mine for years before that—walked into the room more or less at the same time as entrepreneur Mark Cuban, a "shark" investor on the popular *Shark Tank* television show since 2011 and the owner of the Dallas Mavericks basketball team. Like many other events around the country, this night was about borrowing the basic premise of *Shark Tank*, in which aspiring entrepreneurs pitch their ideas to five titans of industry (the sharks) whose potential investment could help make the aspiring entrepreneurs' dreams a reality. Doing a local version of the show would prove to be a great way to get people who cared about their community to invest in local entrepreneurs who couldn't get traditional funding despite a viable idea.

I had agreed to be one of the sharks for the event, which the mayor and The Real Estate Council (TREC), the Dallas organization that created the Community Fund, had put together. This particular event would focus on real estate-related enterprises in Southern Dallas, an area that has always lagged behind in economics and overall development for decades. The goal? To raise awareness of Dallas's economically challenged southern region and to get successful local real estate companies to invest in and mentor southern-sector companies.

Before the event started, Mark Cuban joked with me about events from many years past, including how I had failed to invest in an idea of his that turned out to be huge. Oh well! At least I could be a part of this event. Following a terrific interview with Mark and the mayor, several hundred people cheered on their favorite presenters as the sharks, all prominent Dallas commercial real estate investors, asked the entrepreneurs questions and ultimately decided on whether to invest or not. I wondered whether those petitioners realized that the prior year, three entrepreneurs had landed $2.1 million in funding in the first-ever TREC Shark Tank event.

As it turned out, all three of the 2018 competitors received investments, although not necessarily the complete amounts they were looking for. I offered deals to two of the three, whom I likely never would have met otherwise.

The first was a dentist, an African American woman who had put herself through college and then dental school, which is both expensive and very difficult. She had a dental practice with two locations and was looking to buy a building and remodel it into a multifaceted health clinic in an underserved area of Dallas.

The other entrepreneur, Rodney Burchfield,[1] a young man with whom a few of the sharks had invested years before, had worked for the Dallas Department of Aviation. He understood city incentives for projects there. With the facility he planned, the airport in the southern sector of Dallas would be able to service more people, which would result in greater economic opportunity and jobs for the area, as more goods and services would be required.

Rodney knew he needed advice as much as capital, and he came prepared to make sure he would get both. During an impressive presentation that covered everything related to projected costs and revenues and more, he also informed us about the local tax break that would be part of a development deal. After we got things rolling with him, those incentives would almost prove to be a deal breaker, as they ultimately had to go through the city council for passage.

It turns out that even in areas that are progressive, you'll find tension in local politics. Some people wrap themselves up in the idea of "Why should we, who pay taxes in a nicer neighborhood, incentivize a developer in a bad neighborhood to get a tax break and build 70,000 square feet of new facilities that will bring planes to that airport instead of other airports?" The answer is because it brings jobs, it brings stability, and it helps raise up communities, which increases everyone's safety and well-being. But having to contend with vocal people adamantly against incentives is a very real thing.

In this case, you would have thought that there might be one or two out of fifteen city council members that would have voted with that latter group. The number was shockingly higher. After a lot of hard work and politicking by the developer, the incentives that he needed to make this plan work won eight to seven. With a different mayor, the effort could have easily failed.

It takes a lot of active day-to-day involvement to be a successful mayor, and we are very lucky in Dallas to have Mayor Mike Rawlings at the helm. I knew Mike when he was in the private sector and have been amazed at the difficulties he has endured during his time as mayor of Dallas. He did not run as a career politician. He had been a successful CEO at two large companies, and he took a substantial pay cut in order to make a difference. His leadership, hard work, and passion have put Dallas on the world stage, and we in Dallas owe a great deal of our progress to him. He is one of many good people elected to office who support entrepreneurship throughout their programs.

Whether or not the deal with Rodney comes to fruition, without our local Shark Tank program and the equity from us as investors, this new development likely would have had only a sliver of a chance. While these kinds of nonprofit efforts are hard and don't always work, they are absolutely worth the effort.

Don't Forget the Real *Shark Tank*

The real *Shark Tank* TV show, which was started in 2009, has had a lot of positives when it comes to raising excitement, awareness, and respect for entrepreneurship. The format is simple. Just as in our knockoff event, aspiring entrepreneurs pitch their ideas to five shark investors who have made it big by turning their own ideas into hugely profitable enterprises. A successful pitch results in one or more of the sharks' investing money and time in the entrepreneur's idea.

As Mark Cuban told a group of us the night of our Shark Tank, the shows are actually shot in a much longer format and then cut to fit the television timing. The participants are always interesting and work hard to show why their ideas should be funded. So the six million people who watch the show's episodes, which hit the two hundred mark in 2018 (along with all those reruns), are getting a weekly education about the ins and outs of entrepreneurship.

Teaching the Basics of Entrepreneurship

For better or worse, the success of entrepreneurship on the national front is not determined solely by people's succeeding despite on- or off-screen challenges. Indeed, the environment in which the startups either occur or do not occur is critical. Thanks to a massive ramp-up of higher education entrepreneurial programs and nonprofits across the country, this kind of solid support is increasingly available to would-be entrepreneurs, even if they don't live in those very few, heavily capitalized areas.

Fifty years ago, it was unheard of for prominent universities to offer programs in entrepreneurship. Today, more than five thousand higher education courses on entrepreneurship—attended by some four hundred thousand students—are taught each year in the United States.

If that's not testimony to entrepreneurship's increasing popularity, I don't know what is. Even more interesting, Babson College's *The State of Small Business in America 2016* report found that while small businesses tend to receive less than half of the funding amounts they request, entrepreneurs "receiving a business and management education are more likely to obtain capital and secure a greater portion of their requests."[2]

Realizing the importance and impact of educating future entrepreneurs, the private sector has stepped into the educational arena. Goldman Sachs's 10,000 Small Businesses program provides entrepreneurs "greater access to education, capital and business support services," according to the company's website. "To date, the program has served over 6,700 small business owners across all fifty states and has resulted in immediate and sustained business growth for the alumni of the program."[3]

Along with the International Finance Corporation (IFC), a member of the World Bank Group, Goldman Sachs has also invested $1 billion[4] in its 10,000 Women global initiative, which "fosters economic growth by providing women entrepreneurs around the world with a business and management education, mentoring and networking, and access to capital."[5]

JPMorgan Chase has focused its efforts on entrepreneurs of color, pumping millions of dollars into underserved neighborhoods in Detroit, New York City, San Francisco, and most recently Chicago. In addition to the $3 million the company is putting into the Entrepreneurs of Color Fund in Chicago, for example, an additional "$1 million will fund mentoring programs for minority entrepreneurs at the University of Chicago and Northwestern University," according to CNN.[6]

So far, so great. Now add in the fact that an exciting new focus on entrepreneurship is really on the ascent in many universities.

Dallas's SMU, like several other universities, has offered entrepreneurship classes and programs for more than twenty years. That said, Steven Currall, who became provost at SMU a couple of years ago, has established a whole new approach to entrepreneurship education at the university. From business to the arts to engineering, interdisciplinary groups that include deans, associate deans, professors, a wide range of SMU folks, and people like me talk about how entrepreneurship in the education system can work within different disciplines to help students learn about risk-taking and starting businesses. It's exciting to see all these different disciplines coming together to think about entrepreneurship. I believe that being creative and/or involved in the arts, which has always entailed a certain amount of risk when done professionally, can be very entrepreneurial. It's great to see that embraced by the education system.

On the other hand, I'm not sure that the people currently in entrepreneurship programs are actually going out and starting businesses, as that's so much more difficult in terms of capitalization than it used to be. That's part of why I'm excited about the partnership that Scottsdale, Arizona, has cultivated with Arizona State University (ASU) to create a one-stop shop for would-be entrepreneurs and startups.

SkySong, the ASU Scottsdale Innovation Center, which opened in 2009, works to incubate and fast-track entrepreneurial startups within the university and from around the world. It does this in part by encouraging interactions between three ecosystems—the university (including students, alumni, and staff) and its backers; the startup ecosystem (including startups, angel and venture capital investors, mentor groups, and other incubators); and the wider ecosystem (including big companies, local and federal government, and international connections).[7] As SkySong's website explains, "The project's success is a direct result of a focus on innovation and technology that attracts companies ranging from some of the world's best known brands to one- or two-person startups.... The goal of SkySong is to attract cutting-edge and innovative companies and their base of knowledge workers from around the world, integrating the resources of ASU with the opportunities of the private sector."[8]

Now let's talk specifics. ASU Venture Catalyst, a joint venture with ASU's Tech Transfer Operations that is housed in the SkySong center, provides help with business plans, management, business contacts, and more to startups with great promise. The result? The National League of Cities reports in its 2012 *Supporting Entrepreneurs and Small Business* publication that "48 spinout companies based on ASU intellectual property have been established. Eight ASU companies have been acquired or merged, and there have been two IPOs. AzTE portfolio companies have received more than $100 million in investments and funding, and the valuation of ASU spinout companies and sub-licensees is estimated at more than $200 million."[9]

Considering these kinds of results, I was thrilled to find out that other institutions, including one right in my backyard, have adopted this public institution-private sector model.

A mutual friend recently invited me to breakfast with Dr. Joe May, the chancellor of the Dallas County Community College District. It was an eye-opening breakfast. We covered so many things so quickly, I didn't have time to tell him about Carrie Kelleher Stein and how Dallas Country Community College District had changed her life. But then, that won't be the last time Joe and I get together. He's a very impressive person who has dedicated his life to higher education and really makes a difference.

I asked Joe about entrepreneurship programs. Of course, like many higher education schools of all different levels, the colleges in his district are now embracing entrepreneurship as part of their education. As with the colleges' other programs, he explained, the key to their entrepreneurship efforts lies in trying to find people or organizations they can collaborate with in order to improve the students' experience. In this case, they work closely with the Goldman Sachs programs mentioned previously. Goldman has a real commitment to entrepreneurship and to helping provide support to those interested in potentially becoming entrepreneurs.

Seeing the private sector and the public sector work together in this way is most impressive. I find it interesting that instead of these efforts being spearheaded by the SBA or the U.S. Department of Education, a partnership between large private sector companies that care and local government and/or education organizations is creating such positive programs.

It takes leadership of people like Joe May to make that happen. Luckily those leaders are stepping up across the country. A number of communities across the country, including New Haven, Connecticut; San Diego, California;[10] and Ann Arbor, Michigan,[11] have also made efforts to encourage public-private partnerships among entrepreneurs, existing businesses, and local universities. They understand not only that a startup, along with any spinoff companies, can positively impact the economy, but that a startup that receives local assistance while it's trying to get going is more likely to stay put once it has made it.[12]

I admit there was a time when I wondered if entrepreneurship in higher education was really viable. To me, entrepreneurs were doers rather than students. That said, there are different kinds of entrepreneurs. In my view today, anything that can help aspiring entrepreneurs improve their skills and create the confidence necessary to start businesses is a good thing.

These days there are so many entrepreneurship programs throughout so many schools and universities that it's downright amazing. From the Ivy League to community colleges, entrepreneurship is being taught in many ways and styles. Like the entrepreneurial nonprofits and local government programs, these educational programs are part of the effort being made to get us back on track. That's the American way.

American Entrepreneurship in the Former Eastern Bloc

U.S. entrepreneurship really is different than entrepreneurship around the rest of the world. Pardon the cliché, but it's as American as apple pie. I learned that when Kathryn was appointed by President Clinton to be the ambassador to Austria, a role she continued under President George W. Bush. Her time as U.S. ambassador allowed me to really see things from a totally different perspective.

Among the many things I learned was the importance of entrepreneurship as an integral part of democracy. In seeing what did not exist in the former Eastern Bloc countries adjacent to Austria, I was able to see firsthand the lack of a free capital market for entrepreneurship in a communist government. Even a number of years after the fall of communism, it was obvious that change isn't as easy as turning a switch and saying that you're free.

So Kathryn and I decided to work with the Fulbright program, an international educational exchange program started by the State Department to increase understanding between the U.S. and other nations. In this case, we formed a program to help pay for a professor in entrepreneurship from one of our many universities to go teach entrepreneurship in Central and Eastern Europe.

While we have no involvement in the selection process (that's done by the Fulbright organization in Washington, D.C., and Austria), as mentioned in the acknowledgments, I have met some of the selected professors. As also noted, one has become a friend and is the only professor to have been selected twice: Dr. Garry Bruton from Texas Christian University in Fort Worth. Garry has had me talk with his class, and he and I have compared notes on this book and many aspects of entrepreneurship.

Ironically, as I've talked about and thought about this subject and delved more deeply into the research, I've become increasingly convinced that while it's important to focus on encouraging American-style entrepreneurship worldwide, it's also important to figure out ways to focus right here at home. That, of course, is the whole purpose of this book.

Accelerated Support

Overall, starting a business is tougher than it was when I started out, but today's entrepreneurs don't have to go it alone. Incubators and mentors are providing startups with everything from business expertise and office space to monitoring operations and, in some cases, securing funding. This kind of mentoring that helps people develop and grow in the business arena is an important part of the solution when it comes to reversing the startup decline and reigniting American free enterprise.

Just consider Airbnb,[13, 14] which received financing of a billion to a billion and a half dollars and is now valued at $25 billion. This unicorn didn't gallop onto the scene without help. Roommates Brian Chesky and Joe Gebbia came up with the idea to rent out a room in 2007, when they couldn't afford their San Francisco lease. With a big design conference coming to San Francisco and a related shortage of hotel rooms, they figured that people might need places to flop. So they invested in three air mattresses and found three takers.

This could work! they decided.

Teaming up with former roommate Nathan Blecharczyk, they attempted to turn their idea into a company. They failed, not once but twice.

When an advisor suggested they try to get accepted to Y Combinator, a respected startup accelerator that provides money and training for the small percentage of companies they help, the founders of Airbnb (as it's called now) reacted negatively. The company wasn't a startup, they argued. They had been launched, not once but twice. When the advisor pointed out the obvious, that they were still absolutely broke, the three aspiring entrepreneurs realized they might need a little assistance.

Their admission to Y Combinator provided them with $20,000 in seed funding and cost them a 6 percent stake in the company. In April 2009, after three months, they received their first real investment of $600,000. Two years later, Airbnb could boast more than one million bookings in eighty-nine countries, as well as additional funding to the tune of $112 million. Y Combinator had delivered on its stated mission to get the company through the first phase and to a point where what it had built was impressive enough to pique the interest of investors to whom Y Combinator could introduce the company's founders.

Since 2005 (and as of this writing), Y Combinator has funded more than 1,900 startups, according to its website, for a combined valuation of more than $100 billion.[15] Around the country, plenty of other accelerators and incubators are helping startups to actually start up. According to the International Business Innovation Association (InBIA)—in its words the "go-to organization for business incubators, accelerators, coworking spaces and other entrepreneurship support organizations who are dedicated to nurturing the unique startups in their communities"—87 percent of incubated businesses succeed past the six-year mark compared to only 40 percent for non-incubated businesses.[16] That could be in part because incubators, 93 percent of which are nonprofit organizations,[17] reduce startup costs by 40 to 50 percent on average.[18] Even more important, successful incubators start by helping would-be businesses validate their market opportunities and ascertain whether their products or services actually meet that need.

Whether incubators and accelerators focus on specific groups, such as women or people of color, on developing businesses in a particular sector—such as food manufacturing, pharmaceuticals, or even art—or just on helping promising startups to succeed, they often provide make-or-break support. So do many nonprofit organizations around the country, a handful of which I have the honor of being affiliated with.

One of those is the Entrepreneurs' Organization (EO), formerly known as the Young Entrepreneurs' Organization. It offers mentoring, peer networking, and educational opportunities to members—entrepreneurs who are the "owner, founder or majority stakeholder of a business earning a minimum of US$1 million in the most recent fiscal year."[19] I love this one-of-a-kind global network, which helps entrepreneurs learn and grow through peer-to-peer learning and connections to experts, whether someone is a first-stage entrepreneur looking to catapult a business to the next level or an experienced entrepreneur looking to up his or her game by working with a mentor. As great as it is, however, this program hasn't helped to increase the numbers of women entrepreneurs.

Forget the Glass Ceiling—We Need a New Building

"Where are all the women?" Heather Wentler and Amy Gannon of Madison, Wisconsin, found themselves asking again and again. Finally, they decided that rather than complain about the obvious gender gap in the entrepreneurial community, they would do something about it. So they started Doyenne, a 501c3 nonprofit organization run by the founders, a board of directors, and five volunteer committees.[20]

Doyenne operates with a set of guiding principles that you can find on its website:

- The ecosystem is broken, not the women.

- Women are powerful, and we take their ideas seriously.

- Entrepreneurship happens within a life, not the other way around.

- Entrepreneurship is a messy, iterative process. We all learn by doing.

- Vulnerability is a source of strength and necessary for personal growth.

The organization's mission includes building entrepreneurial ecosystems that invest in the power and potential of women entrepreneurs by helping women to expand their entrepreneurial skills, build and mobilize networks, raise and invest dollars, and partner to change the ecosystem. Doyenne's tagline: "Be Audacious."

Despite the fact that women receive only a tiny fraction of available funding, research on women entrepreneurs shows that they want to build companies that are going to last and would rather build them slowly and thoughtfully. It also shows that because they underestimate their own competence, they're more conservative and overdeliver instead of overestimating and inflating their bottom lines. All of which makes them a pretty darn good investment if they can just get the skills and support they need to jump in.

That's where nonprofits like Doyenne are invaluable. I could paraphrase what members get from the organization, but I'd rather let Doyenne's founders speak for themselves:

> To some being part of Doyenne means finding a group of people who understand what you're going through as an entrepreneur when no one else in your life does. Others look to Doyenne for programming to help them enhance their skills as a business leader and space to comfortably say "I don't know" and find the answers to move them forward.

That last bit was Katie Brenner's story. "We were at a very early stage of development when we joined Doyenne, but we knew there was a huge need for better hormone measurements for women," says Brenner. "Doyenne helped us to get our big idea off the ground… [by helping] us with credibility, publicity, and funds at a crucial time. We won the Doyenne 5×5×5 competition [five women-led businesses deliver five-minute pitches in the hopes of winning a $5,000 grant], which not only gave us credibility and publicity, but a grant to move forward as well. We used the funds to de-risk a piece of our business strategy that enabled us to raise our seed round of capital."[21]

In just four years, Doyenne has begun to build the community's first network of entrepreneurs and is inspiring more women to come forward and start their own companies. Those kinds of results are exactly what we need when it comes to boosting entrepreneurship in this country.

But that's just the start for Doyenne. The organization's long-term goal isn't helping women to break into the system—because, according to cofounder Amy Gannon, that system is broken.

"How do you break through a glass ceiling when the whole set of rules are designed in such a way that keep you out of the process?" she points out. "I hate the expression 'glass ceiling,' because it presumes that the building was built correctly. But the building wasn't built correctly. The whole way we deploy capital and the whole way we support entrepreneurs and the whole way we decide what's worthy or not worthy, it's totally broken. Why don't we just build a new building instead of talking about the glass ceiling and continuing to try and figure out how we get women to navigate through these broken systems that are not built for women or for people of color?"

That's why Doyenne is working not just to get more women into business but to transform the entrepreneurial ecosystem itself, so that it becomes inclusive and, as a result, better for everyone, thereby improving our economy and our planet.

"We need to think differently about how we fund, how we deploy capital, who we deploy capital to, for what purposes, what kind of growth do we need," Gannon points out.

Part of that rethink needs to focus on the rural part of our country.

Center On Rural Innovation

As we have explained in earlier chapters, the American communities experiencing relative success in entrepreneurship startups are urban areas. The rural part of America is dramatically lagging. As with other niche areas involved with the entrepreneurship challenges, nonprofit organizations are being established by caring people who want to address this rural American challenge.

One group trying to increase opportunity in rural America is the Center on Rural Innovation, run by Matt Dunne, a former Google executive with a huge interest in philanthropy, community affairs, and technology. Matt is originally from Vermont, where the Center on Rural Innovation has embarked on its first project. A team of equally passionate individuals has joined Matt in this effort to provide a variety of solutions to help grow America's future work. Luke McGowan, for example, has an MBA from the Harvard Kennedy School and helped build Thumbtack, a San Francisco-based tech startup that matches customers with local professionals.

Luke, who moved his wife and son to Vermont, told me about the Center on Rural Innovation's plan for an entrepreneurship center that will provide access to mentors and seed capital. He and the team are bringing in construction in the form of broadband internet connections. They're providing unemployed or underemployed people with training for midlevel coding work and helping people secure remote employment, so they can work for companies in urban areas throughout the U.S. while remaining in Vermont. Their program also includes creating coworking spaces, creating apartments for people to live in, and just creating a sense of community.

When I asked Luke how the Center on Rural Innovation had been started and was funded, he indicated that successful LinkedIn founder Reid Hoffman was the primary funder and Matt the key starter. The Schmidt Family Foundation has also contributed. Now they're looking to broaden the base.

The Center for Rural Innovation is a very aggressive program that plans to expand to several rural cities to add to its early-round tests and then continue from there. It will be worth watching and hopefully can produce some great results, both for entrepreneurship and the broader-based rural-area challenges.

Seeing the commitment of people like Reid Hoffman, Matt Dunne, and Luke McGowan to give back and make a difference makes me feel very good about the future of America. So do thousands of people behind all the nonprofits supporting entrepreneurship in this country.

Turnaround

A few of those nonprofit endeavors have popped up in the unlikeliest of places, turning around lives in the process.

Private foundations and individual donations, for example, fund the Prison Entrepreneurship Program (PEP) in Houston, which offers privately run, three-month entrepreneurship courses that teach inmates the ins and outs of creating and operating a business. Then it follows up with mentoring from local successful businesspeople once the course participants have been released and are ready to launch the business of their dreams. In a state where almost a quarter[22] of those released from prison find their way back there within three years, only 7 percent of the more than 1,500 program graduates haven't made good. Although the program clearly has a life-altering impact and has resulted in 100 percent postprison employment,[23] not everyone who goes through the program winds up starting a business. But since its inception in 2004, more than three hundred former convicts have spearheaded startups. One of those is Orlander Johnson.

As a young man, Johnson had a promising-looking future. Athletic scholarships and financial aid had allowed him to go to a junior college, where he played football for a year before getting picked up by Ottawa University in Kansas. During his third year in college, however, all that was taken away. When his perceived financial status changed following his mother's marriage, the school's financial aid program deemed him ineligible, even though the family's income was not enough to cover his college tuition.

"I lost everything," he said. "I felt like the world had been snatched from under my feet."

He turned to dealing drugs, an entrepreneurial activity that's often all too readily available.

It would take nineteen years and treatment for substance abuse while in prison for him to stop blaming others for the life he wound up falling into. PEP would teach him everything from business basics to dinner etiquette and would provide a path to a new life. As soon as he was able to ditch the leg monitor he was forced to wear for two months after his release from prison, he got a job with a restoration insurance business doing roof repairs on homes damaged in storms and tornados. During that first year, he saved all his money, as the owner provided Johnson and his family with room and board. Two years after regaining his freedom, he started the business that would eventually become Urban Stylez.

"We took a table we found from the side of the road and put it in the living room and covered it with a blanket," he recalls. "We put the jewelry on it and tried to sell it for ten dollars. We kept doing it and found our first location of four hundred square feet at $450 a month. Now we look at the cash register and get $1,300 a day, but at the time we had to make twelve dollars to thirteen dollars a day to stay in business, and most days we didn't make it. Most days or weeks, we didn't make anything. I had to find money to pay rent."

That's when LiftFund came through with a loan for $5,000. LiftFund is a nonprofit organization funded by government grants and private sector entities, including JPMorgan Chase, that has provided seventeen thousand small-business loans totaling more than $210 million since its inception in 1994.[24]

After paying that loan back, Johnson secured another for $10,000, shifted to selling urban clothes when market testing helped him figure out that would be a better bet, and relocated his storefront.

"The last location we were at cost half of the price of this place," he says. "We took a chance, and I had to give all my money to get everything in here."

The gamble paid off. A year after reopening, average sales doubled. Johnson, however, is not ready to hit the cruise control button.

"People always say, 'You've come a long way,' but there is still work to do," he says. "The potential to grow is here. We are trying to save and cut back on spending. We've been doing $100,000 so far, but we want to do a quarter of a million next year."

What a change from Johnson's early days as a drug dealer. His metamorphosis hasn't helped just him; it has helped his community. Not only is he not perpetuating the scourge of drugs that afflicts so many neighborhoods, but he's contributing to the local and federal tax base instead of costing taxpayers by being incarcerated, all while setting an inspiring example for up-and-coming entrepreneurs and startups in his community.

Leveling the Playing Field

Sometimes, just giving individuals a chance to become entrepreneurs along with the support they need is all it takes. As we've seen, getting that chance is a lot tougher in certain parts of the country. But Revolution's Rise of the Rest initiative, a nationwide effort led by entrepreneur and AOL cofounder Steve Case that showcases and invests in entrepreneurs from startup ecosystems that don't usually get funding, is looking to change that. The Rise of the Rest team tours cities around the country, investing at least $100,000 per city in one local startup selected through a pitch competition.[25] The program is now run on a day-to-day basis by J.D. Vance, author of the bestseller *Hillbilly Elegy* (with 2.5 million copies sold). I got to see Rise of the Rest in action when it hit Dallas in May 2018.

The Pecan Room at Oak Park filled up quickly that day with the Who's Who of the city's business community, most of whom I knew and many of whom are friends. The invitation said breakfast would be served at 8 a.m.; I got there five minutes before and took my seat at one of the ten round tables set for what was clearly going to be a relatively formal meal.

My table of eight was hosted by Harlan Crow, the actual host of the breakfast itself, and included Trey Bowles, the executive chairman of the Dallas Entrepreneur Center and a really terrific promoter of entrepreneurship both in Dallas and throughout the country. Also at my table was the head of the Dallas chapter of United Way, Jennifer Sampson, who would share information with the entire group about her organization's efforts to help social entrepreneurs, and Anurag Jain, who heads Perot Jain, L.P., a Dallas-based venture capital investing company that my company and I have worked with on two deals.

Case started the speeches fairly quickly after the food was served, and one by one a number of locals—including Rob Kaplan, the president of the Dallas Federal Reserve Bank; Ron Kirk, past mayor of Dallas and U.S. cabinet trade representative under President Barack Obama; Dale Petroskey, head of the Dallas Regional Chamber, and many others—spoke briefly but powerfully about what was going on in the Dallas-Fort Worth (DFW) area. It turns out that, according to *Forbes*, DFW is one of the country's fastest-growing tech markets[26] behind Silicon Valley, New York, and Boston. It was pointed out that Jack Kilby invented the microchip in Dallas, and to my surprise that the city is home to Microsoft's second-largest U.S. campus.

Actually, Dallas is doing so well that it took Trey Bowles a long time to convince Steve to add the city to the list of thirty-eight that Rise of the Rest will have toured by the end of 2018. Over the four years that those on the team have been doing these annual five-city bus tours, they've focused on obvious cities in need, such as Detroit, Michigan; York, Pennsylvania; Madison, Wisconsin; Lancaster, Pennsylvania; Albuquerque, New Mexico, and so on. These are just a fraction of the places that haven't received the same levels of capital—and, accordingly, success—of startups based in Silicon Valley, New York, and Massachusetts. On that front, Dallas met the criteria, which Steve acknowledged in his opening statements when he said that in 2017, more than 75 percent of venture capital money had gone to California, Massachusetts, and New York, with only 2 percent coming into the entire state of Texas.

The speeches moved from focusing on Dallas to covering broader topics related to entrepreneurship. Rob Kaplan spoke about his efforts related to incubating social venture capital, along with his concerns about the aging population and the slowing productivity and related slow growth he sees the country moving towards over the next few years.

"Not enough money is being invested in entrepreneurship," he concluded.

Additional speakers revealed a lot about how engaged Dallas's private sector is when it comes to shoring up entrepreneurship in the area. The president of the University of Texas at Dallas talked about the university's efforts to grow education programs that could help entrepreneurship. The head of AT&T Labs talked about the company's outreach efforts to find new entrepreneurs who can create the innovation that will help AT&T's business. In fact, AT&T Labs creates five new patents every day, for a total of 12,500 active patents.[27]

By the time Steve began to speak, I realized that I was hearing a lot about the facts and themes that had prompted me to write this book. He talked about how Detroit has declined 60 percent over the years, the very trend that had driven me to relocate from there to Dallas. His discussion about how most of those with investment capital "focus on why things can't work rather than what if they do work" also hit a chord.

Bingo!

That day, a Dallas startup that provides turnkey furnishings and décor for millennial apartment renters won a $100,000 investment from Rise of the Rest,[28] and Dallas earned an accolade from Steve.

"There's no question it could emerge as one of the great startup cities," he told the *Dallas Business Journal*. Then he added a caveat that we would all do well to heed: "But it's going to require the community to rally around the entrepreneurs—and champion them—and create a culture that's more focused on innovation and risk-taking."

Steve and fellow investors in the Rise of the Rest Seed Fund—people like Eric Schmidt, Jeff Bezos, Henry Kravis, Howard Schultz, Meg Whitman, Jim Breyer, John Doerr, and many others—aren't just getting money to deserving startups and encouraging entrepreneurship in many overlooked parts of our country. They're demonstrating that those of us who care about our country and who have been lucky enough to do well need to put our time and money where our mouths are.

Part of how I do that is through my involvement with the Network for Teaching Entrepreneurship (NFTE).

Inspiring the Future of U.S. Entrepreneurship

Considering the years I spent from ages eight to eighteen doing paper routes, stocking doctors' and dentists' offices with instant coffee and soup, and selling everything from Green River soda to Cutco knives, I have a soft spot for kids who already aspire to become entrepreneurs. And when it comes to encouraging and helping entrepreneurs who want to get started as young as I did, NFTE is great. The organization was founded by Steve Mariotti in 1987[29] after he got beaten up by what can be described as some disenfranchised youth. Most people would have gotten angry. Some might have tried to get even. Steve, whom I met many years ago when he was in the MBA program at the University of Michigan and became a tenant in one of my apartment buildings, decided to try and help the kind of desperate juveniles who would do something like that. Ultimately, he founded NFTE to reach some of the 71 million young people[30] who are unemployed.

As the NFTE founder, Steve has really done a lot for many people.

"Youth are not prepared to seize the opportunities of the 21st century," reads the NFTE website. "Teaching entrepreneurship changes mindsets, changes lives, changes the world. We must equip young people with an innovator's eye and a founder's grit—the skills to excel in an innovation economy. And with economists predicting the jobs of tomorrow don't even exist today, entrepreneurial skills are skills for life."

NFTE goes into schools with a unique combination of high-impact student programs coupled with teacher training and support. These entrepreneurship programs—which help kids come up with business ideas, develop and pitch ensuing business plans, and develop and market their products[31]—wind up changing many young people's lives.

NFTE's impact is so impressive that after Kathryn and I got back from Austria in 2001, I founded an NFTE chapter in Dallas. We put together a board, raised money, and started as a satellite office of the national office located in New York. To this day, NFTE Dallas is very effectively working with the Dallas Independent School District to teach entrepreneurship in classrooms throughout the school system.

Of course, there are plenty of other organizations across the country that are helping youngsters who have already been bitten by the entrepreneurial bug. Junior Achievement (JA), a nonprofit youth organization founded in 1919, provides kids with what is often their only exposure to business and entrepreneurial education, in order to prepare them for the global economy.[32] This granddaddy program may have been around for a century, but its programs sure don't reflect that.

"About two years ago, we decided the business model kids were experiencing through JA was more of a 1970s corporate environment,"

CEO Jack Kosakowski told *Inc.* magazine in 2017. "So we began to re-imagine it based around the current entrepreneurial landscape. They chase capital and learn about things like crowdfunding. They research products to bring to market and learn about lean methodology. In many cases, they produce the product. It ranges from tech services to more mundane household goods that they sell, door to door or online."[33] Last year, JA's Georgia chapter partnered with a school district in the Atlanta area to create the JA Academy, a school within a school where the curriculum revolves around solving business problems. The chapter is hoping to take the pilot program nationwide.

Jan Muirfield, a certified fundraising executive and the president of JA Dallas,[34] has gotten the business community to support Junior Achievement in a big way by creating a Hall of Fame award and getting an incredible Who's Who of Dallas to be honorees. In turn, each honoree spends time at the Dallas public schools that participate in the Junior Achievement programs, with role models and mentoring creating a virtuous cycle of support.

The lineup of worthy kids' programs is way too long for even a cursory exploration of who's doing what in this book. But I would be remiss if I didn't mention BizWorld.org, a nonprofit organization and the largest teacher-led entrepreneurial program in the world, which focuses on inspiring children to do extraordinary things. "We know that tomorrow's jobs and economy are going to be created by leaders and entrepreneurs we foster today," reads its website. "Not every child will be an entrepreneur when he or she grows up, but we can inspire every child to have an entrepreneurial spirit: to lead confidently, think critically and creatively, be financially responsible, and understand the value of teamwork."

Over the past twenty years, the organization's entrepreneurship programs have taught more than six hundred thousand elementary and middle school children across the U.S. and in one hundred countries around the world how to run a business. Using innovative, real-world experiences, they work to reach students before they hit middle school, a period that often proves difficult for so many. Again, from the website:

"Our mission is to empower children to become 21st century thinkers by awakening their entrepreneurial spirit, inspiring them to become the architects of their futures, and giving them the confidence to transform their world."[35]

Horatio Alger Association of Distinguished Americans

Perhaps the greatest organization that celebrates the free market system and how it provides opportunity is the Horatio Alger Association of Distinguished Americans, which was started in 1947. Each year on average, ten Americans with the best self-made, rags-to-riches stories of overcoming adversity are chosen to be honored and are inducted as lifetime association members.

While the organization has provided many great role models, about thirty-five years ago a group of the association's members decided to help empower entrepreneurially minded youth in the form of educational scholarships based on need. Since 1984, the association has provided more than $143 million in scholarship funds, with more than $16 million going to two thousand students in 2018 alone, making the association the largest needs-based scholarship organization in the U.S.[36] The members and friends of the organization provide the funding. An endowment of over $250 million has been raised, which guarantees the organization's ability to make a positive difference for years to come.

I love everything that the Horatio Alger Association of Distinguished Americans represents. One of the proudest moments in my entire career was being inducted into this network when I received the Horatio Alger award in 2007.

Celebrating Entrepreneurship

As different as all these nonprofit programs are, the one thing they absolutely have in common is their focus on encouraging entrepreneurship. EY's Entrepreneur of the Year program does that in spades. Since its founding in 1986, this program—which recognizes entrepreneurs on regional, national and even international levels—has spread to more than sixty countries.

Seventeen years ago, I remember attending an awards ceremony in Dallas, which is always a very prestigious and well-organized evening gala, as a nominee for the 2002 Southwest Real Estate Entrepreneur of the Year award. In hindsight, it was very awkward because two of my best friends had also been nominated. We didn't know until that evening who would win. As it turned out, I was the lucky one that year, even though both of my friends equally deserved the award.

Years later, Kathryn and I were awarded the 2017 Southwest Master Entrepreneur of the Year award (we were also finalists in the national real estate category). The following year, I was one of the judges for the national awards. So while I may be biased, I know from experience that EY is the real deal.

As I was completing this book, I was asked to speak at the national EY awards program in Palm Springs, California, also called their Strategic Growth Forum. I chose to take two full days to go and listen to the great programs they had lined up for the four-day event. It turned out to be an incredible seminar with a wide range of terrific speakers, as well as a fun networking event with some wonderful social programs. One of those included a program to recognize female entrepreneurs. They started the EY Entrepreneurial Winning Women program ten years ago after conversations with the EY partners in charge of the national conference and program prompted the realization that women remain underrepresented in entrepreneurship and deserve an additional boost.

In addition to recognizing deserving female entrepreneurs at a luncheon, they produce a booklet about them and share more information about the program. As part of ongoing efforts to encourage entrepreneurship among women, the program connects these entrepreneurs with an elite national business network, one-on-one guidance and support, and helps them identify key potential partners as well as prospective funding sources. They would be the first to say that the reason they are doing this is because this kind of assistance is, in fact, needed.[37]

EY deserves a lot of credit for promoting entrepreneurship through its award programs and bringing entrepreneurs from all regions, backgrounds and industries together. What makes the EY award program, which is nationally sponsored by SAP, Merrill Corporation, and the Kauffman Foundation, so special is the criteria used for both nominees and winners. In EY's words:

> We honor and recognize the men and women whose boldness drives them to do things differently and change our world in the most unexpected ways. We're excited about the many significant achievements of these incredible entrepreneurs, applauding them for taking the road less traveled to launch new companies, open new markets and fuel job growth.

In short, this program is recognizing everything that makes entrepreneurship so exciting, so special, and so critical.

One of EY's key partners and sponsors for these events is the Kauffman Foundation. The Kauffman Foundation and I did a lengthy interview on this book's topic about the challenges facing traditional entrepreneurship today. They thoroughly understand these issues and share my belief that we need to shine a light on these challenges for all Americans so that we can band together to do something to provide more opportunities to a broader base of potential entrepreneurs. They also get that despite the many positive efforts out there that are providing benefits and making great contributions, we need so much more.

What Next?

The terrific programs I've written about in this chapter don't begin to represent a complete list of positive efforts to help entrepreneurs. Educational and nonprofit programs like these are everywhere today, each with a slightly different twist on how to help entrepreneurship. One thing is clear from all of these efforts. Entrepreneurship is far more popular and respected than it used to be. Add to that so many people who want to help entrepreneurs, and you have the potential for some real progress. Still, as exciting as this is, it has not yet moved the needle when it comes to reversing the country's declining startup numbers. Despite all the best efforts of nonprofits and some great state and local government actions on a broad basis, we are seeing the big get bigger and the small get squeezed out.

Do all of these organizations play a critical role in helping move us closer to leveling the playing field and growing U.S. entrepreneurship? Absolutely. By publicizing what they're doing, we can help entrepreneurs plug into the programs that will help them. By sharing best practices, these programs can get better and better. But even that's not enough.

However laudable, all the efforts by nonprofits, even when coupled with what local and state governments are doing, can do only so much. If we are to free U.S. entrepreneurship to really soar, we have to tackle those tough challenges that have contributed to its tanking in the first place. So we need to augment what's happening on the local, state, education, and nonprofit fronts with a combination of serious public and private backing to really encourage successful entrepreneurial ecosystems everywhere. And that starts with encouraging public policy initiatives and elected officials to heed this groundswell of entrepreneurial concern and support. They need to, because if we as a country don't decide that startups and small businesses are important and do something about it, nature is going to run its course and make them extinct.

The Time Is Now

We've lost sight of the impact of investing in individuals, the community, and our country at large, just as we've lost sight of how important it is to level the playing field and help small businesses and startups get a solid foothold on the economic ladder.

While we clearly need the one-on-one help that nonprofits provide, along with the policies of forward-thinking local and state governments to help trigger a tipping point, we can't wait for those to dramatically increase capital flow into startup investments. The federal public sector can absolutely make a huge difference on that front, and that needs to start now. For that to happen, the issues defined in this book need to lead to a dialogue and subsequent actions. The driving attitude behind this movement to materially grow the number of new traditional start-ups has to be a vociferous commitment to bridging the opportunity gap and creating a fair, level playing field.

Conclusion

Entrepreneurs worthy of the name aren't going to—and shouldn't—sit around and wait for the entrepreneurial environment to improve. But to succeed, they have to have the willingness and the incentive to put themselves on the line, as risk-taking is a critical ingredient if you want to step out of the business comfort zone and forge something new. That's not easy.

Even though as Americans we have always been encouraged to take risks and try new ideas—which is the whole essence of entrepreneurship—from the time we're little kids, we start learning what we can't do. Instead of being encouraged in creative free thinking, we learn what we're not supposed to do or what's supposedly not possible. That wasn't my problem. In fact, Kathryn says risk is my middle name.

As an entrepreneur, you do what you have to do. I've done that all my professional life, starting with managing properties that no one else would.

"Call Rudy and see if this guy's legit," the oversized thug who had pinned me against the wall and put a gun to my head said to the other guy in the room.

Rudy, luckily happening to be close to his phone, vouched for me.

"Okay. Sorry, boy," the thug said when he set me back down.

Any normal person would have run out of there, grateful to be alive. Instead, I unwittingly ended up managing the building for the mafia.

"How much money did you steal this month?" Rudy and his sidekick, Sam, would ask me every time I turned in the rent money I'd collected.

"You guys are the last people I'd ever steal from," I'd always reply. "Believe me."

Luckily, they always did.

Being an inveterate—some would say incorrigible—risk taker doesn't mean that I'm impervious to the stress that comes with business challenges. Like the time I watched the wheels come off in 1985. Having made my first million at age twenty-two, I lost my first billion that year at age thirty-five.

Yes, that was a "b."

"Craig, it looks like if you sell all the assets you control in an orderly liquidation, at the end you would be about $1 billion short of paying all the mortgage debts off on the properties," my financial turnaround advisor, Ken Leventhal, announced.

"You mean I'm broke," I said.

"Broke would be an upside from where you are. You are super broke."

OMG, I thought. *How do I get out of this mess?*

It was as if Ken had read my mind. "Son, my advice is to declare Chapter 7 bankruptcy. Walk away and start your life over again."

"That is not happening. Someone will have to drag me out of here kicking and screaming. I'm staying and fighting to make this right. I'm going to fix this for my ten thousand investors and 4,500 employees. They are depending on me, and I won't let them down."

"Well, if that is how you feel, then I'll have my team see if we can help work on survival and turnaround plans."

Six months later, the day-to-day struggles hadn't lessened. I talked to Ken and his partner or members of their restructuring team several times a day. Reorganizing a financial mess in the middle of a U.S. financial crisis in the S&L business and trying to keep my team together were daunting. As the second-largest owner of apartments in the world, what my company did mattered to communities.

I was now thirty-six years old, part owner of the Dallas Cowboys, and in the eye of the storm. As you already know, I did not escape unscathed. Looking back, I realize that my willingness to keep pushing the boundaries, even when I was down, allowed me to rebuild HALL Group. You never really fail as long as you keep on keeping on and fighting the good fight.

Although I pride myself on being a guy who doesn't panic when things are rough, it's hard to stay unemotional when everything is hurtling to the ground and your parachute won't open. The physical impact of the stress resulted in a heart attack, followed by a round of kidney stones two years later.

So yes, stuff happens. Bad stuff. You could even say that I'm the quintessential poster child for surviving failure.

Although I'm an example of how you can turn that kind of financial disaster around, it should be clear by now that the recession of 2008 to 2009 was not a typical one. That partly explains why today's would-be entrepreneurs are scared and risk averse. The millennial generation, along with the rest of us, saw all these terrible things that happened to people during that time. While that paled to what we experienced in Texas in the mid-1980s, it was nonetheless extremely difficult.

When those kinds of downturns occur, unless the government encourages people to invest and spend through tax laws or fiscal stimulation, the recovery ends up being very slow and difficult. Fiscal stimulation can encourage potential entrepreneurs to jump into the fray. U.S. monetary policy, however, which has dictated the bulk of what is now the third-longest recovery in history, doesn't give people much incentive to take risks. So they sit on the sidelines and play it safe, which dramatically and negatively impacts national growth.

Over the years, I've come to realize that most people need more of a security net than I do. An article titled "1 Million Missing Entrepreneurs" published by the Center for American Progress states that "mitigating certain risks can encourage entrepreneurship. Individuals with access to employer-provided health insurance through a spouse—a situation much more common in middle-class families than in low-income families—are significantly more likely to become self-employed." That same article points to a study by economist Robert Fairlie, who found that sixty-five-year-old men who could access Medicare were more apt to own a business than younger men who did not have that kind of buffer. "In other words," concludes the article, "changing just one risk—health care access—led to an increase in entrepreneurship."

We can do that through policies that encourage people to become first-time entrepreneurs—or to get back out there—if we simply make starting a company ever so slightly less risky.

Most people are afraid of going broke. That said, whether they admit it or not, they're also afraid of the personal embarrassment of failing. To me, failure is relative and just part of the continuum of life. You've never failed until you give up and say you're a failure. Otherwise, it's just the ups and downs of trying to make a difference as you do your best to survive until you thrive.

Entrepreneurship will never be a smooth ride. There is no such thing as a level playing field in the short run. There are always bumps, and things that aren't fair will always occur, whether in business or any other part of life. That said, having the faith to leap—and the tenacity to fight for what's needed to level out the playing field—can do more than just bring back U.S. entrepreneurship. We can help fashion a world that it is faster, cheaper, and on many levels better for business today than it was in the past. And we can all play a part in that.

A Challenge to Us All

How much difference can one person or one company make?

Think about Henry Ford. When asked why he had raised the compensation of his assembly line workers to an unheard-of five dollars a day, his response boiled down to the fact that in addition to retaining his workers, they would now be able to afford the cars being made by the Ford company. That one move ensured the company's survival, increased its sales, and helped create our country's middle class.

Turning around U.S. entrepreneurship starts with awareness, followed by willingness. Even though I was a youngster at the time, I still remember what John F. Kennedy said in his inauguration speech:

"Ask not what your country can do for you. Ask what you can do for your country."

Right now, one of the best things we can do for our country is to safeguard American entrepreneurship by reversing the trends that have stymied it and by increasing investments in startups. We need more Americans to have the kind of opportunity that I did so many years ago. So to mark HALL Group's 50th anniversary, $1 million in grants from the Craig and Kathryn Hall Foundation will be distributed to nonprofit partners so that they can invest in and support entrepreneurs who are most impacted by our country's opportunity gap.

This first grant will provide underserved entrepreneurs with critical access to capital, mentorship, and other resources. I can only hope that it will also inspire other successful companies to follow suit.

When I grew up, the notion that greed was bad and helping one another was good was pretty much a given. It seems as if this belief has been eroding over the past few decades, with too many greedy people, even entrepreneurs, across the country opting for financial success over supporting a system in which anyone with a viable business can thrive.

It's time that changed. Big is not always better. U.S. entrepreneurship does not need to be a zero-sum game. It can be an additive, everybody-wins game if we can increase the success of the United States versus other countries. Our personal freedoms as Americans will flourish when we can provide opportunities in a fair, level environment that fuels individuals' hopes and enables them to take advantage of the ability to start and own a business.

Let's make that happen.

Appendix A

Starter List of Organizations Supporting Entrepreneurship

Federal Agency

U.S. Small Business Administration
409 3rd St SW
Washington, DC 20416
(800) 827-5722
answerdesk@sba.gov
www.sba.gov

National Organizations

Several of these national organizations, such as EO, Junior Achievement, YPO, NAWBO and NTFE, have local chapters around the country. I encourage you to seek them out in your community.

America's SBDC (Small Business Development Center)
8990 Burke Lake Rd, 2nd Floor
Burke, VA 22015
(703) 764-9850
https://americassbdc.org/

Ewing Marion Kauffman Foundation
4801 Rockhill Rd
Kansas City, MO 64110
(816) 932-1000
www.kauffman.org

Center for American Entrepreneurship
info@startupusa.org
www.startupsusa.org

Young Presidents' Organization (YPO)
600 East Las Colinas Blvd, Suite 1100
Irving, Texas 75039
(972) 587-1500
askypo@ypo.org
www.ypo.org

National Venture Capital Association
25 Massachusetts Ave NW, Suite 730
Washington, DC 20001
(202) 864-5920
info@nvca.org
www.nvca.org

The National Association of Women Business Owners (NAWBO)
601 Pennsylvania Ave NW
South Building, Suite 900
Washington, DC 20004
(800) 556-2926
www.nawbo.org

Hamilton Project
1775 Massachusetts Ave NW
Washington, DC 20036
(202) 797-6484
info@hamiltonproject.org
www.hamiltonproject.org/

The Heritage Foundation
214 Massachusetts Ave NE
Washington, D.C. 20002-4999
(202) 546.4400
info@heritage.org
www.heritage.org

SCORE
1175 Herndon Pkwy, Suite 900
Herndon, VA 20170
(800) 634-0245
www.score.org

The Indus Entrepreneurs (TiE)
3975 Freedom Cir, Suite 230
Santa Clara, CA 95054
(408) 567-0700
global@tie.org
www.tie.org

Endeavor
900 Broadway, Suite 301
New York, NY 10003
(212) 352-3200
contact@endeavor.org
www.endeavor.org

Women's Venture Fund
154 Christopher St, Suite 3C
New York, NY 10014
(212) 563-0499
www.womensventurefund.org

WEConnect International
1100 H St NW, Suite 1100
Washington, DC 20005
(202) 810-6000
www.weconnectinternational.org

Young Entrepreneur Council (YEC)
745 Atlantic Ave
Boston, MA 02110
(484) 403-0736
info@yec.coi
www.yec.co

EO (Entrepreneurs' Organization)
500 Montgomery St, Suite 700
Alexandria, VA 22314
(703) 519-6700
www.eonetwork.org

NTFE (Network for Teaching Entrepreneurship)
120 Wall St, 18th Floor
New York, NY 10005
(212) 232-3333
www.nfte.com

Junior Achievement
One Education Way
Colorado Springs, CO 80906
(719) 540-8000
www.juniorachievement.org

Ashoka
1700 North Moore St, Suite 2000
Arlington, VA 22209
(703) 527-8300
www.ashoka.org

Rising Tide Capital
384 Martin Luther King Dr
Jersey City, NJ 07305
(201) 432-4316
info@risingtidecapital.org
www.risingtidecapital.org

Valley Economic Development Center, Inc. (VEDC)
5121 Van Nuys Blvd, Suite 300
Sherman Oaks, CA 91403
(800) 304-1755
info@vedc.org
vedc.org

Small Business Majority
1101 14th St NW, Suite 950
Washington, DC 20005
(202) 828-8357
www.smallbusinessmajority.org

Y Combinator
www.ycombinator.co

Fast Forward
info@ffwd.org
www.ffwd.org

500 Startups
814 Mission St, 6th Floor
San Francisco, CA 94103
www.500.co

Dreamit Ventures
33 Irving Pl, Floor 10
New York, NY 10003
www.dreamit.com

TechStars
www.techstars.com

AngelPad
www.angelpad.org

Capital Innovators
4240 Duncan Ave
St. Louis, MO 63110
(314) 669-5832
info@CapitalInnovators.com
www.capitalinnovators.com

Entrepreneurs Roundtable Accelerator
415 Madison Ave, 4th floor
New York, NY 10017
info@eranyc.com
www.eranyc.com

Rise of the Rest© Seed Fund
1717 Rhode Island Ave NW, Suite 1000
Washington, DC 20036
(202) 776-1400
www.revolution.com/entity/rotr/

Children International
2000 E. Red Bridge Rd
Kansas City, MO 64121
(800) 888-3089
children@children.org
https://www.children.org/

Kiva
875 Howard St, Suite 340
San Francisco, CA 94103
(828) 479-5482
www.kiva.org

Heifer International
1 World Ave,
Littlerock, AR 72202
855.9HUNGER (855) 948-6437
www.heifer.org
Bright Ideas Trust
Miltel,11 Pilgrim St
London, EC4V 6RN, UK
enquiries@brightideastrust.com
www.brightideastrust.com

Select Corporate Entrepreneurial Funds

Goldman Sachs – 10,000 Small Businesses
www.goldmansachs.com

JP Morgan Chase & Co. – Small Business Forward
www.jpmorganchase.com

Tory Burch Foundation
(866) 480-8679
info@toryburchfoundation.org
www.toryburchfoundation.org

Ernst & Young – Entrepreneurship of the Year Program
www.ey.com

Dell for Entrepreneurs
www.dell.com

Google for Entrepreneurs
www.googleforentrepreneurs.com

Microsoft – 500 Million Program
https://startups.microsoft.com

Mass Challenge
contact@masschallenge.org
www.masschallenge.org

Local Organizations by State

ALABAMA

The Economic Development Partnership of Alabama Foundation
1320 1st Ave S
Birmingham, AL 35233
(205) 943-4700
www.edpa.org

Alabama Launchpad
1320 1st Ave S
Birmingham, AL 35233
(205) 943-4700
launchpad@edpa.org
https://alabamalaunchpad.com

Innovation Depot
1500 First Ave N
Birmingham, AL 35203
(205) 250-8000
info@innovationdepot.org
https://innovationdepot.org/

Shoals Business Incubator
3115 Northington Ct
Florence, AL 35630
(256) 760-9014
www.shoalsbusinessincubator.com

The Catalyst Center for Business & Entrepreneurship
515 Sparkman Dr
Huntsville, AL 35816
(256) 428-8190
info@catalystcenter.org
http://catalystcenter.org/

ALASKA

The Alaska Small Business Development Center
1901 Bragaw St, Room 199
Anchorage, AK 99508
(907) 786-7201
info@aksbdc.org
www.aksbdc.org

ARIZONA

StartupAZ Foundation
515 E Grant St
Phoenix, AZ 85004
generosity@startupaz.org
www.startupaz.org

ARKANSAS

Innovate Arkansas
2101 Riverfront Dr
Little Rock, AR 72202
(501) 280-3025
admin@innovatearkansas.org
www.innovatearkansas.org

CALIFORNIA

Renaissance Entrepreneurship Center
275 5th St
San Francisco, CA 94103
(415) 541-8580
info@rencenter.org
www.rencenter.org

Nasdaq Entrepreneurial Center
505 Howard St
San Francisco, CA 94105
hello@theCenter.nasdaq.org
https://thecenter.nasdaq.org/

Code2040
785 Market St, Suite 850
San Francisco, CA 94103
info@code2040.org
www.code2040.org

Women In Consulting
905 South Bascom Ave, Suite 1113
San Jose, CA 95128
(408) 266-9658
admin@womeninconsulting.org
www.womeninconsulting.org

StartX
2627 Hanover St
Palo Alto, CA 94304
www.startx.com

California SBCD
26455 Rockwell Canyon Rd
Santa Clarita, CA 91355
(661) 362-5900
www.cocsbdc.org

COLORADO

Rocky Mountain Innovation Partners
1227 Lake Plaza Dr, Suite B
Colorado Springs, CO 80906-7402
(719) 685-7877
www.rmipartners.org

Colorado Enterprise Fund
1888 Sherman St, Suite 530
Denver, CO 80203
(303) 860-0242
info@coloradoenterprisefund.org
www.coloradoenterprisefund.org

NextFifty Initiative
950 S Cherry St, Suite 510
Denver, CO 80246
(303) 547-1800
info@next50initiative.org
www.next50initiative.org

BIBA
2525 Arapahoe Ave #E4-121
Boulder, CO 80302
(720) 565-3854
www.boulderiba.org

CONNECTICUT

reSET
1429 Park St, Suite 114
Hartford, CT 06106
(860) 560-9120
www.resetco.org

Connecticut Non Profit Alliance
865 Brook St
Rocky Hill, CT 06067
(860) 258-7858
connect@ctnext.co
www.ctnext.com

Innovation Destination Hartford
jshemo@metrohartford.com
www.innovationhartford.com

The Connecticut Technology Council
222 Pitkin St, Suite 113
East Hartford, CT 06108
(860) 289-0878
info@ct.org
www.ct.org

Empower Business Connection
(860) 375-0348
www.empowerbusinessconnection.com

DELAWARE

Delaware Small Business Development Center (SBDC)
1 Innovation Way, Suite 301
Newark, Delaware 19711
Phone: (302) 831-1555
delaware-sbdc@udel.edu
https://delawaresbdc.org/

FLORIDA

Enterprise Development Corporation Florida
3250 NE 1st Ave, Third Floor
Miami, FL 33137
(800) 588-7194
edcinfo@edc-tech.org
www.enterbusiness.org

Domi Station
914 Railroad Ave
Tallahassee, FL 32310
getstarted@domistation.com
www.domistation.com

National Entrepreneur Center
3201 E. Colonial Dr, Suite A-20
Orlando, FL 32803
(407) 420-4848
www.nationalec.org

Orlando Entrepreneurs
1 S Orange Ave, Suite 502
Orlando, FL 32801
www.orlandoentrepreneurs.org

DGIT
14311 Biscayne Blvd #614101
Miami, FL 33181
nfo@digigrass.com
www.digigrass.com

GEORGIA

Georgia Minority Supplier Development Council (GMSDC)
759 W Peachtree St NE, Suite 107
Atlanta, GA 30308
www.gmsdc.org

WEI Atlanta
84 Peachtree St NE, 11th Floor
Atlanta, GA 30303
(404) 546-4065
info@weiatlanta.com
www.weiatlanta.com

ACE Women's Business Center
10 College St NW
Norcross, GA 30071
(678) 335-5600
info@aceloans.org
https://aceloans.org/

Atlanta Tech Village
3423 Piedmont Rd NE
Atlanta, GA 30305
(404) 445-1525
hello@atlantatechvillage.com
https://atlantatechvillage.com/

Startup Atlanta
www.startupatlanta.com

HAWAII

Entrepreneurs Foundation of Hawaii
2800 Woodlawn Dr, Suite 265
Honolulu, Hawaii 96822
www.efhawaii.org

IDAHO

Innovation Collective
418 East Lakeside Ave #7
Coeur D'Alene, ID 83814
(208) 269-5545
info@innovationcollective.co
www.innovationcollective.co

ILLINOIS

Chicagoland Entrepreneurial Center (CEC)
222 W. Merchandise Mart Plaza, Suite 1212
Chicago, IL 60654
(312) 239-0310
contact@1871.com
www.1871.com

Women's Business Development Center (WBDC)
8 S. Michigan Ave, 4th Floor
Chicago, IL 60603
(312) 853-3477
wbdc@wbdc.org
www.wbdc.org

UCWBG
5250 Grand Ave, Suite 14
Gurnee, IL 60031
(847) 223-1234
www.ucwbg.clubexpress.com

BLUE1647
2150 S Canalport Ave
Chicago, IL 60608
www.blue1647.com

Opportunity International
550 West Van Buren St
Chicago, IL 60607
(800) 793-9455

INDIANA

The Venture Club of Indiana
3656 Washington Blvd
Indianapolis, IN 46205
(317) 926-2723
info@ventureclub.org
www.ventureclub.org

NIIC
3201 Stellhorn Rd
Fort Wayne, IN 46815
(260) 407-6442
info@niic.net
www.theniic.org

Start Fort Wayne
111 W Berry St, Suite 211
Ft. Wayne, IN 46802
(260) 969-9393
contact@startfortwayne.com
www.startfortwayne.com

IOWA

Iowa Venture Capital Association
1280 Financial Center
Des Moines, IA 50309
info@iowaventure.org
www.iowaventure.org

Solidarity Microfinance
607 Forest Ave
Des Moines, IA 50314
info@solidaritymicrofinance.org
www.solidaritymicrofinance.org

Square One DSM
700 Locust St, Suite 100
Des Moines, IA 50309
(515) 286-4950
info@DSMpartnership.com
www.dsmpartnership.com

KANSAS

NetWork Kansas
P.O. Box 877
Andover, KS 67002-0877
(877) 521-8600
info@networkkansas.com
www.networkkansas.com

Kansas City Startup Foundation
1712 Main St #426
Kansas City, MO 64108
(913) 937-7494
info@kcstartupfoundation.org
www.kcstartupfoundation.org

ECJC
4220 Shawnee Mission Pkwy, Suite 350B
Fairway, KS 66205
(913) 438-2282
info@ecjc.com
www.ecjc.com

KENTUCKY

Awesome Inc
348 E. Main St
Lexington, KY 40507
(859) 960-4600
founders@awesomeinc.org
www.awesomeinc.org

XLerateHealth
300 E Market St, Suite 260
Louisville, KY 40202
(270) 901-3490
admin@xleratehealth.com
www.xleratehealth.com

The Vogt Awards
614 W Main St, Suite 6000
Louisville, KY 40202
(502) 625-0000
info@enterprisecorp.com
www.vogtawards.com

LOUISIANA

Propeller
4035 Washington Ave
New Orleans, LA 70125
(504) 322-3282
www.gopropeller.org

The Idea Village
900 Camp St, Suite 308
New Orleans, LA 70130
(504) 291-2563
info@ideavillage.org
www.ideavillage.org

Landing Zone
625 Celeste St
New Orleans, LA 70130
(504) 500-7597
info@lznola.com
www.lznola.com

New Orleans BioInnovation Center
1441 Canal St
New Orleans, LA 70112
(504) 680-2973
info@neworleansbio.com
www.neworleansbio.com

MAINE

The Maine Center for Entrepreneurs
63 Federal St, Suite 7
Portland, ME 04101
info@mced.biz
www.mced.biz

Creative Portland
P.O. Box 4675
Portland, ME 04112
(207) 370-4784
info@creativeportland.com
www.creativeportland.com

Startup Portland
startupportland@gmail.com
http://startupportland.com/

Maine Angels
contact@maineangels.org
www.maineangels.org

MARYLAND

Eastern Shore Entrepreneurship Center
8737 Brooks Dr, Suite 101
Easton, MD 21601
(410) 770-9330
info@esec.md
www.ventureahead.org

Maryland Women's Business Center
51 Monroe St, PE-20
Rockville, MD 20850
(301) 315-8091
info@marylandwbc.org
https://marylandwbc.org/

Maryland Center for Entrepreneurship (MCE)
9250 Bendix Rd
Columbia, MD 21045
(410) 313-6550
www.hceda.org

Startup Maryland
www.startupmd.org

MASSACHUSETTS

The Possible Project
17 Sellers St
Cambridge, MA 02139
(617) 492-9200
info@possibleproject.org
www.possibleproject.org

BUILD Greater Boston
745 Atlantic Ave, 8th floor
Boston, MA 02111
(617) 600-0532
greaterboston@build.org
www.buildinboston.org

Entrepreneurship for All
175 Cabot St, Suite #100
Lowell, MA 01854
info@eforall.org
www.eforall.org

Boston Entrepreneurs' Network
info@boston-enet.org
www.boston-enet.org

Early Investors Inc
22 Joseph Rd
Braintree, MA 02184
(617) 446-3946
info@earlyinvestors.org
http://earlyinvestors.org

MICHIGAN

Michigan Association for Female Entrepreneurs (MAFE)
12245 Beech Daly Rd
Redford, MI 48240
(844) 490-6233
www.mafedetroit.org

Detroit Entrepreneurship Network
(734) 531-9247
www.detroitden.com

Automation Alley
2675 Bellingham Dr
Troy, MI 48083-2044
(248) 457-3200
info@automationalley.com
www.automationalley.com

Finance Michigan
1380 East Jefferson Ave
Detroit, MI 48207
(313) 259-6900
info@trowbridgehouse.com
www.financemichigan.com

Build Institute
2701 Bagley Ave
Detroit, MI 48216
(313) 265-3590
hello@buildinstitute.org
www.buildinstitute.org

Start Garden
hello@startgarden.com
www.startgarden.com

MINNESOTA

Women Entrepreneurs of Minnesota
info@wemn.org
www.wemn.org

Meda
1256 Penn Ave N, Suite 4800
Minneapolis, MN 55411
(612) 332-6332
info@meda.net
www.meda.net

MISSISSIPPI

Mississippi Minority Business Alliance, Inc.
1230 Raymond Rd, Box 600
Jackson, MS 39204
(601) 965-0366
info@mmba.us
www.mmba.us

Innovate Mississippi
121 N State St, Suite 500
Jackson, MS 39201
(601) 960-3610
info@innovate.ms
www.innovate.ms

MISSOURI

EQ
editors@eqstl.com
www.eqstl.com

Prosper Women Entrepreneurs
aimee@prosperstl.com
www.prosperstl.com

Center for Emerging Technologies
20 South Sarah St
St. Louis, MO 63108
(314) 615-6300
cmaxfield@cortexstl.com
www.cetstl.com

SixThirty
911 Washington Ave, Suite 844
St. Louis, MO 63101
(314) 669-6803
hello@sixthirty.co
www.sixthirty.co

T-Rex
911 Washington Ave, 5th Floor
St. Louis, MO 63101
(314) 241-7500
kathleen@downtowntrex.org
www.downtowntrex.org

Innovative Technology Enterprises at UMSL
1 University Blvd
St. Louis, MO 63121
(314) 516-4700
itemanager@ite-stl.org
www.ite-stl.org

MONTANA

Innovate Montana
27 N 27th St
Billings, MT 59101
(406) 444-5634
business@mt.gov
www.innovatemontana.com

NEBRASKA

Lincoln Score
285 S. 68th St Pl, Suite 208
Lincoln, NE, 68510
(402) 437-2409
infolincoln@scorevolunteer.org
https://lincoln.score.org

NEVADA

StartUpNV
450 Sinclair St
Reno, NV 89501
(775) 393-9701
info@startupnv.org
https://startupnv.org

Nevada's Center for Entrepreneurship and Technology (NCET)
5441 Kietzke Ln, 2nd floor
Reno, NV 89511
(775) 453-0130
info@ncet.org
https://ncet.org/

Rural Nevada Development Corporation
1320 E Aultman St
Ely, NV 89301
(775) 289-8519
info@rndcnv.org
www.rndcnv.org

NEW HAMPSHIRE

Alpha Loft
P.O. Box 3730
Manchester, NH 03105
(603) 629-9511
info@alphaloft.org
www.alphaloft.org

Center for Women & Enterprise (CWE) New Hampshire
30 Temple St, Suite 610
Nashua, NH 03060
(603) 318-7580
info.NewHampshire@cweonline.org
www.cweonline.org

Entrepreneurs' Fund of New Hampshire
37 Pleasant St
Concord, NH 03301
(603) 225-6641
https://www.nhcf.org

NEW JERSEY

UCEDC
75 Chestnut St
Cranford, NJ 07016
(908) 527-1166
info@ucedc.com
https://ucedc.com

Regional Business Assistance Corporation
3111 Quakerbridge Rd, 2nd floor
Mercerville, NJ 08619
(609) 587-1133
info@rbacloan.com
www.rbacloan.com
EANJ
30 W Mount Pleasant Ave, Suite 201
Livingston, NJ 07039
(973) 758-6800
www.eanj.org

NEW MEXICO

STARTUP New Mexico
5901 Indian School Rd NE
Albuquerque, NM 87110
info@startupnm.org

The Loan Fund
423 Iron Ave SW
Albuquerque, NM
(505) 243-3196
info@loanfund.org
www.loanfund.org

New Mexico Community Capital
219 Central Ave NW, Suite 200
Albuquerque, NM 87102
(505) 924-2820
info@nmccap.org
www.nmccap.org

NEW YORK

The Knowledge House
1231 Lafayette Ave, 2nd Floor
Bronx, NY 10474
info@theknowledgehouse.org
www.theknowledgehouse.org

Business Outreach Center Network
85 S Oxford St, 2nd Floor

Brooklyn, NY 11217
(718) 624-9115
info@bocnet.org
www.bocnet.org

NYPace
P.O. Box 1044
New York, NY 10014
info@NYPACE.org
www.nypace.org

Pencils of Promise
37 West 28th St, 3rd Floor
New York, NY 10001
(212) 777-3170
team@pencilsofpromise.org
https://pencilsofpromise.org

NORTH CAROLINA

CED
600 Park Offices Dr, Suite 100
Research Triangle Park, NC 27709
(919) 549-7500
www.cednc.org

Packard Place
222 S Church St
Charlotte, NC 28202
(980) 500-8288
office@packardplace.us
www.packard.place

Economic Development Partnership of North Carolina
15000 Weston Pkwy
Cary, NC 27513
(919) 447-7777
www.edpnc.com

NORTH DAKOTA

UND Center for Innovation
4200 James Ray Dr
Grand Forks, ND 58203
(701) 777-3132
info@innovators.net
www.innovators.net

Center for Technology & Business
2720 E Broadway Ave
Bismarck, ND 58501
(701) 223-0707
http://trainingnd.com

OHIO

Economic & Community Development Institute (ECDI)
1655 Old Leonard Avenue
Columbus, OH 43219
614-559-0115
www.ecdi.org

Stark Entrepreneurship Alliance
400 3rd St SE
Canton, OH 44702
(330) 453-5900
https://www.starkentalliance.com

Growth Capital
1360 E Ninth St, Suite 950
Cleveland, OH 44114
(216) 592-2332
www.growthcapitalcorp.com

Cincinnati Minority Business Collaborative
1776 Mentor Ave, Suite 100
Cincinnati, OH 45212
(513) 631-8292
www.hcdc.com

OKLAHOMA

I2e
840 Research Pkwy, Suite 250
Oklahoma City, OK 73104
(405) 235-2305
www.i2e.org

Startup OK
http://www.startupok.com/

36 Degrees North
36 E Cameron St
Tulsa, OK 74103
(918) 884-3550
website@36n.co
www.36degreesnorth.co

The Forge
125 W 3rd St
Tulsa, OK 74103
(918) 560-0265
www.theforgetulsa.com

OREGON

Economic Development for Central Oregon (EDCO)
705 Southwest Bonnett Way Suite 1000
Bend, OR 97702
(541) 388-3236
https://edcoinfo.com/

Oregon Entrepreneurs Network (OEN)
309 SW Sixth Ave, Suite 212
Portland, OR 97204
(503) 222-2270
info@oen.org
www.oen.org

Cascade Angels: Elevating Oregon
48 SE Bridgeford Blvd, Suite 210
Bend, Oregon 97701
info@cascadeangels.com
https://cascadeangels.com/

PENNSYLVANIA

ASSETS
100 S Queen St
Lancaster, PA 17603
(717) 393-6089
info@assetspa.org
www.assetspa.org

Economic Development Company of Lancaster County
115 E King St
Lancaster, PA 17602
(717) 397-4046
www.edclancaster.com

Philly Startup Leaders
engage@phillystartupleaders.org
https://phillystartupleaders.org

Entrepreneur Works
400 Market St, Suite 210
Philadelphia, PA 19106
(215) 545-3100
www.myentrepreneurworks.org

RHODE ISLAND

CWE Rhode Island
132 George M. Cohan Blvd
Providence, RI 02903
(401) 277-0800
info.RhodeIsland@cweonline.org
www.cweonline.org

SOUTH CAROLINA

Central Carolina Community Foundation
2711 Middleburg Dr, Suite 213
Columbia, SC 29204
(803) 254-5601
www.yourfoundation.org

The Harbor Entrepreneur Center
1505 King St Ext, Suite 200
Charleston, SC 29405
(843) 972-4070
harborec@gmail.com
www.harborec.com

South Carolina Department of Commerce Office of Innovation
1201 Main St, Suite 1600
Columbia, SC 29201
(803) 737-0400
info@sccommerce.com
www.sccommerce.com

YES Carolina (Youth Entrepreneurship South Carolina)
171 Church St, Suite 212
Charleston, SC 29401
(843) 805-4901
yes@yescarolina.com
http://yescarolina.com

SOUTH DAKOTA

Grow South Dakota
104 Ash St E
Sisseton, SD 57262
(605) 698-7654
info@growsd.org
www.growsd.org

Enterprise Institute
2301 Research Park Way, Suite 114
Brookings, SD 57006
(605) 697-5015
info@sdei.org
www.sdei.org

Zeal Center for Entrepreneurship
2329 N Career Ave, Suite 1
Sioux Falls, SD 57107
(605) 275-8000
info@realzeal.com
www.realzeal.com

TENNESSEE

Nashville Entrepreneur Center
41 Peabody St
Nashville, TN 37210
(615) 873-1257
www.ec.co

Launch Tennessee
211 7th Ave, Suite 200
Nashville, TN 37219
(615) 673-4419
info@launchtn.org
https://launchtn.org

TEXAS

The Dallas Entrepreneur Center (DEC)
3102 Oak Lawn Ave
Dallas, TX 75219
(469) 480-4466
info@thedec.co
www.thedec.co

PeopleFund
2921 E 17th St Building D, Suite 1
Austin, TX 78702
(888) 222-0017
www.peoplefund.org

Prison Entrepreneurship Program (PEP)
P.O. Box 836617
Richardson, TX 75083
(214) 575-9909
info@pep.org
www.pep.org

Women@Austin
701 Brazos St, Suite 1601
Austin, TX 78701
info@womenataustin.com
www.womenataustin.com

BiGAUSTIN Business Investment Growth
8000 Centre Park Dr, Suite 200
Austin, TX 78754
(512) 928-8010
info@bigaustin.org
www.bigaustin.org

Entrepreneurs Foundation of Central Texas
701 Brazos St, Suite 501
Austin, TX 78701
(512) 482-8894
info@efctx.org
www.entrepreneursfoundation.org

Tech Fort Worth
1120 South Fwy
Fort Worth, TX 76104
(817) 984-9841
hayden@techfortworth.org
www.techfortworth.org

The Real Estate Council Community Fund
3100 McKinnon St, No. 1150
Dallas, TX 75201
(214) 692-3600
http://recouncil.com/

UTAH

Grow Utah
450 S Simmons Way, Suite 500
Kaysville, UT 84037
(801) 593-2269
info@growutah.com
www.growutah.com

The Women's Business Center of Utah
175 E 400 S, #600
Salt Lake City, UT 84111
(801) 328-5066
info@wbcutah.com
https://wbcutah.com

Church & State
370 S 300 E
Salt Lake City, UT 84111
info@cs1893.com
www.cs1893.com

Beehive Startups
1656 E Bay Blvd #300
Provo, UT 84606
cbetts@beehivestartups.com
www.beehivestartups.com

VERMONT

Vermont Small Business Development Center
1540 Vermont Rte 66
Randolph, VT 05060
(800) 464-7232
www.vtsbdc.org

VBSR (Vermont Businesses for Social Responsibility)
255 South Champlain St, Suite 11
Burlington, VT 05401
(802) 862-8347
info@vbsr.org
www.vbsr.org

Center for Women & Enterprise (CWE) Vermont
431 Pine St, Suite 101
Burlington, VT 05401
(802) 391-4870
info.Vermont@CWEonline.org
www.cweonline.org

VIRGINIA

Venture Forum RVA
(804) 840-6600
RHogge@VentureForumRVA.com
http://ventureforumrva.com

Virginia is For Entrepreneurs (VA4E)
3704 Pacific Ave, Suite 200
Virginia Beach, VA 23451
(757) 362-0436
http://va4e.org

UnBound RVA
2920 W. Broad St, Suite 224
Richmond, VA 23230
(804) 332-6892
info@unboundrva.org
http://unboundrva.org

NAWBO Richmond
P.O. Box 3632
N. Chesterfield, VA 23235
(804) 346-5644
info@nawborichmond.org
http://nawborichmond.org

WASHINGTON

Ventures
2100 24th Ave S, Suite 380
Seattle, WA 98144
(206) 352-1945
www.venturesnonprofit.org

Technology Alliance
1301 Fifth Ave, Suite 1500
Seattle, WA 98101
(206) 389-7261
info@technology-alliance.com
www.technology-alliance.com

Startup 425
www.startup425.org

Economic Development Council of Seattle & King County
701 5th Ave, Suite 2510
Seattle, WA 98104

Business Impact NW
1437 S Jackson St
Seattle, WA 98144
(206) 324-4330
info@businessimpactnw.org
www.businessimpactnw.org

WEST VIRGINIA

TechConnect West Virginia
1740 Union Carbide Dr, Room 4203
South Charleston, WV 25303
(304) 444-2918
info@techconnectwv.com
www.techconnectwv.org

WISCONSIN

Doyenne Group
7 N Pinckney St, Suite 218
Madison, WI 53703
(608) 620-3479
info@thedoyennegroup.com
www.doyennegroup.com

Wisconsin Women Entrepreneurs Southcentral, Inc.
contact@wwesouthcentral.org
www.wwesouthcentral.org

The Commons
313 North Plankinton Avenue, Suite 213
Milwaukee, WI 53203
www.thecommonswi.com

Startup Milwaukee
www.startupmke.org

Milwaukee Economic Development Corporation
757 N. Broadway, Suite 600
Milwaukee, WI 53202
(414) 269-1440
www.medconline.com

WYOMING
Wyoming Women's Business Center
710 Garfield St, Suite 323
Laramie, WY
(307) 460-3943
wwbc@uwyo.edu
www.wyomingwomen.org

WTBC
1000 E. University Ave
Laramie, WY 82071
(307) 766-1121
www.uwyo.edu/wtbc

Appendix B

Starter List of University Programs Supporting Entrepreneurship

Alfred University: Family Business and Entrepreneurship Minor
1 Saxon Dr
Alfred, NY 14802
(607) 871-2111
https://alfred.edu/academics/undergrad-majors-minors/family
-business-entrepreneurship.cfm

Arizona State University: Entrepreneurship + Innovation
1475 N. Scottsdale Rd, Suite 200
Scottsdale, AZ 85257
(480) 884-1860
https://entrepreneurship.asu.edu/

Babson College: The Arthur M. Blank Center for Entrepreneurship
231 Forest St
Babson Park, MA 02457
(781) 235-1200
blankcenter@babson.edu
http://www.babson.edu/Academics/centers/blank-center/Pages/home.aspx

Ball State University: Entrepreneurship Center
2000 W. University Ave
Muncie, IN 47306
(800) 382-8540
entrepreneur@bsu.edu
https://www.bsu.edu/academics/centersandinstitutes/entrepreneurship
/about-us

Barry University: Entrepreneurial Institute
11300 NE 2nd Ave
Miami Shores, FL 33161
(305) 899-3500
jkleban@barry.edu
http://www.barry.edu/biced/entrepreneurial-institute/

Baylor University: Entrepreneurship at Baylor
One Bear Pl
Waco, Texas 76798
(800) 229-5678
https://www.baylor.edu/business/entrepreneurship/

Belmont University: Center for Entrepreneurship
1900 Belmont Blvd
Nashville, TN 37212
(615) 460-6000
http://www.belmont.edu/business/undergrad_soba/soba_programs
/entrepreneurship.html

Bentley University: Entrepreneurship and Innovation
175 Forest St
Waltham, MA 02452
(781) 891-2000
https://www.bentley.edu/academics/departments/management
/major-concentrations#Entrepreneurship

Bernard Baruch College, The City University of New York;
Entrepreneurship
One Bernard Baruch Way, Box B2-255
New York, NY 10010
(646) 312-2128
academy@baruch.cuny.edu
https://www.baruch.cuny.edu/academy/entrepreneurship.html

Black Hills State University: Entrepreneurial Studies
1200 University St
Spearfish, SD 57799
(605) 642-6398
Jeffrey.Wehrung@BHSU.edu
http://www.bhsu.edu/Academics/Business/Entrepreneurial-Studies

Boise State University: Entrepreneurship Management
1910 University Dr
Boise, ID 83725
(208) 426-1000
regmail@boisestate.edu
https://registrar.boisestate.edu/undergraduate/program-list/p-entrep-bba/

Boston College: Edmund H. Shea Jr. Center for Entrepreneurship
140 Commonwealth Ave
Chestnut Hill, MA 02467
(617) 552-1384
shea.center@bc.edu
https://www.bc.edu/bc-web/schools/carroll-school/sites/shea-center.html

Boston University: Innovation and Entrepreneurship Graduate Certificate
One Silber Way
Boston, MA 02215
(617) 353-2000
http://www.bu.edu/academics/programs/innovation-entrepreneurship/

Bradley University: Turner Center for Entrepreneurship
1501 W Bradley Ave
Peoria, IL 61625
(309) 676-7611
https://www.bradley.edu/turnercenter/

Brigham Young University: Rollins Center for Entrepreneurship & Technology
730 TNRB
Provo, UT 84602
(801) 422-4285
msb_advisement@byu.edu
https://marriottschool.byu.edu/cet/

Brown University: Program in Innovation Management and Entrepreneurship
Sayles Hall, Suite 015, Box 1922
Providence, Rhode Island 02912
(401) 863-1000
http://brownentrepreneurship.com/

California State University Long Beach: Institute for Innovation & Entrepreneurship
1250 Bellflower Blvd
Long Beach, CA 90840
(562) 985-4111
https://www.csulb.edu/institute-innovation-entrepreneurship

California State University Monterey Bay: Entrepreneurship Concentration
5108 Fourth Ave
Marina, CA 93933
(831) 582-3000
https://csumb.edu/business/entrepreneurship

Canisius College: Entrepreneurship Program
2001 Main St
Buffalo, NY 14208
(716) 883-7000
info@canisius.edu
https://www.canisius.edu/academics/programs/entrepreneurship

Carnegie Mellon University: Swartz Center for Entrepreneurship
5000 Forbes Ave
Pittsburgh, PA 15213
swartzcenter@andrew.cmu.edu
https://www.cmu.edu/swartz-center-for-entrepreneurship/

Central Michigan University: Entrepreneurship Program
1200 S. Franklin St
Mount Pleasant, MI 48859
(989) 774-3124
cba@cmich.edu
https://go.cmich.edu/academics/Undergraduate/Find_Program/Pages
/Entrepreneurship.aspx

Chapman University: The Ralph W. Leatherby Center for Entrepreneurship and Business Ethics
One University Dr
Orange, CA 92866
(714) 997-6815
https://www.chapman.edu/research/institutes-and-centers/leatherby
-center/index.aspx

Chatham University: Center for Women's Entrepreneurship
6585 Penn Avenue
Pittsburgh, PA 15206
(412) 365-1253
womens-entrepreneurship@chatham.edu
https://www.chatham.edu/cwe/

Clarkson University: Reh Center for Entrepreneurship
8 Clarkson Ave
Potsdam, NY 13699
(315) 268-6400
rehcenter@clarkson.edu
https://www.clarkson.edu/entrepreneurship

College of Charleston: Center for Entrepreneurship
66 George St
Charleston, SC 29424
(843) 805-5507
http://sb.cofc.edu/centers/centerforentrepreneurship/index.php

Colorado State University: Institute for Entrepreneurship
501 W. Laurel St
Fort Collins, CO 80523
(970) 491-6471
ieinfo@business.colostate.edu
https://biz.colostate.edu

Columbia University: Entrepreneurship Innovation & Design
622 W 113th St
New York, NY 10025
entrepreneurship@columbia.edu
https://entrepreneurship.columbia.edu/contact-us/

Cornell University: Pillsbury Institute for Hospitality Entrepreneurship
Statler Hall Cornell University
Ithaca, NY 14853
607-255-1576
sha_dean@cornell.edu
https://sha.cornell.edu/faculty-research/centers-institutes/pihe/

Creighton University: Social Entrepreneurship Track
2500 California Plaza
Omaha, NE 68178
(402) 280-2700
http://catalog.creighton.edu/undergraduate/business/
marketing-management/social-entrepreneurship/

Dartmouth: Engineering Entrepreneurship Program
14 Engineering Dr
Hanover, NH 03755
(603) 646-2230
Thayer.Receptionist@Dartmouth.edu
https://engineering.dartmouth.edu/about/dartmouth-difference/deep

DePaul University: Coleman Entrepreneurship Center
1 E. Jackson Blvd
Chicago, IL 60604
(312) 362-8000
admission@depaul.edu
https://business.depaul.edu/about/centers-institutes/coleman-entrepre-
neurship-center/Pages/default.aspx

Drexel University: Entrepreneurship Degree
3141 Chestnut St
Philadelphia, PA 19104
(215) 895.2000
http://drexel.edu/difference/entrepreneurship/

Duke University: Innovation & Entrepreneurship Initiative
215 Morris St, Suite 300
Durham, NC 27701
(919) 681-9165
entrepreneurship@duke.edu
https://entrepreneurship.duke.edu/

Eastern Michigan University: Center for Entrepreneurship
473 Gary Owen Building
300 W. Michigan Ave
Ypsilanti, MI 48197
(734) 487-4140
cob_dean@emich.edu
https://www.emich.edu/cob/centers-institutes/center-for
-entrepreneurship.php

Florida Atlantic University: Adams Center for Entrepreneurship
777 Glades Rd
Boca Raton, FL 33431
(561) 297-3654
adamscenter@fau.edu
https://business.fau.edu/centers/adams-center/

Florida State University: Jim Moran School of Entrepreneurship
644 West Call St
Tallahassee, FL 32306
(850) 644-7158
info@jimmoranschool.fsu.edu
http://jimmoranschool.fsu.edu/

Fordham University: Entrepreneurship Concentration
441 E. Fordham Rd
Bronx, NY 10458
(718) 817-1000
https://www.fordham.edu/info/24491/undergraduate_business_majors
_concentrations_and_minors/3052/entrepreneurship/1

George Mason University: Entrepreneurship and Innovation
4400 University Dr
Fairfax, VA 22030
entrepreneurship@gmu.edu
https://startup.gmu.edu/

Georgia State University: Entrepreneurship and Innovation
55 Park Pl, Suite 250
Atlanta, GA 30303
(404) 413-7910
eni@gsu.edu
https://robinson.gsu.edu/academic-departments/entrepreneurship-and
-innovation/

Georgia Tech: Entrepreneurship Education
North Avenue
Atlanta, GA 30332
(404) 894-2000
https://www.gatech.edu/innovation-ecosystem/education

Georgetown University: Leadership & Innovation Major
37th and O Streets NW
Washington, DC 20057
(202) 687-4750
startuphoyas@georgetown.edu
http://startuphoyas.com/

George Washington University: Innovation and Entrepreneurship
2201 G Street NW
Washington, DC 20052
https://business.gwu.edu/academics/programs/undergraduate/bba
/innovation-and-entrepreneurship

Harvard University: Arthur Rock Center for Entrepreneurship
117 Western Ave
Boston, MA 02163
rockcenter@hbs.edu
https://entrepreneurship.hbs.edu/

Illinois State University: Entrepreneurship and Business Management
Campus Box 5500
Normal, IL 61790
(309) 438-2251
cobinfo@ilstu.edu
https://business.illinoisstate.edu/management/sequences
/entrepreneurship.shtml

Indiana University: Johnson Center for Entrepreneurship & Innovation
1275 E Tenth St, Suite 2050
Bloomington, IN 47405
(812) 855-4248
jcei@indiana.edu
https://kelley.iu.edu/faculty-research/centers-institutes/entrepreneurship
-innovation/index.cshtml

Iowa State University: Entrepreneurship Studies
2167 Union Dr
Ames, IA 50011
(515) 294-8300
undergrad@iastate.edu
https://www.business.iastate.edu/undergraduate/majors-minors
/entrepreneurship/

John Carroll University: Edward M. Muldoon Center for Entrepreneurship
1 John Carroll Blvd
University Heights, OH 44118
(216) 397-4391
http://boler.jcu.edu/centers-excellence/edward-m-muldoon-center
-entrepreneurship

Johns Hopkins University: Entrepreneurship and Management Minor
3400 N Charles St
Baltimore, MD 21218
(410) 516-8000
https://entrepreneurship.jhu.edu/

Lehigh University: Minor in Entrepreneurship
27 Memorial Dr W
Bethlehem, PA 18015
(610) 758-3000
http://catalog.lehigh.edu/coursesprogramsandcurricula
/businessandeconomics/entrepreneurship/

Loyola Marymount University: Fred Kiesner Center for Entrepreneurship
1 LMU Dr
Los Angeles, CA 90045
(310) 338-2700
https://cba.lmu.edu/centers/fredkiesnercenterforentrepreneurship/

Marquette University: Kohler Center for Entrepreneurship
1225 W. Wisconsin Ave
Milwaukee, WI 53233
(800) 222-6544
http://www.marquette.edu/business/about/centers-programs-index.php/
kohler-center-for-entrepreneurship

Miami University: Farmer School of Business Entrepreneurship
2078 Farmer School of Business
800 E High St
Oxford, OH 45056
entrepreneurship@miamioh.edu
http://miamioh.edu/fsb/academics/entrepreneurship/

Michigan State University: Entrepreneurship & Innovation
426 Auditorium Rd
East Lansing, MI 48824
517-353-0644
https://entrepreneurship.msu.edu

Missouri State University: Entrepreneurship Major or Minor
901 S National Ave
Springfield, MO 65897
(417) 836-5415
managementandinformationtechnology@missouristate.edu
https://mit.missouristate.edu

North Carolina State University: Entrepreneurship
381 Initiative Way
Raleigh, NC 27695
(919) 513.3676
entrepreneurship@ncsu.edu
https://entrepreneurship.ncsu.edu/

New York University: Entrepreneurial Institute
16 Washington Pl
New York City, NY 10003
(212) 992-6070
entrepreneur@nyu.edu
http://entrepreneur.nyu.edu/

Northeastern University: Centre for Entrepreneurship Education
212 Hayden Hall
360 Huntington Ave
Boston, MA 02115
ma.meyer@northeastern.edu
https://entrepreneurship.northeastern.edu/

Northern Michigan University: Entrepreneurship Concentration
1401 Presque Isle Ave
Marquette, MI 49855
(906) 227-1000
https://www.nmu.edu/business/entrepreneurship-major-and-minor

Northwestern University: Innovation and Entrepreneurship
633 Clark St
Evanston, IL 60208
(847) 491-3741
https://www.northwestern.edu/innovation/

Notre Dame: Innovation & Entrepreneurship Concentration
Mendoza College of Business
Notre Dame, IN 46556
(574) 631-7236
Info.mendoza@nd.edu
https://mendoza.nd.edu/research-and-faculty/academic-departments
/management-organization/academics/innovation-entrepreneurship/

Ohio State University: Center for Innovation & Entrepreneurship
2100 Neil Ave
Columbus, OH 43210
(614) 688-1037
reeder.6@osu.edu
https://fisher.osu.edu/centers-partnerships/cie

Ohio University: Center for Entrepreneurship
Athens, OH 45701
(740) 593-1000
https://www.ohio.edu/entrepreneurship

Oklahoma State University: School of Entrepreneurship
Business Building
Stillwater, Oklahoma 74078
(405) 744-5064
https://business.okstate.edu/entrepreneurship/

Penn State: Corporate Innovation & Entrepreneurship
210 Business Building
University Park, PA 16802
(814) 863-0448
https://undergrad.smeal.psu.edu/majors/
corporate-innovation-and-entrepreneurship

Princeton University: Entrepreneurship Council
34 Chambers St
Princeton, NJ 08544
pecinfo@princeton.edu
https://entrepreneurs.princeton.edu/

Purdue University: Burton D. Morgan Center for Entrepreneurship
1201 West State St
West Lafayette, IN 47907
(765) 494-1314
entrcert@purdue.edu
https://www.purdue.edu/entr/

Rice University: Education Entrepreneurship Program
1900 Rice Blvd
Houston, TX 77005
(713) 348-3816
kari.a.mullen@rice.edu
https://business.rice.edu/
rice-university-education-entrepreneurship-program

Rutgers: Center for Urban Entrepreneurship & Economic Development
1 Washington Park
Newark, NJ 07102
http://www.business.rutgers.edu/cueed

Saint Louis University: Entrepreneurship Concentration
1 N Grand Blvd
St. Louis, MO 63103
(800) 758-3678
https://www.slu.edu/programs/undergraduate/entrepreneurship.php

Salem State University: Center for Entrepreneurship
352 Lafayette Street
Salem, MA 01970
admissions@salemstate.edu
https://www.salemstate.edu/academics/bertolon-school-business/centers

San Francisco State University: Innovation & Entrepreneurship Fellows Program
1600 Holloway Ave
San Francisco, CA 94132
(415) 338-1276
cob@sfsu.edu
https://cob.sfsu.edu/innovation-fellows

Savannah State University: Entrepreneurship & Creativity Concentration
3219 College St
Savannah, GA 31404
https://www.savannahstate.edu/coba/entrepreneurship.shtml

South Dakota State University: Entrepreneurial Studies Major
1175 Medary Ave
Brookings, SD 57006
(605) 688-4141
rita.voeller@sdstate.edu
https://www.sdstate.edu/economics/entrepreneurial-studies-major

Southern Methodist University: Caruth Institute for Entrepreneurship
6212 Bishop Blvd
Dallas, TX 75275
(214) 768-3689
caruth@smu.edu
https://www.smu.edu/cox/degrees-and-programs/bba/curriculum
/academics/majors/entrepreneurship

Stanford University: Center for Entrepreneurial Studies
655 Knight Way
Stanford, CA 94305
(650) 723-2146
https://www.gsb.stanford.edu/faculty-research/centers-initiatives/ces

Syracuse University: Entrepreneurship and Emerging Enterprises
721 University Ave
Syracuse, NY 13244
(315) 443-3751
https://whitman.syr.edu/programs-and-academics/academics/eee
/index.aspx

**Texas Christian University: Neeley Institute for Entrepreneurship
& Innovation**
2805 W Lowden, Suite 309
Fort Worth, TX 76109
(817) 257-6544
neeleyentrepreneurshipcenter@tcu.edu
http://www.neeley.tcu.edu/Entrepreneurship/

Temple University: Entrepreneurship and Innovation
1801 N Broad St
Philadelphia, PA 19122
robert.mcnamee@temple.edu
http://bulletin.temple.edu/undergraduate/fox-business-management
/entrepreneurship/

Thomas College: Harold Alfond Institute for Business Innovation
180 West River Rd
Waterville, ME 04901
(207) 859-1159
haibicoor@thomas.edu
https://www.thomas.edu/academics/institute/

Trinity Christian College: Entrepreneurship Concentration
6601 W College Dr
Palos Heights, IL 60463
(708) 597-3000
https://www.trnty.edu/academic-program/business/major-minors
/entrepreneurship/

Tufts University: Entrepreneurship Center
200 Boston Ave, Suite 2400
Medford, MA 02155
(617) 627-3110
jack.derby@tufts.edu
https://gordon.tufts.edu/entrepreneurship-center/

Tulane: Albert Lepage Center for Entrepreneurship & Innovation
6823 St. Charles Ave
New Orleans, LA 70118
(504) 865-5000
https://entrepreneurship.tulane.edu/

The University of Alabama: Entrepreneurial Institute
2627 10th Ave
Tuscaloosa, AL 35401
205-722-5179
aei@cba.ua.edu
https://aei.culverhouse.ua.edu/

The University of Arizona: McGuire Center for Entrepreneurship
1130 E Helen St
Tucson, AZ 85721
(520) 621-2576
entre.net@eller.arizona.edu
https://entrepreneurship.eller.arizona.edu/

The University of Arkansas: Office of Entrepreneurship & Innovation
1 University of Arkansas
Fayetteville, AR 72701
479-575-6220
https://entrepreneurship.uark.edu/

The University of Baltimore: Center for Entrepreneurship & Innovation
11 W Mt. Royal Ave
Baltimore, MD 21201
410-837-4892
http://www.ubalt.edu/merrick/centers/
center-for-entrepreneurship-and-innovation/

The University of Buffalo: Center for Entrepreneurial Leadership
77 Goodell St, Suite 201
Buffalo, NY 14203
(716) 885-5715
mgt-cel@buffalo.edu
http://mgt.buffalo.edu/entrepreneurship/center-for-entrepreneurial
-leadership-cel.html

The University of California Berkeley: Entrepreneurship Program
Haas School of Business #1930, Room F450
Berkeley, CA 94720
(510) 642-4255
entrepreneurship@haas.berkeley.edu
https://entrepreneurship.berkeley.edu/

The UC Davis: Mike and Renee Child Institute for Innovation and Entrepreneurship
One Shields Ave
Davis, CA 95616
(530) 752-7658
innovation@gsm.ucdavis.edu
https://gsm.ucdavis.edu/entrepreneurship

The University of Chicago: Polsky Center for Entrepreneurship and Innovation
5807 S. Woodlawn Ave, Suite 207
Chicago, IL 60637
(773) 834-9767
polsky@uchicago.edu
https://polsky.uchicago.edu/

The University of California San Diego: Rady School of Management Entrepreneur and Innovation Minor
9500 Gilman Dr
La Jolla, CA 92093
(858) 534-9000
https://rady.ucsd.edu/programs/undergraduate-programs
/entrepreneurship-and-innovation-minor/

The University of Colorado Boulder: Innovation & Entrepreneurship Initiative
99 UCB, Suite 1B29
Boulder, CO 80309
mailto:innovate@colorado.edu
https://www.colorado.edu/innovate/

The University of Colorado Denver: Jake Jabs Center for Entrepreneurship
1475 Lawrence St
Denver, CO 80202
(303) 315-8500
jakejabs.center@ucdenver.edu
https://jakejabscenter.org

The University of Dayton: Entrepreneurship
300 College Park
Dayton, OH 45469
937-229-1000
info@udayton.edu
https://udayton.edu/business/index.php

The University of Denver: Office of Entrepreneurship
2101 S University Blvd
Denver, CO 80208
(303) 816-3924
https://daniels.du.edu/entrepreneurship/

The University of Florida: Center for Entrepreneurship & Innovation
1384 Union Rd
Gainesville, FL 32611
(352) 273-0330
cei@warrington.ufl.edu
https://warrington.ufl.edu/entrepreneurship-and-innovation-center/

The University of Georgia: Entrepreneurship Program
3475 Lenox Rd
Atlanta, GA 30326
(404) 842-4825
http://www.terry.uga.edu/academics/entrepreneurship/

The University of Hartford: Entrepreneurial Center
& Women's Business Center
222 Pitkin St
East Hartford, CT 06108
(860) 768-5681
http://www.hartford.edu/ec/

The University of Hawaii: The Pacific Asian Center for
Entrepreneurship
2404 Maile Way
Honolulu, HI 96822
(808) 956-5083
pace@hawaii.edu
http://pace.shidler.hawaii.edu/

The University of Houston: The Wolff Center for Entrepreneurship
4742 Calhoun Rd
Houston, TX 77204
(713) 743-4752
wce@uh.edu
https://www.bauer.uh.edu/centers/wce/

The University of Iowa: John Pappajohn Entrepreneurial Center
108 Pappajohn Business Building
Iowa City, IA 52242
(319) 335-0862
tippie-business@uiowa.edu
https://tippie.uiowa.edu/about-tippie/centers-institutes/iowa
-entrepreneurship

The University of Idaho: Vandal Innovation and Enterprise Works
875 Perimeter Dr
Moscow, ID 83844
(208) 885-6111
info@uidaho.edu
https://www.uidaho.edu/cbe/hands-on-learning-opportunities
/idaho-entrepreneurs

The University of Kansas: KU Center for Entrepreneurship
1654 Naismith Dr, Room 1030E
Lawrence, KS 66045
(785) 864-7583
wmeyerjr@ku.edu
https://entr.ku.edu/

The Univeristy of Kentucky: Von Allmen Center for Entrepreneurship
107 ASTeCC
Lexington, KY 40506
(859) 218-6557
http://vace.uky.edu/

The University of Louisville: Entrepreneurship Concentration
College of Business, Harry Frazier Hall
Louisville, KY 40292
(502) 852-6440
http://business.louisville.edu/graduate-programs/entrepreneurship-mba/

The University of Maryland: Master's in Telecommunication Program
2433 A.V. Williams Building
College Park, Maryland 20742
(301) 405-3682
telecomprogram@umd.edu
http://www.telecom.umd.edu/entrepreneurship

The University of Massachusetts Boston: Entrepreneurship Center
100 Morrissey Blvd
Boston, MA 02125
(617) 652-0352
https://www.umb.edu/entrepreneurship_center

The University of Michigan—Ann Arbor: Entrepreneurship
t Michigan Ross
701 Tappan Street
Ann Arbor, MI 48109
(734) 615-5002
https://michiganross.umich.edu/programs/entrepreneurship-minor

The University of Minnesota: Entrepreneurial Management
321 19th Ave S
Minneapolis, MN 55455
(612) 625-0027
csom@umn.edu
https://carlsonschool.umn.edu/degrees/undergraduate/majors-and-minors
/entrepreneurial-management

The University of North Carolina at Chapel Hill:
Entrepreneurship Minor
107 Gardner Hall, CB# 3305
Chapel Hill, NC 27599
(919) 966-2383
patrick_conway@unc.edu
http://catalog.unc.edu/undergraduate/programs-study/entrepreneurship
-minor/

The University of Oklahoma: Price College of Business Tom Love
Center For Entrepreneurship
201 David L. Boren Blvd
Norman, OK 73019
(405) 325-7632
entrepreneurship@ou.edu
http://www.ou.edu/entrepreneurship/contact

The University of Oregon: Lundquist Center for Entrepreneurship
1208 University of Oregon
Eugene, OR 97403
(541) 346-4122
lcblce@uoregon.edu
https://business.uoregon.edu/centers/lce

The University of Pennsylvania: Penn Wharton Entrepreneurship
220 S 40th St
Philadelphia, PA 19104
(215) 898-4856
entrepreneurship@wharton.upenn.edu
https://entrepreneurship.wharton.upenn.edu/

The University of Rochester: Ain Center for Entrepreneurship
P.O. Box 270360
(585) 276-3500
aincfe@rochester.edu
https://www.rochester.edu/aincenter/

The University of South Carolina: Faber Entrepreneurship Center
1014 Greene St
Columbia, SC 29208
(803) 777-3176
kressd@moore.sc.edu
https://sc.edu/study/colleges_schools/moore/business_solutions
/research_and_partnership_centers/faber_entrepreneurship_center
/index.php

The University of South Florida: Center for Entrepreneurship
4202 E. Fowler Ave
Tampa, FL 33620
(813) 974-1550
entrepreneurship@usf.edu
https://www.usf.edu/entrepreneurship/

The University of Texas at Austin: Entrepreneurship and Innovation
110 Inner Campus Dr
Austin, TX 78705
(512) 471-3434
https://www.utexas.edu/campus-life/entrepreneurship-and-innovation

The University of Texas at Dallas: Institute for Innovation and Entrepreneurship
2830 Rutford Ave
Richardson, TX 75080
(972) 883-2705
innovation@utdallas.edu
https://innovation.utdallas.edu

The University of Utah: Entrepreneurship
1655 East Campus Center Dr
Salt Lake City, UT 84112
(801) 581-7676
MC@Eccles.Utah.edu
https://eccles.utah.edu/programs/undergraduate/academics/majors
/entrepreneurship/

The University of Virginia: Batten Institute for Entrepreneurship and Innovation
P.O. Box 6550
Charlottesville, VA 22906
(434) 924-1335
batten@darden.virginia.edu
https://www.darden.virginia.edu/batten-institute/

The University of Washington: Arthur W. Buerk Center for Entrepreneurship
227 Dempsey Hall, Box 353223
Seattle, WA 98195
(206) 616-0734
uwbuerk@uw.edu
https://foster.uw.edu/centers/buerk-ctr-entrepreneurship/

The University of Wisconsin Madison: Weinert Center for Entrepreneurship
975 University Avenue
Madison, WI 53706
(608) 263-2882
weinertcenter@bus.wisc.edu
https://bus.wisc.edu/centers/weinert

The Utah State: The Center for Entrepreneurship
3500 Old Main Hill
Logan, UT 84322
(435) 797-1107
andy.thunell@usu.edu
https://huntsman.usu.edu/ecenter/index

Vanderbilt University: The Wond'ry
2414 Highland Ave, Suite 102
Nashville, TN 37212
(615) 343-1501
thewondry@vanderbilt.edu
https://www.vanderbilt.edu/thewondry/

Villanova University: Innovation, Creativity, and Entrepreneurship Institute
800 Lancaster Ave
Villanova, PA 19085
ice@villanova.edu
http://www.villanovaice.com/

Washington University of St. Louis: Skandalaris Center for Interdisciplinary Innovation and Entrepreneurship
6465 Forsyth Blvd
St. Louis, MO 63105
(314) 935-9134
sc@wustl.edu
https://skandalaris.wustl.edu/

Wake Forest University: Center for Entrepreneurship
1834 Wake Forest Rd, Suite 230
Winston-Salem, NC 27106
(336) 758-3153
barretsf@wfu.edu
http://entrepreneurship.wfu.edu

Western Michigan University: Entrepreneurship Major
1930 W Michigan Ave
Kalamazoo, MI 49008
(269) 387-5860
https://wmich.edu/entrepreneurship

Wichita State University: Center for Entrepreneurship
1845 Fairmount St
Wichita, Kansas 67260
(316) 978-3456
cfe@wichita.edu
https://www.wichita.edu/academics/business/entrepreneurship/

William & Mary: Alan B. Miller Entrepreneurship Center
101 Ukrop Way
Williamsburg, VA 23186
(757) 221-2949
millerec@wm.edu
https://millercenter.mason.wm.edu/

Xavier University: Entrepreneurial Studies
3800 Victory Pkwy
Cincinnati, OH 45207
(513) 745-3000
https://www.xavier.edu/entrepreneurial-studies/

Yale University: Program on Entrepreneurship
165 Whitney Ave
New Haven, CT 06511
https://som.yale.edu/faculty-research-centers/centers-initiatives/program
-on-entrepreneurship

Endnotes

Introduction

1 *Merriam-Webster Online Dictionary.* "Entrepreneur." Merriam-Webster, Incorporated. 2015. https://www.merriam-webster.com/dictionary/entrepreneur.

2 Kauffman Foundation (website). "Kauffman Foundation: Entrepreneurship is on the Rise but Long-Term Startup Decline Leaves Millions of Americans Behind." kauffman.org, Newsroom. February 6, 2017. https://www.kauffman.org/newsroom/2017/2/entrepreneurship-is-on-the-rise-but-long-term-startup-decline-leaves-millions-of-americans-behind.

3 United States Census Bureau. "Business Dynamics Statistics (BDS)." 2016. https://www.census.gov/ces/dataproducts/bds/.

4 Kauffman Foundation (website). "Kauffman Foundation: Entrepreneurship is on the Rise but Long-Term Startup Decline Leaves Millions of Americans Behind." kauffman.org, Newsroom. February 6, 2017. https://www.kauffman.org/newsroom/2017/2/entrepreneurship-is-on-the-rise-but-long-term-startup-decline-leaves-millions-of-americans-behind.

5 Robehmed, Natalie. "What Is a Startup?" *Forbes* (website). December 16, 2013. https://www.forbes.com/sites/natalierobehmed/2013/12/16/what-is-a-startup/#70766e840440.

6 Kauffman Foundation (website). "The Importance of Startups in Job Creation and Job Destruction." kauffman.org, Firm Formation and Growth Series. September 9, 2010. https://www.kauffman.org/what-we-do/research/firm-formation-and-growth-series/the-importance-of-startups-in-job-creation-and-job-destruction.

Part I

1 Porter, Eduardo. "Where Are the Start-ups? Loss of Dynamism Is Impeding Growth." *New York Times* (website), Economic Scene. February 6, 2018. https://www.nytimes.com/2018/02/06/business/economy/start-ups-growth.html.

Chapter 1

1 Kilcullen, Timothy, and Salim Furth, Ph.D. "Starting a New Business Shouldn't Be This Hard." The Heritage Foundation (website), Commentary. October 16, 2017. https://www.heritage.org/jobs-and-labor/commentary/starting-new-business -shouldnt-be-hard.

2 Eaton-Cardone Monica. "VC Funding Favors Men Despite Proven Potential of Female Founders." *PRWeb*, News Center. May 29, 2018. http://www.prweb.com/ releases/2018/05/prweb15518158.htm.

3 Saxena, Anoop. "The Rise of Women Entrepreneurship." *Entrepreneur India*, an international franchise of Entrepreneur Media (website). March 2, 2016. https:// www.entrepreneur.com/article/271784.

4 McManus, Michael. "Minority Business Ownership: Data from the 2012 Survey of Business Owners." U.S. Small Business Administration Office of Advocacy, Issue Brief. September 14, 2016. https://www.sba.gov/sites/default/files/advo- cacy/Minority-Owned-Businesses-in-the-US.pdf.

5 Palia, Darius. "Differential Access to Capital from Financial Institutions by Minority Entrepreneurs." *Journal of Empirical Legal Studies*, Volume 13, Issue 4 (December 2016): 756–785. http://andromeda.rutgers.edu/~dpalia/papers/ JELS_2016.pdf.

6 https://www.mbda.gov/page/executive-summary-disparities-capital-access-be- tween-minority-and-non-minority-businesses.

7 Kauffman Foundation (website). "2017 State of Entrepreneurship Address." kauffman.org, Resources. February 17, 2017. https://www.kauffman.org/ what-we-do/resources/state-of-entrepreneurship-addresses/2017-state-of -entrepreneurship-address.

8 Kauffman Foundation (website). "Kauffman Foundation: Entrepreneurship is on the Rise but Long-Term Startup Decline Leaves Millions of Americans Behind." kauffman.org, Newsroom. February 6, 2017. https://www.kauffman.org/ newsroom/2017/2/ entrepreneurship-is-on-the-rise-but-long-term-startup-de- cline-leaves-millions-of-americans-behind.

9 Koetsier, John. "There Are Now 229 Unicorn Startups, with $175B in Funding and $1.3T Valuation." *Venture Beat* (website). January 18, 2016. https:// venturebeat.com/2016/01/18/there-are-now-229-unicorn-startups-with -175b-in-funding-and-1-3b-valuation/.

10 Kauffman Foundation (website). "The Importance of Startups in Job Creation and Job Destruction." kauffman.org, Firm Formation and Growth Series. Septem- ber 9, 2010. https://www.kauffman.org/what-we-do/research/firm-formation -and-growth-series/the-importance-of-startups-in-job-creation-and-job -destruction.

11 McCain, John. "John McCain: It's Time Congress Returns to Regular Order." *Washington Post* (website), Opinions. August 31, 2017. https://www.washing- tonpost.com/opinions/john-mccain-its-time-congress-returns-to-regular-order

/2017/08/31/f62a3e0c-8cfb-11e7-8df5-c2e5cf46c1e2_story.html?utm_term=. b1b7467ac5e4.

12 Casselman, Ben. "A Start-Up Slump Is a Drag on the Economy. Big Business May Be to Blame." *New York Times* (website). September 20, 2017. https://www. nytimes.com/2017/09/20/business/economy/startup-business.html.

13 Guidant Financial (website). "Current Small Business Trends and Statistics: Business Confidence Remains High During Political Turbulence." guidantfinan-cial.com, Small Business Trends. Accessed December 31, 2018. https://www. guidantfinancial.com/small-business-trends/.

14 Guidant Financial (website). "Current Small Business Trends and Statistics: Business Confidence Remains High During Political Turbulence." guidantfinan-cial.com, Small Business Trends. Accessed December 31, 2018. https://www. guidantfinancial.com/small-business-trends/.

15 Thompson, Derek. "The Myth of the Millennial Entrepreneur." *The Atlantic* (website), Business. July 6, 2016. https://www.theatlantic.com/business/ archive/2016/07/the-myth-of-the-millennial-entrepreneur/490058/.

16 Yang, Andrew. "The Surprising Truth About Young Entrepreneurs – They're Fewer Than Ever." *Techonomy* (website). September 1, 2015. https://techonomy. com/2015/09/the-surprising-truth-about-young-entrepreneurs-theyre-fewer-than-ever.

17 Hobbes, Michael. "FML: Why Millennials Are Facing the Scariest Financial Future of Any Generation Since the Great Depression." *Huffington Post* (website), Highline. Accessed December 31, 2018. https://highline.huffingtonpost.com/ articles/en/poor-millennials-print/.

18 Ambrose, Brent W., Larry Cordell, and Shuwei Ma. "The Impact of Student Loan Debt on Small Business Formation." Social Science Research Network (website). Last modified July 21, 2015. https://papers.ssrn.com/sol3/papers. cfm?abstract_id=2417676.

19 Lettieri, John. "America Without Entrepreneurs: The Consequences of Dwin-dling Startup Activity." Testimony before Committee on Small Business and Entrepreneurship, U.S. Senate, June 29, 2016. https://www.sbc.senate.gov/ public/_cache/files/0/d/0d8d1a51-ee1d-4f83-b740-515e46e861dc/7F-75741C1A2E6182E1A5D21B61D278F3.lettieri-testimony.pdf.

20 Azoulay, Pierre, Benjamin Jones, J. Daniel Kim, and Javier Miranda. "Age and High-Growth Entrepreneurship." National Bureau of Economic Research (website). April 2018. http://www.nber.org/papers/w24489.

21 Kauffman Foundation (website). "Kauffman Foundation: Entrepreneurship is on the Rise but Long-Term Startup Decline Leaves Millions of Americans Behind." kauffman.org, Newsroom. February 16, 2017. https://www.kauffman.org/ newsroom/2017/2/entrepreneurship-is-on-the-rise-but-long-term-startup-de-cline-leaves-millions-of-americans-behind.

22 U.S. Geological Survey (website). "How Many Counties Are There in the United States?" usgs.gov, Mapping, Remote Sensing, and Geospatial Data. Accessed December 31, 2018. https://www.usgs.gov/faqs/how-many-counties-are-there -united-states.

23 Kauffman Foundation (website). "2017 State of Entrepreneurship Address." kauff-man.org, Resources. February 17, 2017. https://www.kauffman.org/what-we-do/ resources/state-of-entrepreneurship-addresses/2017-state-of-entrepreneurship -address.

24 Michigan Live Media (website). "George A. Wild Jr." *Ann Arbor News*. August 2, 2015. http://obits.mlive.com/obituaries/annarbor/obituary.aspx?n=george -a-wild&pid=175403398&fhid=5988.

25 Thompson, Derek. "The Myth of the Millennial Entrepreneur." *The Atlantic* (website), Business. July 6, 2016. https://www.theatlantic.com/business/archive /2016/07/the-myth-of-the-millennial-entrepreneur/490058/.

Chapter 2

1 Solomon, Dan. "The First Self-Driving Car Service in America Is Launching in Frisco." *Texas Monthly* (website), The Culture. May 8, 2018. https://www.texas-monthly.com/the-culture/self-driving-car-frisco-launch/.

2 Chui, Michael, James Manyika, and Mehdi Miremadi. "Where Machines Could Replace Humans—and Where They Can't (Yet)." *McKinsey Quarterly* (website). July 2016. https://www.mckinsey.com/business-functions/digital-mckinsey/ our-insights/where-machines-could-replace-humans-and-where-they-cant-yet.

3 Paquette, Danielle. "Robots Could Replace Nearly a Third of the U.S. Workforce by 2030." *Washington Post* (website), Wonkblog. November 30, 2017. https:// www.washingtonpost.com/news/wonk/wp/2017/11/30/robots-could-soon-replace-nearly-a-third-of-the-u-s-workforce/?utm_term=.cc34603187ff.

4 Manyika, James, Susan Lund, Michael Chui, Jacques Bughin, Jonathan Woetzel, Parul Batra, Ryan Ko, and Saurabh Sanghvi. "Jobs Lost, Jobs Gained: What the Future of Work Will Mean for Jobs, Skills, and Wages." McKinsey Global Insti-tute, Report. November 2017. https://www.mckinsey.com/featured-insights/ future-of-organizations-and-work/Jobs-lost-jobs-gained-what-the-future-of-work-will-mean-for-jobs-skills-and-wages.

5 Leopold, Till Alexander, Vesselina Ratcheva, and Saadia Zahidi. "Chapter 1: The Future of Jobs and Skills." World Economic Forum (website), Reports. Accessed December 31, 2018. http://reports.weforum.org/future-of-jobs-2016/ chapter-1-the-future-of-jobs-and-skills/.

6 AllTrucking.com. "Truck Drivers in the USA." Accessed December 31, 2018. http://www.alltrucking.com/faq/truck-drivers-in-the-usa/.

7 1millioncups.com. "About 1 Million Cups." Accessed December 31, 2018. https:// www.1millioncups.com/about.

8   Kauffman Foundation. "Kauffman Fasttrac." fasttrac.org. Accessed December 31, 2018. https://fasttrac.org/.

9   North, Aaron. "A Playbook for Building Entrepreneurial Ecosystems." kauffman. org, Currents. October 24, 2017. https://www.kauffman.org/currents/2017/10/a-playbook-for-building-entrepreneurial-ecosystems.

Chapter 3

1   Ward, Jason. "How Microsoft's Technological and Social Impacts Have Changed the World." Windows Central (website). September 8, 2017. https://www.windowscentral.com/microsoft-has-had-profound-technological-and-social-global-impact.

2   Small Business Administration Office of Advocacy (website). "Frequently Asked Questions." sba.gov. March 2014. https://www.sba.gov/sites/default/files/FAQ_March_2014_0.pdf.

3   Small Business & Entrepreneurship Council (website). "Facts & Data on Small Business and Entrepreneurship." sbecouncil.org. Accessed December 31, 2018. http://sbecouncil.org/about-us/facts-and-data/.

4   Small Business & Entrepreneurship Council (website). "Facts & Data on Small Business and Entrepreneurship." sbecouncil.org. Accessed December 31, 2018. http://sbecouncil.org/about-us/facts-and-data/.

5   Small Business & Entrepreneurship Council (website). "Facts & Data on Small Business and Entrepreneurship." sbecouncil.org. Accessed December 31, 2018. http://sbecouncil.org/about-us/facts-and-data/.

6   U.S. Department of Labor, Bureau of Labor Statistics (website). "Employment Projections—2016-26." bls.gov, News Release. October 24, 2017. https://www.bls.gov/news.release/archives/ecopro_10242017.pdf.

7   Wiens, Jason, and Chris Jackson. "The Importance of Young Firms for Economic Growth." kauffman.org, Entrepreneurship Policy Digest. September 13, 2015. https://www.kauffman.org/what-we-do/resources/entrepreneurship-policy-digest/the-importance-of-young-firms-for-economic-growth.

8   Casselman, Ben. "A Start-Up Slump Is a Drag on the Economy. Big Business May Be to Blame." *New York Times* (website). September 20, 2017. https://www.nytimes.com/2017/09/20/business/economy/startup-business.html.

9   Institute for Local Self-Reliance (website). "Locally Owned vs. Chain: The Local Premium." ilsr.org. July 21, 2006. https://ilsr.org/locally-owned-vs-chain-local-premium/.

10 Rivera, Roberto. "Post-traumatic Growth is When People Grow from the Pain, and End Up Empowered." *Love Wisconsin* (website), Stories. Accessed January 1, 2019. http://www.lovewi.com/roberto.

11 Dallas County Community College District (website). "Lets Get Started." dcccd. edu. Accessed January 3, 2019. https://www.dcccd.edu/pages/default.aspx?utm_source=local&utm_medium=organic&utm_campaign=gmb&utm_content=do.

12 Zipkin, Nina. "The Tax Break That Small Businesses Need to Know About (Info-graphic)." *Entrepreneur* (website), Startup Basics. October 14, 2016. https://www.entrepreneur.com/article/270128.

13 Taulli, Tom. "What Entrepreneurs Need to Know About Deductions." *Forbes* (website). February 16, 2016. https://www.forbes.com/sites/tomtaulli/2016/02/16/what-entrepreneurs-need-to-know-about-deductions/#3cb3bd7463c5.

14 Mitchell, Nina. "Smart Financial Strategies for Women Entrepreneurs." wtop.com, Business & Finance. September 20, 2017. https://wtop.com/business-finance/2017/09/smart-financial-strategies-women-entrepreneurs/.

15 AARP The Magazine. "Daniel Lubetzky and His 'Must-Do Attitude.'" aarp.org, Events & History. August/September 2018. https://www.aarp.org/politics-society/history/info-2018/daniel-lubetzky-hispanic-heritage-month.html.

16 Center for American Entrepreneurship (website). "Center for American Entrepreneurship Releases New Study on the Immigrant Founders of Companies in the 2017 Fortune 500." startupusa.org, News. December 3, 2017. http://www.startupsusa.org/press-releases/center-american-entrepreneurship-releases-new-study-immigrant-founders-companies-2017-fortune-500/.

17 Webpage for United States Senator for Kansas Jerry Moran. "Sens. Moran, Warner Introduce Bipartisan Startup Act." moran.senate.gov, News Releases. September 28, 2017. https://www.moran.senate.gov/public/index.cfm/news-releases?id=2A5982C7-CD7D-4102-95C1-9AB60DB5991B.

18 Center for American Entrepreneurship (website). "Center for American Entrepreneurship Releases New Study on the Immigrant Founders of Companies in the 2017 Fortune 500." startupusa.org, News. December 3, 2017. http://www.startupsusa.org/press-releases/center-american-entrepreneurship-releases-new-study-immigrant-founders-companies-2017-fortune-500/.

19 Center for American Entrepreneurship (website). "Center for American Entrepreneurship Releases New Study on the Immigrant Founders of Companies in the 2017 Fortune 500." startupusa.org, News. December 3, 2017. http://www.startupsusa.org/press-releases/center-american-entrepreneurship-releases-new-study-immigrant-founders-companies-2017-fortune-500/.

Chapter 5

1 Kelliher, Fiona. "How NIMBY Lawsuit Sank This Redwood City Development." *San Francisco Business Times* (website), Residential Real Estate. August 13, 2018. https://www.bizjournals.com/sanfrancisco/news/2018/08/13/nimby-redwood-city-sobrato-pauls-housing-crisis.html.

2 Kelliher, Fiona. "How NIMBY Lawsuit Sank This Redwood City Development." *San Francisco Business Times* (website), Residential Real Estate. August 13, 2018. https://www.bizjournals.com/sanfrancisco/news/2018/08/13/nimby-redwood-city-sobrato-pauls-housing-crisis.html.

3 Albright, Matthew. "Neighborhood's Italian Food Fight Highlights Delaware's NIMBY Pandemic." *Delaware News Journal* (website). July 20, 2018. https://www.delawareonline.com/story/opinion/columnists/matthew-albright/2018/07/20/neighborhoods-italian-food-fight-shows-delawares-nimby-pandemic/804150002/.

4 Jedra, Christina. "War Escalates between Wilmington Neighbors, Italian Restaurant." *Delaware News Journal* (website). July 19, 2018. https://www.delawareonline.com/story/news/local/2018/07/19/war-escalates-between-wilmington-neighbors-italian-restaurant/769578002/.

5 Albright, Matthew. "Neighborhood's Italian Food Fight Highlights Delaware's NIMBY Pandemic." *Delaware News Journal* (website). July 20, 2018. https://www.delawareonline.com/story/opinion/columnists/matthew-albright/2018/07/20/neighborhoods-italian-food-fight-shows-delawares-nimby-pandemic/804150002/.

Chapter 6

1 Amadeo, Kimberly. "Deregulation Pros, Cons, and Examples." *The Balance* (website), Hot Topics. Last modified February 22, 2018. https://www.thebalance.com/deregulation-definition-pros-cons-examples-3305921.

2 Center for American Entrepreneurship (website). "Regulation." startupusa.org. Accessed January 2, 2019. http://www.startupsusa.org/regulation/.

3 Center for American Entrepreneurship (website). "Regulation." startupusa.org. Accessed January 2, 2019. http://www.startupsusa.org/regulation/.

4 Wilonsky, Robert. "Thirty Years after Sasaki Plan created Dallas Arts District, a Call for a New Vision—and Fast." *Dallas Morning News* (website). June 2015. https://www.dallasnews.com/news/dallas-city-hall/2015/06/19/thirty-years-after-sasaki-plan-created-dallas-arts-district-a-call-for-a-new-vision-and-fast.

5 The Dallas Arts District: Connect. "The Dallas Arts District Master Plan." dallascityhall.com. June 7, 2017. http://dallascityhall.com/departments/pnv/Documents/170608_DRAFT_DAD%20Master%20Plan_v7.pdf.

6 Sarbanes-Oxley Act 2002. "A Guide to the Sarbanes-Oxley Act." soxlaw.com. 2006. http://www.soxlaw.com/.

7 Kenton, Will. "Dodd-Frank Wall Street Reform and Consumer Protection Act." *Investopedia* (website), Law Regulations. Last modified May 23, 2018. https://www.investopedia.com/terms/d/dodd-frank-financial-regulatory-reform-bill.asp.

8 Incfile.com. "Why Form a Limited Liability Company (LLC) in New York?" Accessed January 2, 2019. https://www.incfile.com/new-york-llc/.

9 World Bank Group (website). "Ease of Doing Business in United States." doingbusiness.org, Data. Accessed January 2, 2018. http://www.doingbusiness.org/data/exploreeconomies/united-states.

10 Ficklin, Patrice. "African-American and Hispanic Borrowers Harmed by Provi-
    dent Will Receive $9 Million in Compensation." Consumer Financial Protection
    Bureau (website), Blog. November 2, 2017. https://www.consumerfinance.
    gov/about-us/blog/african-american-and-hispanic-borrowers-harmed-provi-
    dent-will-receive-9-million-compensation/.
11 Consumer Financial Protection Bureau (website). "Bureau of Consumer Financial
    Protection Settles with TCF National Bank." consumerfinance.gov, Newsroom.
    July 20, 2018. https://www.consumerfinance.gov/about-us/newsroom/bureau
    -consumer-financial-protection-settles-tcf-national-bank/.
12 McCord, Roisin, Edward Simpson Prescott, and Tim Sabilik. "Explaining the
    Decline in the Number of Banks Since the Great Recession." richmondfed.org,
    Economic Brief. March 2015. https://www.richmondfed.org/~/media/richmond
    fedorg/publications/research/economic_brief/2015/pdf/eb_15-03.pdf.
13 Kenton, Will. "Small Business Investment Company (SBIC)." *Investopedia*
    (website), Entrepreneurship. Last modified December 13, 2017. https://www.
    investopedia.com/terms/s/smallbusinessinvestmentcompanysbic.asp.
14 Washington Post Staff. "What Trump Proposed Cutting in His 2019 Budget."
    The Washington Post (website), Politics. Last modified February 16, 2018.
    https://www.washingtonpost.com/graphics/2018/politics/trump-budget-2019
    /?utm_term=.1f613ed1665a.
15 Washington Post Staff. "What Trump Proposed Cutting in His 2019 Budget."
    The Washington Post (website), Politics. Last modified February 16, 2018.
    https://www.washingtonpost.com/graphics/2018/politics/trump-budget-2019
    /?utm_term=.1f613ed1665a.
16 Securities and Exchange Commission (website). "Crowdfunding." sec.gov.
    Accessed January 2, 2019. https://www.sec.gov/rules/final/2015/33-9974.pdf.

Chapter 7

1 Demers, Jayson. "Small Business Growth Has Stalled and That's Bad for All of
   Us." *Time* (website), Ideas. March 23, 2017. http://time.com/4709959/small
   -business-growth/.
2 Canal, Emily. "Why Amazon, Facebook, and Google May Have Caused a Startup
   Slump." *Inc.* (website), Wire. September 21, 2017. https://www.inc.com/
   emily-canal/why-big-businesses-are-to-blame-for-the-startup-slump.html.
3 Griffith, Erin. "Will Facebook Kill All Future Facebooks?" *Wired* (website), Business. October 25, 2017. https://www.wired.com/story/facebooks-aggressive
   -moves-on-startups-threaten-innovation/.
4 Schechter, Asher. "The White House Acknowledges: The U.S. Has a Concentration
   Problem; President Obama Launches New Pro-Competition Initiative." promar-
   ket.org. April 15, 2016. https://promarket.org/the-white-house-acknowledges
   -the-u-s-has-a-concentration-problem-president-obama-launches-new-pro-com-
   petition-initiative/.

5 Nareit (website). "Reit Industry Financial Snapshot." reit.com, Market Data. Last modified December 31, 2018. https://www.reit.com/data-research/reit-market-data/reit-industry-financial-snapshot.

6 Emert, Carol. "Legendary California Wine Company is Sold/Conglomerate Buys Mondavi for $1 Billion—Deal Will Keep Brands Under One Roof." sfgate.com. November 4, 2004. https://www.sfgate.com/bayarea/article/Legendary-California-wine-company-is-sold-2637611.php.

7 Federal Reserve Economic Data. "Commercial Banks in the U.S." fredstlouisfed.org. Last modified December 13, 2018. https://fred.stlouisfed.org/series/USNUM.

8 Amadeo, Kimberly. "Savings and Loans, Their History and Operations." *The Balance* (website), Real Estate. Last modified December 31, 2018. https://www.thebalance.com/what-are-savings-and-loans-history-and-today-3305959.

9 Federal Reserve Economic Data (website). "Commercial Banks in the U.S." fredstlouisfed.org. Last modified December 13, 2018. https://fred.stlouisfed.org/series/USNUM.

10 YCharts (website). "JPMorgan Chase & Co Total Assets (Quarterly): 2.615T for Sept. 30, 2018." ycharts.com. Accessed January 2, 2019. https://ycharts.com/companies/JPM/assets.

11 YCharts (website). "Wells Fargo & Co Total Assets (Quarterly): 1.873T for Sept. 30, 2018." ycharts.com. Accessed January 2, 2019. https://ycharts.com/companies/WFC/assets.

12 YCharts (website). "Citigroup Inc Total Assets (Quarterly): 1.925T for Sept. 30, 2018." ycharts.com. Accessed January 2, 2019. https://ycharts.com/companies/C/assets.

Chapter 8

1 World Bank Group (website). "Ease of Doing Business in United States." doingbusiness.org, Data. Accessed January 2, 2019. http://www.doingbusiness.org/data/exploreeconomies/united-states.

2 Prindle, David F. *The Paradox of Democratic Capitalism: Politics and Economics in American Thought*, 30-36. Maryland: JHU Press, 2006. https://books.google.com/books?id=3Lkc4bfhV9UC&pg=PA30&lpg=PA30&dq=%E2%80%9Cprudent+aids+and+encouragements+on+the+part+of+government.%E2%80%9D&source=bl&ots=kT_JVt1dIe&sig=s7zD0D5g8907m0fXe8QkGWW-JHCQ&hl=en&sa=X&ved=2ahUKEwjJxrqA3MzcAhUJLXwKHS9-Aw0Q6A-EwAnoECAgQAQ#v=onepage&q=%E2%80%9Cprudent%20aids%20and%20encouragements%20on%20the%20part%20of%20government.%E2%80%9D&f=false.

3 Burton, David. "Building an Opportunity Economy: The State of Small Business and Entrepreneurship." The Heritage Foundation (website), Markets

and Finance. March 13, 2015. https://www.heritage.org/testimony/ building-opportunity-economy-the-state-small-business-and-entrepreneurship.

4 https://apolitical.co/solution_article/government-venture-capitaAl-fund -boosted-israels-start-economy/.

5 https://apolitical.co/solution_article/government-venture-capitaAl-fund -boosted-israels-start-economy/.

6 Olson, Parmy, and Alex Wood. "France's Big Pivot." *Forbes* (website), Feature. May 1, 2018. https://www.forbes.com/feature/france-macron-station-f-entrepreneurship /#fa419d573a4f.

7 Olson, Parmy, and Alex Wood. "France's Big Pivot." *Forbes* (website), Feature. May 1, 2018. https://www.forbes.com/feature/france-macron-station-f-entrepreneurship /#fa419d573a4f.

8 HM Revenue & Customs. "Enterprise Investment Scheme and Seed Enterprise Investment Scheme." gov.uk, Assets Publishing Service. April 27, 2017. https://assets.publishing.service.gov.uk/government/uploads/system /uploads/attachment_data/file/611524/April_2017_Commentary_EIS_SEIS _Official_Statistics_v5.pdf.

9 Lillington, Karlin. "Big Benefits for All from UK's Seed Enterprise Investment Scheme." *The Irish Times* (website), Business, Technology. July 16, 2015. https://www.irishtimes.com/business/technology/big-benefits-for-all-from-uk -s-seed-enterprise-investment-scheme-1.2286245.

10 Sheppard, Emma. "Investment is Down for Businesses Through Government Relief Schemes." *The Guardian* (website), Small Business Network. April 28, 2017. https:// www.theguardian.com/small-business-network/2017/apr/28/investment -down-businesses-government-relief-schemes-seis-eis-crowdcube.

11 Bright Horizons Family Solutions. "What is 30 Hours Funded Childcare?" brighthorizons.co.uk. Accessed January 2, 2019. https://www.brighthorizons. co.uk/30-hours/30-hours-childcare.html.

12 Holtzman, Yair. "U.S. Research and Development Tax Credit." cpajournal.com. October 30, 2017. https://www.cpajournal.com/2017/10/30/u-s-research -development-tax-credit/.

13 Center for American Entrepreneurship (website). "Taxes." startupusa.org. Accessed January 2, 2019. http://www.startupsusa.org/taxes/.

14 Barr, Michael S. Minority and Women Entrepreneurs: Building Capital, Networks, and Skills. The Hamilton Project (website), Policy Proposal. March 9, 2015; p. 3. http://www.hamiltonproject.org/papers/minority_and_women _entrepreneurs_building_capital_networks_and_skills.

15 Barr, Michael S. Minority and Women Entrepreneurs: Building Capital, Networks, and Skills. The Hamilton Project (website), Policy Proposal. March 9, 2015; p. 3. http://www.hamiltonproject.org/papers/minority_and_women _entrepreneurs_building_capital_networks_and_skills.

16 Opportunity Finance Network (website). "What is a CDFI?" ofn.org. Accessed January 2, 2019. https://ofn.org/what-cdfi.

17 Kauffman Foundation (website). "Kauffman Foundation: Entrepreneurship is on the Rise but Long-Term Startup Decline Leaves Millions of Americans Behind." kauffman.org, Newsroom. February 16, 2017. https://www.kauffman.org/newsroom/2017/2/entrepreneurship-is-on-the-rise-but-long-term-startup-decline-leaves-millions-of-americans-behind.

18 Scott, Elfy. "Why is the U.S. the Only Developed Country Without Paid Maternity Leave?" *Buzzworthy* (website). July 18, 2017. https://www.buzzworthy.com/why-is-the-us-so-behind-regarding-maternity-leave-policy/.

19 Woetzel, Jonathan, Anu Madgavkar, Kweilin Ellingrud, Eric Labaye, Sandrine Devillard, Eric Kutcher, James Manyika, Richard Dobbs, and Mekela Krishnan. "How Advancing Women's Equality Can Add $12 Trillion to Global Growth." Mckinsey Global Institute (website), Report. September 2015. https://www.mckinsey.com/featured-insights/employment-and-growth/how-advancing-womens-equality-can-add-12-trillion-to-global-growth.

20 Brown, Emma. "A Nobel Prize Winner Says Preschool Programs Should Start at Birth." *The Washington Post* (website), Education. December 12, 2016. https://www.washingtonpost.com/local/education/a-nobel-prize-winner-says-public-preschool-programs-should-start-at-birth/2016/12/11/2576a1ee-be91-11e6-94ac-3d324840106c_story.html?noredirect=on&utm_term=.a880bb445aea.

21 Fine, Camden R. "No, There Aren't Too Many Banks in the U.S." *American Banker* (website), Opinion. October 25, 2017. https://www.americanbanker.com/opinion/no-there-arent-too-many-banks-in-the-us.

22 Lux, Marshall, and Robert Greene. "The State and Fate of Community Banking." Harvard Kennedy School (website), Mossavar-Rahmani Center for Business and Government. 2015. https://www.hks.harvard.edu/centers/mrcbg/publications/awp/awp37.

23 Shane, Scott. "How the Decline in Community Banks Hurts Small Business." *Entrepreneur* (website). April 2, 2015. https://www.entrepreneur.com/article/244573.

24 Lux, Marshall and Robert Greene. "The State and Fate of Community Banking." Harvard Kennedy School (website), Mossavar-Rahmani Center for Business and Government. 2015. https://www.hks.harvard.edu/centers/mrcbg/publications/awp/awp37.

25 Center for American Entrepreneurship (website). "Capital." startupusa.org. Accessed January 2, 2019. http://www.startupsusa.org/capital/.

26 America's SBDC. "Half of Millennials Plan to Start a Business in the Next 3 Years." prnewswire.com, News Releases. May 31, 2017. https://www.prnewswire.com/news-releases/half-of-millennials-plan-to-start-a-business-in-the-next-3-years-300465835.html.

27 Emmons, William R., Ana H. Kent, and Lowell R. Ricketts. "The Demograph-
    ics of Wealth: How Education, Race and Birth Year Shape Financial Outcomes.
    Federal Reserve Bank of St. Louis (website), Center for Household Financial
    Stability. 2018. https://www.stlouisfed.org/~/media/Files/PDFs/HFS/essays/
    HFS_essay_2_2018.pdf?la=en.
28 Stengel, Geri. "5 More Assists That Will Help Women Entrepreneurs Score
    in 2017." *Forbes* (website). January 5, 2017. https://www.forbes.com/sites/
    geristengel/2017/01/05/5-more-assists-that-will-help-women-entrepreneurs-
    score-in-2017/#777e067050fa.
29 Abramitzky, Ran, and Leah Boustan. "Immigration in American Economic
    History." National Center for Biotechnology Information (website), HHS
    Public Access. February 1, 2018. https://www.ncbi.nlm.nih.gov/pmc/articles/
    PMC5794227/.
30 Center for American Entrepreneurship (website). "Talent." startupusa.org.
    Accessed January 2, 2019. http://www.startupsusa.org/talent/.
31 Center for American Entrepreneurship (website). "Capital." startupusa.org.
    Accessed January 2, 2019. http://www.startupsusa.org/capital/.
32 Babson College (website). "Stimulating Small Business Growth: Progress
    Report on Goldman Sachs 10,000 Small Businesses." goldmansachs.com/10ksb.
    Accessed January 3, 2019. http://www.babson.edu/media/babson/site-assets/
    content-assets/executives-amp-organizations/expanding-entrepreneurship/
    goldman-sachs-10000-small-business-program/10ksb-impact-report-2018.pdf.
33 Babson College (website). "Stimulating Small Business Growth: Progress
    Report on Goldman Sachs 10,000 Small Businesses." goldmansachs.com/10ksb.
    Accessed January 3, 2019. http://www.babson.edu/media/babson/site-assets/
    content-assets/executives-amp-organizations/expanding-entrepreneurship/
    goldman-sachs-10000-small-business-program/10ksb-impact-report-2018.pdf.
34 Webpage of U.S. Congressman John K. Delaney. "Delaney, MacArthur Form
    Entrepreneurship Caucus." delaney.house.gov, Press Releases. February 28,
    2018. https://delaney.house.gov/news/press-releases/delaney-macarthur-form
    -entrepreneurship-caucus.
35 Webpage of U.S. Congressman John K. Delaney. "Delaney, MacArthur Form
    Entrepreneurship Caucus." delaney.house.gov, Press Releases. February 28,
    2018. https://delaney.house.gov/news/press-releases/delaney-macarthur-form
    -entrepreneurship-caucus.
36 Webpage of Oregon Secretary of State Dennis Richardson. "Business." sos.oregon.
    gov. Accessed January 3, 2019. https://sos.oregon.gov/business/Pages/default.
    aspx.
37 Oregon.gov. "Startup Toolkit." Business Xpress page. Accessed January 3, 2019.
    https://www.oregon.gov/business/Pages/toolkit.aspx.

Chapter 9

1 U.S. Geological Survey (website). "How Many Counties Are There in the United States?" usgs.gov, Mapping, Remote Sensing, and Geospatial Data. Accessed December 31, 2018. https://www.usgs.gov/faqs/how-many-counties -are-there-united-states.

2 Young Presidents' Organization (website). "Membership Criteria." ypo.org. Accessed January 3, 2019. https://www.ypo.org/why-join-ypo/membership -criteria/.

3 Livengood, Chad. "Challenges Remain for Detroit 4 Years After Declaring Bankruptcy." *Crain's Detroit Business* (website). July 18, 2017. http://www.crainsdetroit. com/article/20170718/blog026/634131/challenges-remain-for-detroit -4-years-after-declaring-bankruptcy.

4 Niche.com. "Frisco Independent School District." K-12 Schools Dallas-Fort Worth Area. Accessed January 3, 2019. https://www.niche.com/k12/d/frisco -independent-school-district-tx/.

5 Masunaga, Samantha. "Jamba Juice Moving to Texas from Bay Area." *Los Angeles Times* (website). May 6, 2016. http://www.latimes.com/business/la-fi-jamba- juice-20160506-snap-story.html.

6 Webpage of Rock Hill, South Carolina. "Open for Business Program." cityofrock- hill.com, Departments, Planning and Development. Accessed January 3, 2019. http://www.cityofrockhill.com/departments/planning-and-development/ open-for-business.

7 Seattle Council Connection (website). "Citywide Business Advocacy Team Formed." seattle.gov, News Releases. May 23, 2011. http://council.seattle.gov /2011/05/23/citywide-business-advocacy-team-formed/.

8 New York City Economic Development Corporation (website). "Mayor Bloomberg Announces Three New Steps to Make It Easier for Immigrant-Owned Businesses to Start and Grow in New York City." nycedc.com, Press Releases. March 3, 2011. https://www.nycedc.com/press-release/mayor-bloomberg-an- nounces-three-new-steps-make-it-easier-immigrant-owned-businesses.

9 Konz, Paul. "How Boston's Innovation District is Redefining Startup Ecosystems." National League of Cities (website). April 12, 2016. https:// citiesspeak.org/2016/04/12/has-bostons-innovation-district-created-a-new -regional-innovation-ecosystem/.

10 Shaar, Deborah. "Wichita Area Ranked Third in Nation for Export Growth: What's Next Under Trump Trade Policy?" kmuw.org. February 27, 2017. http:// www.kmuw.org/post/wichita-area-ranked-third-nation-export-growth-what-s- next-under-trump-trade-policy.

11 Valley Economic Development Center. "VEDC's Where's the Money? Access to Capital Business Expo in San Diego, CA." youtube.com. May 10, 2011. https:// www.youtube.com/watch?v=UEGYuYhvtH4.

12 Les Schwab Amphitheater (website). "2018 Bend Brewfest, Aug. 16-18." bend-concerts.com. Accessed January 3, 2019. https://www.bendconcerts.com/Bend -Brewfest-Les-Schwab-Amphitheater.html.

13 Economic Development for Central Oregon (website). "The Team." edcoinfo. com. Accessed January 3, 2019. https://edcoinfo.com/team/.

14 Humm Kombucha (website). "The Humm Story." hummkombucha.com. Accessed January 3, 2019. https://hummkombucha.com/the-humm-story/.

15 Feld, Brad. *Startup Communities: Building an Entrepreneurial Ecosystem in Your City.* New Jersey: Wiley, 2012. https://www.amazon.com/Startup-Communities -Building-Entrepreneurial-Ecosystem/dp/1531886035#reader_1531886035.

16 Kauffman Foundation (website). "2017 State of Entrepreneurship Address." kauffman.org, Resources. February 17, 2017. https://www.kauffman.org/ what-we-do/resources/state-of-entrepreneurship-addresses/2017-state-of -entrepreneurship-address.

17 Halbert, Gary D. "Business Startups Flock to Just 20 US Counties—Here's Why." valuewalk.com, Business. June 28, 2016. https://www.valuewalk.com/2016/06/ business-startups-usa/.

18 Economic Innovation Group (website). "Opportunity Zones." eig.org. Accessed January 3, 2019. https://eig.org/opportunityzones.

Chapter 10

1 Texas Real Estate Council Staff. "Everyone Gets Real During Inaugural TREC Shark Tank." TREC Wire (website). November 3, 2017. http://recouncil.com/ trec-news/shark-tank-2017-recap/.

2 Babson College (website). "Stimulating Small Business Growth: Progress Report on Goldman Sachs 10,000 Small Businesses." goldmansachs.com/10ksb. Accessed January 3, 2019. http://www.babson.edu/media/babson/site-assets/ content-assets/executives-amp-organizations/expanding-entrepreneurship/ goldman-sachs-10000-small-business-program/10ksb-impact-report-2018.pdf.

3 Goldman Sachs (website). "Goldman Sachs 10,000 Small Businesses: About the Program." goldmansachs.com. Accessed January 3, 2019. https://www.gold-mansachs.com/citizenship/10000-small-businesses/US/about-the-program/.

4 Goldman Sachs (website). "IFC, Goldman Sachs Initiative Invests $1 Billion in Women Entrepreneurs in Emerging Markets." goldmansachs.com, Press Release. May 18, 2018. https://www.goldmansachs.com/citizenship/10000women/ news-and-events/ifc-gs-investment-article.html.

5 Goldman Sachs (website) "Goldman Sachs 10,000 Women." goldmansachs. com. Accessed January 3, 2019. https://www.goldmansachs.com/citizenship /10000women/#overview.

6 Horowitz, Julia. "JPMorgan Takes Its Fund for Entrepreneurs of Color to Chicago." *CNN Business* (website). July 20, 2018. https://money.cnn.com/2018/07/19/ investing/jpmorgan-chase-entrepreneurs-of-color-chicago/index.html.

7 McConnell, Gordon. "Supporting Small Business and Entrepreneurship presented at the NLC Congress of Cities." November 12, 2011. [LG NOTE: THIS INFO CAME FROM The National League of Cities' "Supporting Entrepreneurs and Small Business" tool kit for local leaders]

8 The ASU Scottsdale Innovation Center (website). "Overview." Skysong.com. Accessed January 3, 2019. http://skysong.com/about-skysong/overview/.

9 National League of Cities, Small Business Toolkit to Support Entrepreneurs and Business, 2012. https://www.nlc.org/supporting-entrepreneurs-and-small-business. If correct, the entries should be: National League of Cities (website). "Supporting Entrepreneurs and Small Business." nlc.org. Accessed January 3, 2019. https://www.nlc.org/supporting-entrepreneurs-and-small-business.)

10 Price, Michael. "A Vision for the Valley." San Diego State University (website), NewsCenter. July 18, 2018. http://newscenter.sdsu.edu/sdsu_newscenter/news_story.aspx?sid=77295.

11 Sugiyama, Jane. "Mobility Startups Join U-M Incubator." University of Michigan Center for Entrepreneurship (website), Blog. October 3, 2017. http://cfe.umich.edu/mobility-startups-join-u-m-incubator-to-pilot-autonomous-and-connected-vehicle-innovations/.

12 Nager, Marc, and Claire Topalian. "With Strong Community Support, Startups Create More Than Jobs." *Forbes* (website). January 10, 2013. https://www.forbes.com/sites/kauffman/2013/01/10/with-strong-community-support-startups-create-more-than-jobs/2/.

13 Gallagher, Leigh. "Airbnb's Surprising Path to Y Combinator." *Wired* (website). February 21, 2017. https://www.wired.com/2017/02/airbnbs-surprising-path-to-y-combinator/.

14 Carson, Biz. "How 3 Guys Turned Renting an Air Mattress in Their Apartment into a $25 Billion Company." *Business Insider* (website). February 23, 2016. http://www.businessinsider.com/how-airbnb-was-founded-a-visual-history-2016-2#the-occasional-rager-and-legislative-wars-have-not-slowed-the-company-from-becoming-a-force-both-within-silicon-valley-and-as-a-steadily-gaining-competitor-of-the-hotel-industry-24.

15 Y Combinator (website). "About." ycombinator.com. Accessed January 3, 2019. http://www.ycombinator.com.

16 Hendricks, Drew. "5 Creative Ways Business Incubators Are Helping Their Startups Succeed." *Forbes* (website). January 23, 2015. https://www.forbes.com/sites/drewhendricks/2015/01/23/5-creative-ways-business-incubators-are-helping-their-startups-succeed/#1940f1c07659.

17 Nicolosi Galluzo, LLP (website). "Whitepaper: Business Incubators." nicgal.com. Accessed January 3, 2019. https://nicgal.com/wp-content/uploads/2016/12/NGbusiness-incubators.pdf.

18 http://innovate.uic.edu/node/13.

19 Entrepreneurs' Organization (website). "Apply for Membership." eonetwork.org. Accessed January 3, 2019. https://www.eonetwork.org/why-join/apply-for-membership/.

20 Doyenne (website). "About Us." doyennegroup.org. Accessed January 3, 2019. https://doyennegroup.org/about-us/.

21 Doyenne (website). "Doyenne Member: Katie Brenner." doyennegroup.org. Accessed January 3, 2019. http://doyennegroup.org/wp-content/uploads/2017/06/Katie_Brenner.pdf.

22 State of Texas Legislative Budget Board (website). "Statewide Criminal and Juvenile Justice Recidivism and Revocation Rates." lbb.state.tx.us. February 2015. http://www.lbb.state.tx.us/Documents/Publications/Policy_Report/1450_CJ_Statewide_Recidivism.pdf.

23 Turner, Allan. "Entrepreneur Program Serves as Ladder Out of Texas Prisons." *Houston Chronicle* (website). Last modified February 25, 2013. https://www.houstonchronicle.com/news/houston-texas/houston/article/Entrepreneur-program-serves-as-ladder-out-of-4304707.php.

24 LiftFund (website). "About." liftfund.com. Accessed January 3, 2019. https://www.liftfund.com/about/.

25 Revolution (website). "Revolution's Rise of the Rest® Seed Fund Announces its First Investments and Next Rise of the Rest Bus Tour Cities." revolution.com, Press Release. https://www.revolution.com/press-release/revolutions-rise-rest-seed-fund-announces-first-investments-next-rise-rest-bus-tour-cities/.

26 Kotkin, Joel. "Tech's New Hotbeds: Cities with Fastest Growth in STEM Jobs Are Far from Silicon Valley." *Forbes* (website). January 11, 2019. https://www.forbes.com/sites/joelkotkin/2018/01/11/techs-new-hotbeds-cities-with-fastest-growth-in-stem-jobs-are-far-from-silicon-valley/.

27 Frank, Scott. "AT&T Patents: Imagining Tomorrow's Experiences Today." att.com, Technology Blog. January 14, 2016. http://about.att.com/innovationblog/011416patents.

28 Womack, Brian. "Dallas Start-Up Focused on Millennial Renters Lands $100,000 at Steve Case Event." *Dallas Business Journal* (website), Technology. May 8, 2018. https://www.bizjournals.com/dallas/news/2018/05/08/dallas-startup-focused-on-millennial-renters.html.

29 Network for Teaching Entrepreneurship (website). "Press Room." nfte.com. Accessed January 3, 2019. https://www.nfte.com/pressroom/.

30 Network for Teaching Entrepreneurship (website). "Entrepreneurship: The Best Preparation for the Innovation Economy." nfte.com. Accessed January 3, 2019. http://www.nfte.com/why-entrepreneurship/.

31 Network for Teaching Entrepreneurship (website). "How We Do It." nfte.com. Accessed January 3, 2019. http://www.nfte.com/our-programs/.

32 Junior Achievement USA (website). "Junior Achievement's Purpose and Values." juniorachievement.org. Accessed January 3, 2019. https://www.juniorachievement.org/web/ja-usa/about.

33 Foster, Tom. "These Nine Organizations Are Turning Kids into Entrepreneurs." *Inc.* (website), Innovate. Accessed January 3, 2019. https://www.inc.com/tom-foster/how-kids-become-entrepreneurs.html.

34 https://www.juniorachievement.org/web/ja-dallas/ja-board;jsessionid =002E7829760BDC6B5F54339F9B9A981B

35 Bizworld.org. "Inspiring Children to Become the Architects of Their Futures." Accessed January 3, 2019. https://www.bizworld.org/About-BizWorld.

36 Horatio Alger Association of Distinguished Americans, Inc. (website). "Our Impact." scholars.horatioalger.org. Accessed January 3, 2019. https://scholars.horatioalger.org/our-impact/.

37 https://www.ey.com/us/en/services/strategic-growth-markets/entrepreneurial -winning-women--about-the-program

Acknowledgments

Believe it or not, books are extremely difficult to write. I wrote my first book at age twenty-eight, titled *The Real Estate Turnaround*. That book was about what I had learned in the real estate business between the ages of eighteen and twenty-eight. What made writing it fun was that my ghostwriter and partner in writing that book was my father. He was a very strong writer, which I am not. Since then, I have written six other books, including this one. Of my six previous books, four are real estate–related, one is focused on entrepreneurship, and the most recent is about our wine business. Writing comes easily to some people, but not to me. For me, it is draft after draft and a lot of hard work. However, I have always considered writing a team sport, so I solicit the help of some very talented people. While the team was just my father and me for book number one, for this book the team really grew.

This book has been a big team effort, with Linden Gross doing a lot of the heavy lifting. She is terrific. My wife and I worked with Linden to write *A Perfect Score*, our *New York Times* bestseller released in 2016. For a variety for reasons, *BOOM: Bridging the Opportunity Gap to Reignite Startups* has been years in the making. This has been an off-and-on project, as I felt like the subject matter was complex and there were a lot of nuances. I did not want to write a book that was unhelpful to this very important national issue. While it is surprising, the fact is, traditional entrepreneurship is in decline. At the same time, a huge groundswell of interest in entrepreneurship is also happening. I found it confusing and difficult to describe these crosscurrents. Ultimately, I hope this book helps readers by clarifying the confusion regarding the good and bad trends happening in tandem for startups and entrepreneurs today. All of this said, without the encouragement and help of many, this book would never have been completed.

Mark Zandi, the chief economist at Moody's, first got me interested in writing on this subject. None of this would have happened without him. As I describe in more detail in the book, he was the inspiration and the "whistleblower" who made me aware of this alarming decline in entrepreneurship. He was also an early manuscript reader and made many great suggestions. Finally, I asked if he would be willing to write the foreword for the book and was thrilled and honored when he agreed to do that as well.

Ellen Marsau Burger, who is the director of communications for HALL Group, my company in Dallas, together with two of our talented then–interns (now full-time associates), Cade Hill and Abby Witkowski, helped put together a lot of research for this book. Between researching, fact checking, building the appendices, and providing feedback and critiques, the three of them made a huge difference. Ellen then acted as the quarterback, really working with Linden and me on revising and perfecting the manuscript piece by piece, page by page. When a book is completed, it seems a lot simpler than when you are creating the pieces that go into it. This one has a lot of pieces, and no doubt we have overlooked something or there will be things we wish we had done differently, but I am extraordinarily proud of my team for their hard work and dedication.

Along my journey, at one point I was planning to coauthor this book with Dr. Garry Bruton, my friend and a great professor of entrepreneurship at Texas Christian University. Garry teaches all over the world. I met Garry after he had been chosen by the Fulbright committee to be the first Fulbright professor for a position in Central and Eastern Europe that my wife and I endowed in the late 1990s. Garry is also the only professor who has been chosen twice, having served in that role previously. Ironically, it was during Garry's second stint that I had a resurgence of energy to write this book and finally pull it together. All of that said, Garry and his associates Dr. Chao Chen and

Jiexia Qian were very helpful in shaping and confirming a lot of the book's original premise.

This book was written off and on over a number of years with countless full drafts. My two assistants, Jan Jones in Dallas and Amy Taylor in Napa, California, are each in their own way terrific at putting up with me. They each helped pull together all the pieces of this lengthy project. Margaux Chauve, my niece, who lives in Paris, also added some valuable research on French entrepreneurship.

As with my previous books, I owe a great deal to my friends and agents, Jan Miller and her great team, Nena Oshman and Austin Miller. In particular, Jan and Nena's guidance over many years kept this project moving. Additionally, thank you to our publishing team at Post Hill Press, led by Debby Englander, and to Elena Vega for her detailed copy editing.

A lot of HALL Group and HALL Wines board members read the manuscript and gave me great feedback and ideas. These board members include Don Braun, Mark Depker, Dick Hyman, Herb Weitzman, Mike Reynolds, Susan Adams, Susan Butenhoff, Mike Bell, Tom Carroll, and Eric Reed. Thank you all!

Additionally, other friends who read this in advance and helped include Congressman Mike Thompson, Gavin Susman, Mark Blocher, Lisa Covey, Bryan Tolbert, Kim Butler, Kymberley Scalia, Mike Jaynes, Stephanie Byrd, Debra von Storch, Trey Bowles, Roger Lee, and many others. I thank all of you for your help and efforts.

I would also like to thank all of the entrepreneurs who inspired this book. Without the insight from your experiences, this would not have been possible. In particular, Carrie Stein, whose feedback and input while writing was also invaluable. So, to Carrie Stein, Orlander Johnson, Patrick Brandt, Roberto Rivera, Daniel Black, Carl Dorvil, Fernando De Leon, Michelle Mitchell, Jamie Danek, Daniel Lubetzky and many others, it is because of you and the difference you have made that I wrote this book and champion this cause.

Last but not least, I'd like to thank my amazing wife, Kathryn, who read and reread the book and provided me with valuable insight and feedback. Brijetta, aka Jet, who runs the storytelling project Love Wisconsin, also helped with interviews, research, reading, and commentary. That said, to our four children, including Jet, Independence, David, and Jennifer; and their spouses/significant others, Parker, Eric, and Vanessa; and my grandchildren, Courtney, Caitlyn, Sebastian, Maximilian, Parker Jr., Ellie, Lola and our newest granddaughter, Montana Rose. I love you all and thank you for your support.